The Islander
A translation of *An tOileánach*

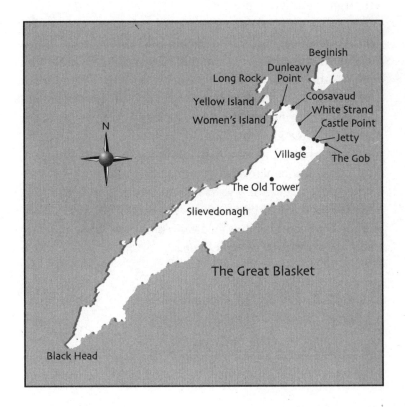

Beginish

Dunleavy
Point

Long Rock

Yellow Island

Women's Island

Coosavaud

White Strand

Castle Point

Jetty

N

Village

The Gob

The Old Tower

Slievedonagh

The Great Blasket

Black Head

The Translators

Garry Bannister was born in Sligo in 1953. He developed a great love for Irish from his teacher, the late Harry Lush. He studied Irish and Russian at Trinity College Dublin, after which he went to Moscow State University where he received an MA in Russian language and literature. It was also in Russia he wrote and successfully defended a PhD in comparative linguistics. Bannister established the first department of Modern Irish at Moscow State University, a department that, over the years, has produced many celebrated Russian scholars of Modern Irish. He has a large number of publications in modern Irish including *The English–Irish Learner's Dictionary* and *Teasáras na Gaeilge*. Bannister's main interest is early twentieth century modern Irish literature and he has collaborated over the past twenty years with Dr David Sowby on various translation projects.

David Sowby was born in the English Lake District and came to Ireland when he was seven years old. He was educated in Dublin, and had the privilege of learning Irish from the inspirational Harry Lush. He studied medicine in Trinity College Dublin and at the University of Toronto, after which he worked in Canada in the field of radiation protection. In 1962 he became the Scientific Secretary of the International Commission on Radiological Protection, and remained in that position until he retired after twenty-three years. A few years later he returned to Ireland and resumed his study of Irish with his former teacher, Harry Lush, during which time he translated *Cúirt an Mheán Oíche* and then began the translation of *An tOileánach*.

Contents

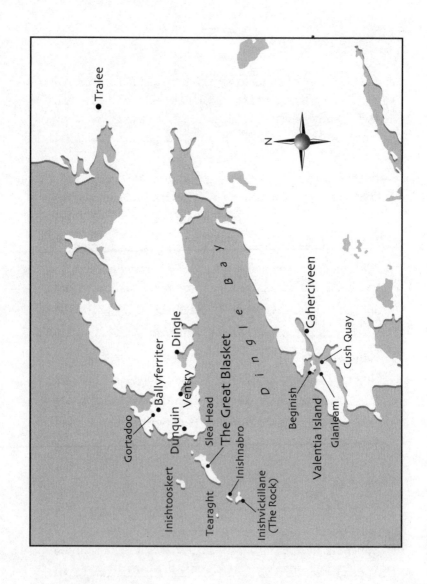

Foreword

by Professor Alan Titley

The opening sentence of Tomás Ó Criomhthain's[1] *An tOileánach* is stark and striking: 'I remember being at my mother's breast.' It would perfectly fulfil the requirements of the formulaic short story looking for a sudden opening. It also gives the lie to the colonised notion that Ireland, and Irish-speaking Ireland in particular, was a land of prissy puritans and pious paddies. There is no book in the English-speaking world which begins with such an admission of the most natural thing in the world. And yet it is a book of which we are a little bit scared. Peasants are meant to stay in their own place, and more than that, to know their place. They are meant to be simple and uneducated, to have limited horizons, to speak a pattery patois, and to be somewhat dense.

The scary thing about *The Islander* is that it subverts every one of those silly and stupid stereotypes. The place of its telling may be in the back of beyond, but the voice that tells is of the always here and now. It is a voice without buckles, without posies, without flowers, without fancies. It is a voice that cuts through all the crap, and gets right down to it beyond yea or nay, or neigh or bay. The shapes that are being thrown in this book are very simple, and obvious even unto the guileless mind.

An tOileánach was a classic from the start. It is not a novel with a happy ending, or an autobiography with a conventional journey.

---

[1] Tomás Ó Criomhthain in the original Gaelic text. We decided to use the traditionally accepted 'O'Crohan' throughout our translation as this anglicised version of Tomás's surname seemed easier for English readers to pronounce.

It is not a story wherein the hero overcomes his background and his family and goes on to greater things. It is not an adventure, as the most exciting active parts have to do with killing innocent seals on the rocky shore. And yet, there was always something about it which set it apart. Even when the other Blasket biographies appeared, *Fiche Bliain ag Fás* in 1933, and *Peig* in 1936, there was a sense that the classic status of *An tOileánach* would not be surpassed. Although those three classics deal with the same island, they are different in outlook, imagination, treatment, acceptance and philosophy. But within these confines we also see the world. It was John McGahern who said that 'unwittingly, through the island frame, we have been introduced into a complete representation of existence.' It does, of course, also tell us of the life of the island and its people, but many others could have done the same. A bland description ticking the required boxes would have given us the necessary information. But this book is about a lot more than giving us information; it is giving us the sense of felt life.

As the translator from English into Irish must avoid the magnet of English idiom, so the translator from Irish into English must escape from the clutches of a very determined Irish rhythm. Translation is always a demanding craft but at its highest it is a haunting art. Douglas Hyde and John Millington Synge beguiled readers of English with the cadences and phrasings of Irish. It was an innovative and poetic turn which opened the mind and brought music to the ear. In the hands of lesser practitioners this idiom soon grew tiresome and clodhopping and paddywhackish. Those who spoke this brogue were not people any more; they were peasants or hayseeds or bumpkins. Anybody translating from the Irish, unless involved in a humorous exercise, would be well warned to avoid this stuff. Not everybody did.

To be fair to Robin Flower, he was well aware of the pitfalls in his translation of this great book, published as *The Islandman* in 1934. He acknowledges the problem: 'Irish and English are so widely separated in their mode of expression that nothing like a literal translation from one language to the other is possible.' And while he notes the 'charm' of the Hiberno-English glue, he realises that 'there is always something slightly artificial about it, and often a suggestion of the pseudo-poetic. This literary dialect could not be used to render the forthright, colloquial simplicity of the original of this book.' In this he largely succeeds, although some echoes and turnings and stray wisps of Irish slip through the net.

Garry Bannister and David Sowby are probably aware of this, and hence their greater determination to provide a 'clear and readable' translation in 'simple understandable language'. There is a sense in which Ó Criomhthain's style was a great help to them, as he writes himself in a plain and uncluttered manner, as hard as the rocks below his house, as clean as the living stream. Despite the fact that the islanders lived close together and shared a common way of living and spoke the same language, it does not in any way follow that they all thought the same way or used their language after the same fashion. It is revealing that the three main autobiographies present us with very different people and with a very different cut of Irish. Peig makes use, for example, of a lot more *seanfhocail* or wise saws than the others, and occasionally a flourish from her large repertoire of folk tales and wisdom; Muiris Ó Súilleabháin, on the other hand, talks to you like a young man you might meet in a bar, cheerfully grabbing you by the elbow and gabbling into your ear. Ó Criomhthain is like neither of these. His prose is scoured of fluff and affectation, picked clean of all fancy, sculled by a mind that brooks no pretence.

This is not the problem. The problem with all translation is one of feeling and echoes. Each language has its own history, which is not the history of any other language, and the taste of a word in one is not the taste of its translation in another. You either get this, or you don't. It may even be easier to successfully translate from some languages into others. One suspects that languages of Latin origin carry some of the great columns and marble edifices of Rome in their innards and resonances can be more readily shared between them. But between Irish and English there are vast shelves of libraries and vast cities and practised bureaucracies and marching troops and technical wrestlings which make the gap of feeling immense.

And yet, this translation is carried off with style. Apart from the sensibility of the translators, and their necessary humility before the original, they had a clear and unambiguous sense of what they were about. They never deviated from this, despite the temptations of the text.

While in no way denigrating Flower's translation, because it is in its own way a fine achievement, the differences are easily seen. On the opening page Ó Criomhthain is telling us how he was the favourite child. He uses the simple word *peata* for 'pet', which is a direct borrowing from English anyway, although one of the few in the island vocabulary. Flower renders the appropriate sentence as 'so that it is little wonder that I was spoilt among them all'. Bannister and Sowby write, 'so that it was no wonder that I was their pet'. Simple, direct, clean, accurate. A more difficult problem arises with direct speech, of which there are many examples in the book. Where Flower translates '"Bad cess to you, you've made a fine muddle of the day for me,"' this translation says, '"You little wretch!" says she. "I suppose you don't care that you've ruined the day for me."' Again, we get the idea. Go straight, no fuss, tell it like an ordinary speaker of a common colloquial English might do.

But ordinary speech can also be a minefield. Fashions change and today's normal chatter grows easily stale. It is most difficult to strike a register that has the common touch but is still neutral enough not to draw attention to itself. Thus 'Cheers' in place of 'Dé do bheathasa' is cheeky, but seems about right, while just after it 'She has indeed — she arrived there yesterday,' is far more accurate in tone and propriety than 'By my soul, she has since last night,' which would be more literal.

They also have the good sense to get around that which might sound corny or false. While Ó Criomhthain rarely employs rhetoric of any kind when he is describing a sea journey he makes use of the formulaic 'runs' which were the stock in trade of the traditional storyteller. Instead of simply trying to imitate this the translators employ their own stratagem acknowledging the origin of the phrases, but merely hinting at its style — 'like the wild Fenians of old, we put out "the four tough, smooth, sturdy, white, broad-bladed oars" and we didn't slow up until we reached the mouth of the cave we were heading for.' This sound judgement marks every page of the translation, and nothing comes between us and the sense of the original, which is what they set out to do.

Garry Bannister and David Sowby have had the good sense to draw on Seán Ó Coileáin's definitive version of the text. Both An Seabhac's 1929 edition, and Pádraig Ua Maoileoin's 1973 one served their purpose in their time, but we are beholden to Ó Coileáin's for making Ó Criomhthain's own words in their complete garb available to us. This translation is homage to both the writer and the editor, but it is also an act of honour to a wonderful book. This is as good as it gets.

Preface

by Professor Seán Ó Coileáin

The task of the translator is an unenviable one, standing as he does in the shadow of the author by whose authority alone he speaks, simultaneously revealing and concealing his original while all the while being himself invisibly present in every word. The effect on the readers may vary greatly, even in respect of the same work, particularly when they themselves are familiar with the primary source and hold it in some considerable regard. In such an event, initial outrage is likely to be followed up with charges of literary vandalism. Here is Myles na Gopaleen, writing in *The Irish Times* on 3 January 1957, speaking of Robin Flower's translation of *An tOileánach*: '*A greater parcel of bosh and bunk than Flower's "Islandman" has rarely been imposed on the unsuspecting public.*'

The distinguished scholar, Professor D.A. Binchy, is far more complimentary: '*Dr Flower is the ideal interpreter … he has risen nobly to the occasion, producing a masterly translation in which the sensitiveness of the poet and the accuracy of the scholar are blended in perfect harmony.*' (*Studies*, December 1934)

On the whole, I am more inclined to agree with Binchy's assessment of Flower's translation, as is John McGahern in his very fine article on the book (*The Irish Times*, 2 November 1991). '*A field is only described as it is reclaimed and cultivated. A strand is there to be crossed, a sea to be fished, a town to be reached, a shore to be gained, walked upon, lived upon. These are all near and concrete realities but so stripped down to their essence, because of the necessities of the action, as to seem free of all local characteristics.*

One conditions the other to the same simplicity of form. So elemental is the vision that it only be rendered into the English we now possess in a weakened half-light.'

That word 'elemental' accords well with the 'gauntness' of which Myles speaks, terms that are immediately defined for us in Bannister's and Sowby's translation.

> 'We were living in a small, narrow house; it was roofed with rushes from the hill above us. There was often a hen's nest to be found up in the roof with a dozen eggs in it. There was a bedstead in the corner, and two other beds at the far end of the house. Inside the house there were two cows, two pigs, hens with their eggs, a donkey ... and of course all of us.' (page 2)

Flower's translation was based on the 1929 edition of An Seabhac who, while he had the considerable advantage of free access to Tomás, was more constrained than the modern editor in certain respects. Some passages in the original manuscript appear to have been omitted on grounds of literary taste; almost invariably, it seems to me, the author's judgement is to be preferred to that of his first editor and they have been restored in the 2002 edition which serves as exemplar for Bannister and Sowby.

It is they who now bring Tomás forward into the present. It is through them he speaks from another world.

Acknowledgements

The authors are greatly indebted to a long list of people from Dún Chaoin and various institutes throughout Ireland, to many scholars who have generously assisted them over the many long years of this translation. Amongst those whose written work and advice have been of considerable assistance, from the very onset of our work in late 2002, are: Professor Seán Ó Coileáin who provided the authors with numerous insights and scholarly advice regarding difficult sections in the original text, Professor Alan Titley whose far-reaching knowledge and intuitive understanding of the life of the Islanders has been a consistently invaluable resource to the authors, Máire Mhac an tSaoi whose deeply personal and intimate acquaintance with this particular part of Ireland has been both informative and helpful throughout. Our sincere thanks also go to Breandán Ó Conaire, Professor Máirín Nic Eoin, Máiréad Nic Craith, Professor Declan Kiberd, Críostóir Ó Floinn, and many others whose books and other publications have been extraordinarily helpful on our long and ambitious venture.

Especial thanks goes to the late Harry Lush who held a deep affection for the people of Dingle and spent many years in Dún Chaoin, visiting the Island and talking with those who lived there before it was evacuated in 1953. In recognition of his huge contribution in helping many generations of young boys and girls to love, foster and speak Irish, we have dedicated this book to our friend and teacher, Mr Harry Lush. Go ndéana Dia trócaire ar a anam.

Harry Lush (1916–2005)

Thanks to Fergal Tobin and his team at Gill & Macmillan for all their dedicated work on the book, but especially to Deirdre Rennison Kunz who ceaselessly showed tremendous patience, professionalism and an extraordinary ability to keep everybody calm and on track.

We would especially like to thank Bassia Bannister and Eve White for their great support over the years. Their love and encouragement have immeasurably contributed to the success of this project.

Finally, the authors alone are solely responsible for any errors, discrepancies or misreadings of the Gaelic text. We do, however, hope that despite any inadequacies, our translation will nonetheless provide the English reader with some meaningful understanding of the enormous achievements of this local fisherman who not only taught himself to read and write in his own language but also taught, impressed and inspired many distinguished writers and scholars of his time. Thanks to this haunting autobiography that celebrates the language, folklore, customs and life on the Great Blasket Island off the west coast of Kerry, generations of readers have continued to enjoy discovering and rediscovering this vibrantly inspiring account of a world that has long since disappeared.

Introduction

In 2002 Professor Seán Ó Coileáin published his definitive edition of *An tOileánach*. This momentous achievement was the final chapter in the illustrious history of great scholarship that has surrounded Tomás O'Crohan's emblematic and foundational masterpiece in the genre of Gaelic autobiographical literature: *An tOileánach*. Later that same year, after reading the Professor Ó Coileáin edition, it was quite clear to David and myself that this unique and outstanding classic should also be made available to an English readership. Little did we realise, however, when we started, that this project would take the best part of ten years to complete.

None of our work, of course, would have been at all possible without the gargantuan achievements of Professor Seán Ó Coileáin, whose lifetime study of the Blasket people and their literature, along with his profound understanding of both the man, Tomás O'Crohan, and his writings, finally concluded in his definitive 2002 publication. Professor Ó Coileáin's incredibly scholarly and informative introduction to the Gaelic text provides essential guidance to anyone attempting to interpret or understand this early masterpiece of the Gaelic autobiographical genre. In fact, Professor Ó Coileáin's preface (*pages xvii–xlii*) is a gripping and stand-alone text in itself. Anyone wishing to read *An tOileánach* in Gaelic would be well advised to acquaint themselves thoroughly with this detailed and illuminating introduction to the book.

Tomás, his family and life on the Great Blasket

Tomás O'Crohan was born in the spring of 1855[2] to Dónal O'Crohan and Cáit O'Shea. Tomás was the youngest of eight children and according to his own account, being the last of the brood, he became the family pet.

The book is an extraordinary account of how people lived on a small, wind-swept island. It holds a fascinating account of a long and lasting friendship between Tomás and his uncle Diarmaid. Indeed it is Diarmaid who introduces Tomás to a young girl of the Ó Dálaigh household from Inishvickillane. This young girl becomes the centre of Tomás's world and she, in turn, becomes equally interested in her young Blasket admirer.

However, this match was not to be, as his older sister Máire intervened by suggesting to her parents that the family's interests would be better served were Tomás to marry a local girl. So a marriage match between Tomás O'Crohan and Mary Keane was eventually arranged and in the year 1878 the two were wed.

The song or lament that Tomás sings at his wedding, *O'Neill's Castle or The Dark Mountain Lass*, gives us some indication of the quiet sorrow he must have felt on this important moment in his life as he bade farewell to his youthful dreams and undertook, as he himself saw it, the responsibilities of adulthood.

Surviving on the Island

It was a hard and unforgiving life on the Island. People mostly lived off fishing and hunting. But some years were extremely lean for the Island people and it was only the odd shipwreck or the arrival of a shoal of porpoises that saved them from starvation and gave them a reasonably comfortable life.

The Islanders' isolated situation had, however, its advantages too as the British and Irish authorities found it rather difficult to

---

[2] Muiris Mac Conghail in his book *The Blaskets — People and literature* suggests that Tomás O'Crohan was born in April 1855 because he had been baptised in the parish church of Ballyferriter on 29 April of the same year. It was generally the custom to have children baptised as quickly as possible due to the high rate of infant mortality in those times.

make them pay their taxes or even keep any track of what livestock the Islanders possessed. There are a number of powerful passages in the book concerning the arrival of state officials to the Island.

Death was a frequent visitor to the Great Blasket but Tomás does not often write in much detail about these catastrophic moments, which he and the Islanders seem to have accepted as part and parcel of their rugged Island existence.

One of the most moving passages in the book is the account of the death of his own parents. First his father, who simply declined one day to go out picking potatoes with Tomás. Then not long afterwards, his mother who also quietly and peacefully passed away after a reasonably short period of illness.

The sometimes shocking tales of survival as related in this autobiography provide a comprehensive overview of life at the end of the 19th and the beginning of the 20th centuries on the exposed slopes of the Great Blasket Island. Apart from the wealth of information concerning both the private and public lives of the Islanders, there is also much to be discovered about the cultural, political, social, economic and religious environment of the Island at that time. The lightly humorous and intimate conversational style of the author makes the book very readable and enjoyable but certainly unlike anything else you are ever likely to read. It is a story that stands apart from those of other books of its time; a book about the life of a vanishing community *'whose likes will never be seen again.'*

A word from the authors

As far as we know, there has been only one previous translation of *An tOileánach*, namely *The Islandman* by Robin Flower, which was published in 1934 by Talbot Press, Dublin and Cork. Flower enjoyed the advantage of having a close personal friendship with Tomás, and was therefore able to discuss the trickier passages in considerable depth with the author himself. Flower's translation, which gives us a magnificent insight into O'Crohan's great work, falls slightly short of providing a comprehensive English translation of its original text. There are several reasons why this may be so, two of which are perhaps worth mentioning here. Firstly, the way in which the text was written in dribs and drabs over an extended period of time, where manuscripts were edited and re-edited by different writers and folklorists, must have caused, and did cause, confusion as to what Tomás exactly intended as a finished text, ready for publication, or what he may have loosely considered to be a preliminary draft which was to be revisited or further developed at some later date.[3] Indeed it wasn't until the beginning of the 21st century that adequate scholarship had been brought to bear on all the original manuscripts so that a definitive version of the Gaelic text could be provided for its Gaelic readership. Another factor that perhaps gave rise to the restricted parameters of the first translation may well have been an understandable reluctance to offend the mores of the time when the book was written, where some of Tomas's more forthright passages could well have been construed as being offensive to the delicate attitudes of an early 20th-century readership. Today these excised details may seem to us to be extraordinarily tame and even mildly amusing.

When in late 2002, early 2003, we originally set out to translate this epic autobiography by Tomás O'Crohan, we attempted to provide a translation in the form of a guide for those who might want to read the original Gaelic text.[4] However, this was doomed to failure as the original syntax of the Gaelic is so far removed

---

[3] It should, perhaps, be pointed out that Tomás seems to have perceived himself more as a provider of material rather than a writer who concerns himself with the details of how his work should be finally edited. In a number of places in his writings, he clearly expresses the view that such matters are outside of his personal control. Cf. *"If I had my way, I'd have included half a dozen fine songs here and there in these writings. However, I have no choice in the matter, and I have to do as I'm instructed by my esteemed editor." (191)*; and again at the end of his book: *"If there is a sentence there that you don't like, leave it out." (329)*

[4] This idea was based on David Sowby's very successful literal translation of 'The Midnight Court' by Brian Merriman (2001) which also provided copious notes for the student who would, it was understood, be using the English translation as a guide to reading the original Gaelic text.

from modern English idiom that our literal translation provided neither adequate clarity nor any real sense of the vibrancy, local colour or wealth of literary expression that is so vividly evident in the original text. All our best efforts and our dogged adherence to the original only ever resulted in an English translation that was unwieldy, bleak and, for the most part, incomprehensible.

In 2004 we decided on a different approach. We began the long process of rewriting the first translation we had cobbled together and to restructure it in such a way as to preserve three critical aspects of the original text. Firstly, although the translation had to be clear and readable, it also, as far as possible, had to reflect the intended meaning of its author. Secondly, the translation needed to convey something of the richness and elegance of O'Crohan's own literary style of expression; thirdly, the language of the English translation was not to lose too much of the essence or feeling of the time in which it was written.

The gap, not only between modern English idiom but even between that of modern Irish, was so wide in certain passages of the book that both the syntax and the vocabulary had to be radically 'renovated' in order to express, with any modicum of clarity, what the author had originally in mind. For example:

> ... *Ní cheapfá go raibh aon teanga in aon duine insa tigh, beag ná mór, nó go raibh sé críochnaithe. Do thug a raibh istigh suas don amhrán déanta é agus, ar an dtaobh eile, don amhrán ráite é.* (page 191)
> ... *Until it was finished you might have thought that everyone in the house had been struck dumb. Everyone was bewitched by the song and the way it had been sung.*

There are a few points we would like to note regarding the final translation as it appears in this book. Firstly, not all the original text has been translated into English as can be seen from the example above. Secondly, the syntax has often been significantly rearranged in order to suit English idiom; and thirdly, the English translation aims, in general, to convey, in simple understandable language, the key sentiments and sense of what is being expressed in the original Gaelic version.

Apart from not deviating too far from the original wording and adhering as closely as possible to the intended meaning, there were a number of other matters that required our continuous, careful consideration. Should repetitions in the original text be included in the English version and if so, should they be modified in any way? Should anachronistic Hibernian English be used in order to convey O'Crohan's personal style? What should the trade-off be between textual clarity and the author's personal, unique style? To whom is our translation being addressed? — to students of Irish who might be studying the original Gaelic or to a much more general readership?

The guiding principle that we decided to adopt in regard to all the above considerations was that of clarity. All other aspects of the text would have to be kept subordinate to the readability of the English translation. In certain situations where anachronistic forms did not interfere with the understanding or the reading of the text, these were left unchanged. Where O'Crohan's personal style of expression did not detract from the lucidity of what was being communicated in English, these idiosyncratic peculiarities were also carefully preserved.

The sheer beauty and poetry of O'Crohan's expression is frequently evident whenever he describes, in general terms, his own personal recollections, images or perceptions of life on the Island:

> ... *some of us had a passion for the sea and the ocean, imbued with the sound of the wind that blew in from the seashore, beating in our ears every morning, clearing our brains and the dust from our skulls.*

As regards the excerpts from the verses, poems or songs quoted in the book, we decided that it would be best to provide metrical translations of the Gaelic. This, we believe, conserves, in form at least, a closer feel of what was being expressed initially in the original:

On the Sunday, on the Sunday, it was bright and summery,
The daughter and the mother are discussing men, but she,
The gentle little darling said, 'oh mother let me be,
For I'll have to marry very soon or leap across the sea.'

'Listen, ugly hussy, don't you moan or lose your head.'
'You haven't listened, mother; since I came of age to wed,
I am thirteen years or fourteen if the truth were only said,
And I'll have to marry very soon or take the boat instead.'

In the text of our translation, marginal numbers have been provided. These refer to the page numbers of Professor Ó Coileáin's 2002 edition. The reader will also note that some words in the book have been placed between square brackets. This is to indicate that these words do not form any part of the original text but have been introduced into our translation solely for the purposes of clarification.

Finally, we have given the English for the place names and people's names with a few iconic exceptions such as, for example, 'Tomás'. Places that have ceased to exist in modern maps have been translated to the best of our ability. Footnotes have also been provided wherever the translation or any part of the text may require additional explanation.

ONE

I can remember being at my mother's breast; I wasn't weaned until I was four years old. You might call me the dregs of the little jug, the last of the brood. That's why I was left so long feeding on my mother's breast.

Page 1

I was also the family pet. I had four sisters, each of them putting morsels of food into my mouth as if I were their very own fledgling bird. My sisters were Mary Donal, Kate Donal, Eileen Donal and Nora Donal, and I also had two brothers, Patrick Donal and Tomás Donal. Mary is still alive today and living here on the Great Blasket. Two others are living in America. Patrick is still alive. However, no sooner had Kate received her quarterly pension than she died. That was our family brood. They were all around while I was an infant, so it was no wonder that I was their pet. Besides, I had appeared quite unexpectedly.

My father wasn't tall but he was strong and well-built. My mother was easily as tall as a policeman. She was a beautiful, vigorous, strong blonde, but by the time I was at her breast there was no nourishment left in her milk. And another thing, I myself was an old cow's calf, and therefore not easy to rear.

And indeed, that rogue death was carrying off many fine plump children, but he seemed to be leaving me till last. Or perhaps he just didn't think it worth his while to take me. I was becoming hardier by the day and going wherever I wanted to, although an eye was still kept on me lest I ventured too close to the edge of the sea. I wore a coat[5] of undyed sheep wool and a knitted cap. My pleasures were simple — a hen's egg, a bit of butter, a bit of fish, some limpets or winkles — titbits of everything from land and sea.

We were living in a small, narrow house; it was roofed with rushes from the hill above us. There was often a hen's nest to be found up in the roof with a dozen eggs in it. There was a bedstead in the corner, and two other beds at the far end of the house. Inside the house there were two cows, two pigs, hens with their eggs, a donkey . . . and of course all of us. In other words, the back of the house was where the family lived. Our door faced north and the door of the other part of the house faced south.

There was another house opposite ours; their door faced us. The people of the two houses used to chat together every day. The woman of the house opposite used to be in and out of our place every minute of the day, and she'd very often come away with something worthwhile for her efforts. This woman was a little scandal-monger, dishevelled, sallow, ugly and shapeless, and she'd go from house to house, gossiping. She often used to say to my mother that Ireland couldn't raise the calf of an old cow. But if you ask me, there never was a cow, old or young in Ireland, that had a calf as miserable as herself.

I was soon growing up quickly and the grey coat was getting far too short for me. That was when I was beginning to understand things better. I soon became accustomed to the old hag and I was giving her as good as I got. A group from the two households used to meet every Sunday in our house for my father's reciting of the Communal Rosary. The woman of the house opposite used to say to my mother:

[5] Also called a petticoat or a smock

"You leave the grey coat on him until you start seeking a wife for him! How well he's growing, may God prosper him!" says she — helping herself to another portion of fresh bream.

My Father
Page 3

My father's family came from Dunquin; he married into this Island. My mother's family came from the parish of Ventry. They truly liked each other, but didn't suffer from the 'affliction' that many of them have these days, that would make you want to take a stick to them. They settled down in a poor cabin with only a small holding of their own, and they eked out a living by fishing and working the land. They were very successful at making a living off the sea and land. There was no donkey on the Island at that time. Instead, every man and woman used to carry a creel on their backs — that is, if the woman wasn't a spoilt pet or a rogue of a woman who would prefer to starve rather than do a decent day's work.

My father was a wonderful hunter and fisherman, and he had a great work attitude. He was a stone-mason by trade, a boat captain, and a handyman too. He did many a job for other people, since at that time most of them were like a herd of mindless donkeys in a field.

That year was great for fishing. I was wearing my grey coat by then, although I was hankering after my mother's milk as I still thought that I should be on my mother's breast, even though I'd probably been weaned for more than a year by that time.

One morning my father was going fishing. We had a fine stack of turf that year, but someone told my parents that the whole stack had been stolen the previous day. As the day was fine my father asked my mother to try bringing some turf back to the house.

So she threw her creel up on her back, and brought six creels home before I had even woken up. My mother then had to put her work to one side to look after me, the pet. She dressed me in my grey coat and gave me a nibble to eat, but then, when I should have been satisfied, I wasn't.

My mother strapped up her creel so that she could head back up the hill again, but now I too wanted to go along with her. So my mother had no option but to take me, and I only able to crawl slowly beside her at that time. Pretty soon I was tired of walking, so she had to put me into her creel and carry me up the hill herself. My mother cursed me a few times that day I can tell you, and who could blame her!

When she'd filled the creel with turf, she warned me to get a move on down the slope, but I was more obstinate coming back than going up. I well remember that she put the point of her foot under me, lifting me off the ground and sending me a fine distance.

"You little wretch!" says she. "I suppose you don't care that you've ruined the day for me."

She had to take me home on her chest, with the creel on her back as full as it ever was.

She dumped me on the floor and told Mary to turn the creel over on top of me and leave me to live or die. In spite of any mischief I might have done, she still managed to bring twenty creels of turf with her that day. By Sunday she had brought home a huge stack of turf. My father had caught five thousand fish that week. My mother used to be telling all this and more to the old woman next door.

The Ship Carrying Yellow Oil

It had been a harsh year before an oil-ship struck the stony cove on the north side of the Island. The ship was ground into matchwood, and lumps of oil went floating all over the sea. It was high-quality oil, and a very little of it would do for a poor person who might need the money to buy a sack of white meal. At that time yellow meal was not available.

There was a coastguard in Dunquin then, and they were certainly needed, because ships were frequently going aground, since they hadn't any form of propulsion other than sails. When the blue-coats (that's what we called the coastguard) heard that the boat had sunk near this Island, and knew what was in it, they didn't sleep day or night, but were all the time cruising around.

They had a beautiful boat in good working-order, and they were very clued-in to whatever was happening. They tormented the heart out of the Islanders who were trying to hide the lumps in cracks and crevices where neither cats nor dogs could get at them. When all is said and done, the people lived very well that year on the Island, in spite of the best efforts of the blue-coats. The Islanders took a lot of oil across Dingle Bay and sold it on the mainland at night. Mind you, the blue-coats got their cut out of it, which helped them to pay their rent.

Page 5

One day a boat came in with only four patrolmen in it. The boat from the Island, with six large lumps of oil in it, had come right up ahead of them. The patrolmen quickly took the lumps into their own boat, and they were really pleased with themselves! There was a young woman on the shore holding a big jagged stone behind her back. She got into her father's boat, but the blue-coats noticed nothing until she threw the rock clean through the bottom of their boat and water started gushing in.

Off went the blue-coats, and off went the lumps of yellow oil, floating again until the women managed to rescue them. The blue-coats had to drag their boat up and put a tin patch on it. When they got it mended they rowed away home as fast as they could go. I don't think they did much sightseeing while there was oil like lumps of putty still floating around.

Some time after that, a few men on a hill noticed that a sheep had fallen down onto the shore. They went down to try and rescue it. One of them caught sight of a brass bolt under a flat, protruding rock. He loosened it and pulled it out. It was at least four feet long. The shore was full of the stuff, partly brass and partly copper. No one knows how much the two of them salvaged, but it was to be found on the beach where the shipwreck had happened, and there were plenty of long crates still there, full of these valuable bolts. No one really knows what the Islanders did with these valuable bolts. They were bad years, and the old folk used to say that if it hadn't been for that shipwreck, no one on the Island would have ever survived. I can still hear the old hag on her doorway saying that it was God who sent these spoils

Page 6

to the poor. The Islanders lived well for a couple of years on account of the flotsam, while those in other regions were living quite precariously, having to endure a considerable amount of deprivation at that time.

Whenever my father used to bring home a load of these bolts in a pack, I wasn't even able to stand one of them up, they were so heavy.

I almost went crazy the day I was dressed in breeches for the first time. I didn't stay still for a minute but rushed around like a hound puppy. I thought there was no need for me to eat anything, and I did nothing but run in and out, to and fro. All the same, someone was keeping an eye on me.

Well, during one of my visits to the fire, my mother looked at me and saw that the grey trousers were soaking wet.

"My little ray of sunshine", said she, "what got your trousers wet? I bet you peed in them."

I admitted it, and said that I'd asked Nora to undo my buttons but that she hadn't done so. That's probably the first lie I ever told, for I hadn't said anything to poor Nora, and my mother gave her a fierce beating because she didn't do as I had asked. It's a great humiliation for someone to be unjustly accused, but look how soon I started getting up to mischief. My father went to work on the trousers again — for it was he who made them in the first place — and he fixed them cleverly, so that it would be easy for me the next time mother nature called.

My mother said I was eight years old that day. The next day off I went, all around the village, with Eileen accompanying me, going from house to house. It was a custom at that time, when a boy got a new garment or a new suit, for him to go to every house, where there'd be a penny or two to put in your pocket. When I came home there were three shillings in my little grey pocket. I gave the money to my father, though I would have preferred to have given it to my mother as it was she who had suffered on my account. However, as my father was a smoker, the pennies were more useful to him.

The Porpoises

Pretty soon the bottoms of my grey trousers were torn, and my shirt was coming out through it. My mother said that she'd have to put a patch on it before she went to sleep, and she did too. The next morning she had my trousers ready for me, all mended and ready to go. She warned me to take care of them and not to tear them again too soon or I'd get a lash of the rod.

It was a very fine day by the time I'd had a hen's egg, plus a cup of milk and something else — potatoes, probably. I didn't eat a thing without the hag next door knowing all about it. But her chatter was changing when she saw that I was becoming sturdier and more hearty.

"Oh, feed him up well, luv!" says she. "He'll grow into a fine man yet."

She wasn't right about that, either, for no one ever saw any resemblance whatsoever in me to any of the great Celtic heroes. She used to be purring selfishly like a cat, hoping to get some of the catch my father brought home with him. Her husband wasn't skilled in such matters. He was a clumsy individual, whether out in the hills or working in the fields. At any rate, the old hag was forever making off with a sizable morsel of one thing or another from our home.

I was full of energy at that time, almost leaping out of my body I was. With my grey trousers pulled right up, and my belly full, I was very proud of myself indeed. If anyone had anything to worry about at that time, it certainly wasn't me.

At noon I was let down to the White Strand with Mary along with me. On my way to the strand I ran as fast as I could. When Mary looked out to sea, she saw a school of porpoises coming round the Gob at the south end of the Island. They didn't stop until they came in front of us out onto the open beach. There were big dorsal fins sticking up on them, and they were as close together as a shoal of fish. Mary had often seen them before, one at a time, but never in such a large school. She figured that they would come right up onto the strand and she got frightened. She put me up on her back and carried me home.

When we arrived, mother announced that there were boats coming and that some of them were circling the porpoises, trying to force them ashore. There were three large seiners on the Island at that time, and seven in Dunquin. Every one of those boats was there to get porpoises. The Island boats were trying to drive the porpoises ashore, while the Dunquin people jeered at them, but not one of them tried to help. In the end, a porpoise landed up on the shore, high and dry. One man, with his wits about him, drew its blood; and when the rest of the porpoises got the scent of the blood, off they went towards it, until they too were all beached.

When the Dunquin boats saw the rich pickings on the beach, and people killing them, in they went to fill up their boats and to get their share of the spoils, but the Islanders wouldn't let them get a single one. It wasn't too long before everyone was covered in blood, as were the porpoises, which the Islanders were driving out along the shore, cut and injured. There was one Dunquin boat that didn't interfere or try to get to the porpoises. The Island people gave the crew of that boat the best porpoise on the strand; the other six boats had to go home without as much as a taste of them, and indeed, for some of them, even getting home was difficult enough.

It was a huge job bringing them home and salting them. But no one shirked from the work, since in those days it'd be difficult to exchange a porpoise for a pig. My father's face was red with his own blood and with that of the porpoises. But I still recognised him as I was a bright lad for my age.

I used to make fun of the old hag when she'd come with a big creel of chopped-up porpoises on her back; you'd think that she herself had come out of one of the porpoises in the creel, she was so covered in blood. But she earned a certain amount of respect that day, for she'd almost killed the captain of a Dunquin boat with a blow of her shovel.

Page 9 There was no shortage of meat for a long time after that, and it would have lasted two years if it hadn't been taken from them by relatives all over the mainland. I'll never forget that day, even if I live to be two hundred: every person could be seen red with blood instead of white or sallow. Another thing, I'm afraid I might very well have been killed by a porpoise or a bonham on the beach, and Mary too, if we had been caught up in that little war with the porpoises. At the end of the day the old hag ate her food at our place.

While I was very small I used to hear talk about the Wheat Ship. This was another example of stuff that used to come in after storms at sea and which used to benefit us even though other people had suffered extreme misfortune.

I don't remember the year this particular vessel foundered at the White Strand, because at the time I hadn't been born or even been expected. But I've heard about what happened and about the number of people that she saved from death during the Great Famine. I'm fully aware of how she was lost with her entire crew. She was wrecked on the beach, and it wasn't possible to save even one of them. I got the story from the woman next door and my mother, because they were often talking together.

There wasn't a shred of a sail on this ship, only one tattered piece of material on the forward mast. The captain tried to bring her in to the White Strand though she'd foundered far out, being heavily loaded. The men on board put a chunk of wood on the end of a rope, but they weren't able to come ashore. People said they'd never seen a stormier day, with the wind blowing right along the whole beach. When all is said and done, part of the ship ended up somewhere on the beach. The men on land and those out on the boat pulled on the rope but, alas, the rope broke, and *Page 10* away went the men through the storm to the south. The Islanders haven't been the same for having witnessed that sight.

The ship broke up a while after that, but even though the men themselves were lost, thousands lived as a result during the worst year of the Famine. The Islanders saved thousands of bags of wheat, which kept them going for a long time. There wouldn't be anyone alive on the Island today if it hadn't been for the ship, and of course the old hag had to say that it was God who had sent it to the poor.

Eileen was only a week old when the ship was wrecked; she's still living in the New World. In that country people of her age have already had a pension for three years. That means that she is now seventy-three years old. My mother was on the beach, even though it was only six days after she had given birth. Patrick, my brother, was tough enough to be there but he did more harm than good because he had to be watched all the time. A lot of stuff was coming in to shore but much of it was driven out to sea by the offshore winds.

As well as that, as soon as the ship broke apart, the wheat poured out of her. I believe that all kinds of bags had been thrown out of her, although it was mostly coal or salt that was being picked up when the tide came in. It took a long time for some of it to come out of the ship — affording the Islanders an opportunity to retrieve it — or that's what people said. They had to wash it in fresh water to get the brine out of it, after which it had to be put out in the sun and then brought in close to the fire. Nobody knows how much was given away to relatives. The wheat was boiled until it softened into a thick porridge. People used to call it flummery.[6] Anything else that they came across helped them to survive.

Page 11 I often used to hear the old hag saying to my mother that out of her whole life this was by far the best part of it. She had a double set of teeth and two jaws to do the grinding. It was said that she chewed the cud like a cow.

At that time I was wearing the grey breeches and going off by myself. I used to go out to meet the boats every afternoon. Pilchards were the commonest fish at that time, and they were full of bones. They're very like herrings. The fishermen had no good word to say for them; they were small fish, and you'd need a lot of them to make up a pound weight. What's more, they used to rot the nets. My father called me into the boat one afternoon while the fish were being thrown out, and put me in the stern. I was peering out, and pretty soon I saw a fishing-line and a bit of

---

[6] Cf. Welsh *llymru*

a pilchard on its hook. What do you think but I threw out the bait! My father saw me doing it, but he paid no heed to it because he thought that any fish so near land wouldn't take the bait.

It wasn't long before a fish took it, and the line became twisted round my foot. The fish lifted me out into the sea. Everyone on the jetty screamed at my father, but by the time he turned round he saw the pet swimming by himself. He put the boat-hook into my grey breeches, above my backside, and pulled me in to the stern of the boat. Then he pulled the fishing-line and took care to bring the fish in — a huge, vigorous conger eel, six feet long. My greatest fear was that my mother would kill me on account of my breeches being wet. The young women were in fits of laughter at me, but I didn't have the savvy at that time to have any feelings of pride about myself. They were big, strongly-built women, out up to their bellies emptying the boats — as strong and sturdy as any girls in Ireland.

On our way home, holding Nora's hand until we reached the house, I started to sulk, and I said to Nora that I wouldn't go any further because my mother would kill me. Another woman was trying to convince me that she wouldn't. As luck would have it, who should come upon us but my father, carrying a creel of fish.

Page 12

"What's up with you, Nora? He's cold and wet. Shouldn't you bring him home?"

"He won't go with me," said she. "He's afraid of Mam."

"Oh, come along with you, Tomás, my boy. It's my fault you're wet, because it was I who brought you along," said my father.

He grabbed hold of my hand, and I set off walking with him. When I went in, I wasn't up to my usual tricks. My mother saw straightaway that there was something the matter with me. She put me sitting beside the fire, because she thought there was something else wrong with me. But soon the whole fire-slab was wet and soaked by me. My father came in.

"Have you taken his clothes off him yet? He's soaking wet," said he.

He was dragging the conger eel behind him. He brought it in and it was as long as the hearth.

"Don't tell me that he fell into the sea?"

"Don't you see the fine big fish he caught? And as it's the first fish he ever caught, didn't he do well!" said my father.

Then he told her the whole story, and that got me off. Everything I had on me was taken off, and dry clothes were put on me. I didn't like the pair of breeches that I got, because it was one I'd already discarded, with patches on it. She didn't give me tea, but a mug of porridge and milk after my dip in the deep.

TWO

The school; The schoolmistress and the apple; The future King beside me; My mother back from Dingle; Alex's boat; Mary's marriage; The schoolmistress married; Good Friday and Woman's Island

The School

There came a very fine day; it was a Sunday. For some reason a large boat came in from Dunquin; nothing was known about currachs at that time, though we were soon familiar with them. When the boat reached the jetty the people waiting there said there was a lady in it; who was she but the schoolmistress. When I heard that news, it didn't please me one little bit, for that was just when I was beginning to go out with a stick, foraging for myself from strand to hill. There was no one watching over me because they thought I was a big hunk of a fellow, carrying my little rod with a hook tied to its end. Each of us boys used to take twenty rocklings out of holes — not much of a catch, but the rocklings were just the thing for our pet seagulls.

Well, one Monday, after breakfast, the lad in the grey trousers wasn't to be found. The girls were ready for school but the wee guy was nowhere. Mary was sent out looking for me, and she told my mother that I was looking for rocklings with two other boys, Seán Mairead and Mick Peg.

"Let him off today, but God help me tomorrow if he slips out without me knowing!" says my mother.

I got to my young seagull and gave her my rocklings.

When I came home I wasn't as bumptious as I was on other days. I realised that my mother had something in store for me. What's more, the little old woman from next door was already in there so that she could see the beating I'd get, for I used to be slagging her off fiercely at that time. But my mother was too clever for her.

When the girls came home from school, my mother asked them about what sort of woman the teacher was, was she easy-going or bad-tempered. Everyone said that she was a fine decent woman, and that she didn't slap or beat them. That was when my mother asked me what I had to say.

"Look at this brat, gadding about all day from morning, in danger of going head-first into some hole, collecting fish for his gull. But let him know that he'd better be ready in the morning to go along with you, God willing," says she.

"Perhaps," says Kate, "since you didn't scare him, he'll pull a fast one on you in the morning." She was a precocious sister, the one I liked the least.

"Oh, he'll be a good boy tomorrow, Kate. The first steps are always the hardest," says my mother.

We were all lovey-dovey with each other until it was time to go to bed. My sisters were talking about the school, and telling my mother the schoolmistress's name, which they couldn't pronounce properly. The whole evening was spent with each of them doing their best to say it, until they started bickering with one another. Then I had as much fun out of them as they had with me earlier that evening. In the end Mary, the eldest, got the name — Nancy O'Donoghue. It was a difficult name for them, as nothing like it had ever been heard on the Island. Finally, everyone went off to get ready for bed.

The next morning everyone was all set for what they had to do. The food was ready fairly early, for the tide waits for no man. Patrick was pretty savvy at this time; he was the second eldest of the brood, Mary being the oldest. My father was going around the house collecting ropes and a sickle, for himself and for Patrick. Mary and my mother were going along with them. It was a spring-tide day, and the season to cut black seaweed for fertiliser. Kate was to look after the house while Eileen, Nora and I went off to school. That was how we were organised that day.

For breakfast we had boiled potatoes and fish, and a drop of milk with them. All of us, old and young, gobbled down our fill. We had no tea in those days, so no one in the Island at that time, or for a long time afterwards, had ever seen a kettle.

When the horn blew, off went the school-children and those working on the strand, while precocious Kate remained at home. "Be well-behaved at school, Tomás, me boy," said my mother to me, and before she went to the beach she wiped the snot from my nose with a cloth. As I set off for school that day, around the year 1866, my mother told me I was ten years old.

On our way to the schoolhouse I was spirited and bold, hand in hand with Nora. Poor Nora thought that I would make a show of her but I didn't. The schoolmistress was at the open door and she handed me a lovely apple. When I went in I was amazed that I didn't see anyone else with an apple. But she wasn't going to give us an apple every day, although I thought at the time that she was. This was a hansel apple, given to every pupil on their first day, and this being my first day I was the one to get it.

I didn't pay much attention until I had munched my apple, and that didn't take me long because I had a fine grinding-mill then, something I can't boast about today. Then I took a good look around the room. I saw books and papers here and there in little piles, a blackboard hanging on the wall, with white marks jotted all over it as if done with chalk. I was intrigued as to what they meant until I saw the schoolmistress calling the biggest girls *Page 16* to the blackboard. She had a little stick in her hand and was pointing out the marks to them, and it began to dawn on me that she was speaking some kind of nonsense-talk to them. I prodded Pats Micky who was beside me on the bench — this is the same Pats Micky who has been King over us long since, and he's also now the postman for this district. I asked him what sort of gibberish talk was going on between the schoolmistress and the girls around the blackboard.

"I haven't the faintest idea," says he, "but I reckon it'll never be understood here." I thought that I'd die of hunger at school, but it wasn't long before the schoolmistress spoke the English word "*Playtime*". This word made me stare in surprise, for I didn't know what it meant. The mob inside was jumping up and rushing out the door. Nora had to take my hand before I'd move off the bench. Every one of us made off for our own homes.

A handful of cold, boiled potatoes was waiting for us. They were placed near the fire. We had fish with them, yellow scad, a fine sweet fish. My mother had broiled limpets, which had come from the strand while we were at school. She had roasted the limpets on the fire, and threw them to us one by one, like a hen with her chickens.

The three of us didn't talk much while we ate, but went on munching until we were full. Then my mother began to ask me about school; she'd been afraid to ask me while I was munching in case I'd choke while trying to answer her.

"Well, Tomás, me boy, isn't it great to be at school," said she. "How did you like the lady?"

"Mary, Mother of God! the grand hearty apple she gave him," said Nora. I wasn't a bit pleased with Nora that she didn't let me answer.

Page 17
"Did you get an apple, Tomás?"

"I did, Mam, but Nora took a chunk out of it, and Eileen another chunk."

"But the apple was very big; there was plenty left of it after we'd taken a bite," says Eileen.

"Off you go, my dears," says Mam to us.

We spent some more time at school; the King used to be beside me on the bench, and he was a fine placid hunk of a chap, and has been ever since. We were the same age. He often pointed his finger at another boy who was being bold, someone screeching, another pair punching each other, a big yellow snot running down from the nose of other hunks here and there. The King didn't like these sights and he was always pointing them out to me. Look at the nature that is innate in a person from early youth and which always remains with him. It was the same with the King, who didn't like to see ugly, dirty sights in school when he was young, sights that others didn't notice at all. It was no wonder, therefore, that when the authorities came round wanting to name a King for the Blasket they concluded that he would be the best person to bear the title.

For me the day passed quickly, and I thought it was a bit early when the schoolmistress said "*Home now*". Some of them got stuck in the door hurrying to get out to the road. At home, there was a chunk of bread for us and a drop of milk with it. There always used to be plenty of cooked fish but we often had an aversion to it. This was because Patrick often had as big a catch as my father and we had abundance and plenty in the cottage, a wonderful fire, and enough delicacies of every possible kind. Then we went off to the White Strand for the rest of the day.

The next day the school had our full attention because the spring-tide for spreading seaweed was over. I saw that my mother had some new clothes for me and that pleased me. She ran over to me and took me by the hand, shook my clothes and gave me a kiss.

"Be a good boy now," she said, "until I come home. I'll bring you sweets from Dingle. Do what Mary and Kate tell you and go to bed when they go." I began to cry but I soon stopped. *Page 18*

I set off for school with Nora and Eileen. Mary and Kate stayed in charge of the house while my mother was away. When we went in, the whole mob was already there, although my pal hadn't come yet; he was the one I liked best. Little books were being given out that day. There was a blackboard with strange things being written on it, and others being rubbed out. There were large gadgets hanging here and there on the wall — I was keenly observing every one of them.

When I'd finished examining all these things, in burst the King, and that pleased me greatly. His own place beside me was waiting for him, and he made straight for it. I saw the way he was elbowing his way along, so that he could sit beside me. And so I gathered that he liked me as much as I him.

"I'm late," he whispers to me.

"Most of them have only just come in," says I to him.

He was so vigorous and healthy-looking that you'd think he was three years older than me, but actually it was only nine months. The schoolmistress summoned us to the blackboard and six times she pointed out the letters that were on it.

That day was Friday, and when we were about to go home, she told us not to come until Monday. Most of them were happy to hear this, but it didn't thrill me one little bit; I preferred to come to school. I don't think it was because of my love of learning but rather that I liked being with my pal the King.

My mother wasn't supposed to come back from Dingle until Sunday, and Mary and Kate thought that I wouldn't go to bed with them under any circumstance. So they started coaxing me and sweet-talking me before bedtime. I fell asleep on my father's knee and he told them to take me to bed with them, and they did that immediately.

It was already noon when the cock woke me. As I hadn't cost them a night's sleep, everyone was enquiring about me and I was getting attention from all of them. Needless to say, I wasn't as big an eejit as they thought.

Page 19

I had my teeth now and was able to chew everything, and I was so big that no one believed I was the age I actually was. A good indication of that was when the old hag across the way stopped teasing me. She dropped calling me 'the pet' and 'the old cow's calf' and things like that, which she had been saying about me to my mother up to then, although you'd have sworn that the cow that had given birth to the old hag couldn't have been less than fifty herself.

My Mother Back from Dingle

On Sunday my mother came home from the town. She had a white bag and a coarse bag. They were full of things but there wasn't a bit of tea or sugar, nor indeed was anything known about them at that time. I myself carried the white bag home with me and it wasn't too heavy for me, since most of the things in it were glad-rags for the girls. The grey hag was ahead of me in the house so that she might hear everything about Dingle from the woman who'd been there.

The first thing my mother took out was a cap with two peaks on it, which she thrust on my head. "Mary, Mother of God!" said my father, "you've made a real policeman out of him!" and everyone in the house burst out laughing.

"Perhaps he'll have a job yet," says she. "He's young and has time to learn; let him stay at school until he learns all there is to be learnt there." I still remember those words well, because, in time, the necessities of life changed all that.

There were apples, sweets and cakes, loaves, tobacco for my father, and a pair of shoes for Patrick, white clothes for the daughters and a lot more as well. The grey woman got a little of everything because she was an ugly wretch who was greedy to boot.

Every day we went off to school, while Patrick, who was big and strong, was out hunting with my father. Mary didn't spend much time at school, for she was a woman by now. There were four of us doing well, and teaching each other.

Alex's Boat   *Page 20*

One day, after we were let out from school at noon, we saw all the people of the district above the jetty. The schoolmistress and all of us were wondering what was going on. One of the boys was looking intently towards Slea Head.

"Mary, Mother of God! look at the boats in the middle of the squall — and what a sea," says he. The boats were given up for lost, and it was feared that no one would ever see those who were in them again.

There was an Island boat tied to the wreck, which it was towing. The sea was going right up over them. The tide was with them, which helped them considerably in finally reaching the jetty.

It was the wreck of a large, strong boat; the captain was in it and two other men, and a boy of about sixteen years, who was only barely alive. He was taken out of the boat and laid on dry land, but he soon died. He was buried at Castle Point — that's where Pierce Ferriter's castle was when he was in authority.

Even with everyone doing their utmost, they couldn't save the wrecked boat, and the ocean took it away again. My father was captain of the boat that found the wreck. The wreck's captain was a man by the name of Alex. He was a big, hearty man. The name Alex is still known in the Blaskets, and will be for some time to come, because many of the Island people alive today were born at the time of the wreck. They got great compensation for saving the crew, and some who gave them hospitality were paid equally well. My father got himself a saw out of it and it's only recently that we've lost it.

Mary's Marriage

My sister Mary was a strapping, capable woman at that time, and as there were three others at home, they decided to send her to some other house. The most important personage on the Island at that time was Paddy Martin. He had had ten milking cows for a long time. However, I never saw him with all ten, because he had two married sons living on the mainland, and undoubtedly he'd had to give them some land and a few cows, which left him with only five. However, his youngest son, Martin Junior, still unmarried, was living with him on the Island.

Page 21

A marriage was arranged between Mary and Martin Junior, because what his parents wanted was a capable woman who knew what would be expected of her and would be able to do it. And that was what Mary was without a word of a lie — and I don't say that just because she was my sister. My father wasn't asked for any money, for they knew that he had none. All the same, even though life wasn't too easy, my parents looked after us well.

Martin, his father and his mother were living in the house at that time — there were four of them after Mary got married. Martin only lived another year, and my sister Mary had to return home to her own family. That was because Martin's brother came to live with the old couple, who didn't want to give anything to Martin's wife, even though she was left with a boy. Mary left the child with us, and set off for America. She spent three years over there, and when she returned she sued Martin's family, and got the father's inheritance for her son.

Soon after that the schoolmistress was called home at Shrovetide to be married. This left the school closed for a while until a tall, thin master, Robert Smith, arrived. He wasn't popular with the mob of pupils seated in front of him, and he certainly didn't please my pal the King. He had a wild appearance, and the King used to whisper to me that he came from Russia. He had a big, sulky mug, bulging eyes, a sallow sleekness and buck-teeth. A bush grew out of his nose, like a goat's beard. The bush wasn't the worst part of him, for it was fair, and it covered his less attractive features.

The Schoolmistress Married

The schoolmistress was married in a village in the Parish of Ballyferriter. Her husband was a blacksmith, and I suppose the parish priest had a soft spot for him because his new wife got a job *Page 22* in a school in that area and spent her life there until she retired on her school- and old-age pensions. Her husband, the blacksmith, as well as getting his old-age pension, also had money coming in from his trade — so they had enough money. Both of them lived into their eighties but are dead now these past few years. And that was the end of the first school-teacher who came to the Great Blasket.

It wasn't long before the boys started whistling, and the girls began laughing at Robert — and, my goodness, what plump and hearty kids they were in our school at that time. Robert realised that he wouldn't be able to do his job with kids like these and only stayed three months before he ran off.

Good Friday

While I was picking at my food one morning, I was also looking this way and that. My mother came through the door carrying an iron spike — a portion of a boat's gripe. She didn't sit down, but started looking for something else. While searching, she came across a bag. I was watching her as a cat watches a mouse, because I realised that she was planning to go to the strand.

"Well," says she, "since it's a fine day would any of you like to go down to the strand?" As is the custom around here, everyone goes down to the strand on Good Friday to get whatever sea-food goodies they can find.

"Mary, Mother of God! I'd love to go with you, Mam," says I, jumping up from the table, although I was still in the middle of eating.

"Sure, there's no reason why not, but eat your fill first, my darling. I'll wait for you," says she.

"I'm coming along too," says Eileen.

"There's nothing stopping you either. But isn't it just as well that the school is closed today," says my mother.

My father and Paddy were digging in the field, Kate was looking after the house, Mary was away, over in the States, and at that time her son was being looked after by Kate.

Page 23 Kate had been instructed by my mother to take good care of Mary's child until Mary returned home.

We rushed out the door and set off towards the strand. If anyone was in good form it was surely me. I was really keen to be paddling in the sea in my grey trousers.

When we reached the strand there wasn't a rock that hadn't a woman, a child or a youngster gathering limpets, shellfish, winkles or some such thing. There was a great ebbing spring tide at that time. To the east was an island which was called Woman's Island. This island was impossible to reach unless the tide was far out. So there used to be limpets and all sorts of good things to be found there, because normally it was so inaccessible to gatherers.

There was a small deep inlet between Woman's Island and the shore, but there wasn't much water in it. I watched my mother gathering her dress together and pulling it between her legs. I was never ashamed of my mother's legs and calves when they were laid bare and seen by other people because she wasn't a fat woman, or a lump, but tall and white-skinned from the crown of her head to her heels. I regret that I didn't take after my mother, but what else would you expect, being the calf of an old cow. The other children in our family were all good-looking.

I kept a close watch on her, looking to see what she was up to. She soon called to the women who were near her to go across to the island. Four answered quickly — the hag from across the way, one of my father's sisters who was married to a man called Kerry, White Joan and Ventry. The water went above their knees, but a big wave surged up over the old hag and my aunt, upending them both. Ventry was up to the challenge; she hooked my aunt and pulled them both up. Anyone would have sworn the old hag and my aunt came out of the same belly — they had the exact same appearance, the same height and indeed, the same demeanour — but the two of them did have the same father.

I myself was snivelling pitifully because I had lost sight of my mother for such a long time. As a matter of fact, Nora was spurring me on but Eileen was trying to get me to stop. Nora was always on my back, and both of us were very ill-humoured with each other.

I understood the reason why this was so when I was a bit older *Page 24* and had more understanding. The old hag often told me that she preferred it when we were up to mischief than when we were supposedly getting along together. Nora was the family pet for five years before I arrived on the scene. I hadn't been expected when I suddenly appeared. When the family saw me, Nora was no longer the pet, and that's the reason she didn't have as much time for me as the others did.

Fairly soon, one woman after another was screaming that the creek had filled with water all around the women on the island and that there wasn't one of them to be seen. Off went everyone to look at the creek, but by then the water was over six feet high and all of the women were carrying full bags. They had to remain where they were and everyone agreed that the women might well be stranded there till morning. I was out of my mind when I heard this.

Off went some of the girls who were on the strand to tell the people in the fields that there were a lot of women stuck on

Woman's Island. The men set off for the strand, all except my father who went straight to the house, looking for a ladder, having heard that something similar had been used to rescue women on a previous occasion. I soon saw him making his way towards me with a twenty-foot ladder on his shoulder. They tried laying it across the creek, but it was too heavy to put it in the right place.

My poor father had to go swimming so that he could grab hold of the top of the ladder and put it in a crevice in the rock. My mother was the first woman to go across on the ladder, and then Ventry; they came over without any difficulty and three others followed them. Two of them were on one side of the ladder and one on the other side. Because it wasn't level, the ladder turned over and down they fell into the sea. I myself was in high spirits when I had my mother back and I was singing a cheery song. But I soon stopped because my father had to go off swimming to bring his sister across to dry land. While he was hooking on to White Joan, he saw that the old hag from next door *Page 25* was going down, so he had to grab her by the hair. I was at my wit's end by the time my father finally got safely back. It was a close shave that the hag didn't pull him under while trying to save herself, just because she had to hold on to her apron-load of limpets!

THREE

*The hag, Bald Tomás and their family; Playing
hurley on the White Strand; The new schoolmistress;
The crab grabs my fingers; I start courting*

etween our house and the one opposite there was a yard, and each of the houses had a single door. The neighbours had the lower part of the yard and we had the upper part. The two doors faced each other. If the old hag had wanted to, she could, without leaving her own door, have scalded my mother with hot water and my mother could have done the same to her. My mother often told me to keep clear of the old hag, because she was a nasty piece of work and because my mother forever had to buy her off in order to keep the peace. And this was certainly true.

My mother used to do everything for the old hag because the hag herself was careless and untidy. Her husband, indeed, was no better. My father had to fix everything for him: his spade, his harness, the roof on his house and all sorts of other things. I never saw a more inept human being.

People used to call him Bald Tomás because he didn't have as much as a strand of hair between his two ears. All the same, he was very bright, and if he'd had a good education he could have easily become the Brain of Ireland. My mother often used to send me over to ask him when this or that holy day was coming up. If they were eating, the pair of them would stand between me and

Page 27

the door and insist that I had a bite to eat with them. There was never a poor cottage that was as hospitable as theirs. Of course, all those who were around in my early lifetime are now with the host of the dead. However, I'm still alive. May God give them a better place than a poor cottage, and indeed, a better place for all of us! Not one of them ever hit any of us.

Page 28

Bald Tomás and the old hag had a son and a daughter. I don't know whether they ever had any other children. The daughter was a small, scruffy person, like her mother, and the son was an insignificant, soulless idler, and, like his father, all fingers and thumbs. He couldn't even handle going out to sea. No sooner would he be in a boat than he'd get sick. That meant that he never did any fishing. The son often worked as a servant boy. Our Paddy was a year older than he was and both of them reached their eighties. As Paddy himself might tell you, the father is dead for three months now, but Paddy the son is still alive and kicking.

There wasn't anyone, young or old, either on the Island or in the parishes on the mainland, that Bald Tom didn't know his age to the day, the year and the hour he was born. Folk used to say that there wasn't such a knowledgeable person in the whole district, even though he was unable to read or write in any language. He often used to tell me that the Christmas loaves were brought forth at the time when I myself was born — that is, on St Thomas's Day, three days before Christmas — when my mother found me on the White Strand.

"Anyway, how old is Tomás now?" the old hag used to ask him.

Bald Tom never failed to give the right answer: "Fourteen years next Christmas," he'd say.

From then on the old hag used to be very chatty with me, since my own house had now appointed me as an errand-boy between the two houses. I took a lot more out of my own house than I used to ever bring back to it. Well, I'm not boasting about this, and perhaps I would have got more from the old hag if she had had it to give.

On Sundays, after a meal of potatoes and bread, every lass and lad would set off for the White Strand, everyone carrying a ball and a hurley-stick. Wanting to find out what was going on, I got myself ready. I put on my clothes — new clean, grey breeches made of undyed sheep's wool, and my policeman's hat with two peaks on it. Then I lowered my head into a basin of water and scrubbed my face clean. It wasn't my mother who was cleaning me at that time, for by then, my boy, I was a tall, lean young fella. Off I went down to the Strand with my hurley-stick — a furze handle that had a crooked shank on it. Nora and Eileen were with me, and we didn't stop running until we came into the middle of where the commotion was taking place. None of them had a shoe or a stocking on their feet. No day was as tough for the young ones as was the day of the Sunday match.

Page 29

Someone saw a boat coming from Dunquin under full sail, and when she made for the jetty every one of us left the strand and went to meet it. There was a woman in its stern, the new schoolmistress, sister of the first one — Kate O'Donoghue. She was a fine, handsome young woman. The priest hadn't managed to find a master. The young mistress wasn't all that keen, although the job wasn't hard to do at that time.

There was no escaping school on Monday, so off we all went, each to his own place, and upon my word, the King sat down right next to me. I was ten years of age when I went to school for the first time, in 1866, so by this time, 1870, I was fourteen. The schoolmistress was giving out small new books. She was busy at the blackboard, erasing and revising everything that had been written on it. Her eyes were wide-open with surprise, and hardly had she written a problem on it before someone had solved it, and so she had to make it harder.

The young people of the Island were very keen on this new work, and from that time on they were hungry to learn. Some of us were passionate about anything to do with the sea or the ocean. We were imbued with the sound of the wind that blew in from the seashore, beating in our ears every morning, clearing our brains and rinsing the dust from our skulls.

The King-to-be sat beside me every day, and the hammers of an iron mill couldn't have separated him from me, even if his attention wasn't on me. He never had any time to help me in class because he'd be constantly looking around the place, pointing out some girl with a dirty nose, or another girl sitting opposite with a smudge on her cheek.

Page 30

He'd point at boys whose appearance he didn't like or he'd whisper to me: "Look at that one over there. Isn't she ugly — she has a nose like a cup!"

That was the only fault I could find in him. He'd be frequently leading me astray at a time when I was just getting into my stride with the work. We were doing well and enjoyed school, but all the same we were always happy when Saturday was approaching so that we'd be free to get off on our own, and go capering about by ourselves, doing whatever we wanted.

I clearly remember one Saturday after St Patrick's Day. It was a fine uneventful year, and fish were scarce in the district. Suddenly my father burst in through the door, having come from the field even though it wasn't time for a meal.

"What brought you home?" asked my mother.

"It's a beautiful calm day," says he. "If I found a crab or two perhaps I might also catch a few rock-fish into the bargain," and he stomped out again. Well, before you know it, out I went after him and when he saw me coming he hollered: "Where do you think you're going?"

"I'm going with you. I'll look after any crabs you find."

Well, he set off from the jetty, out to a nearby island, and began diving and swimming under water. He retrieved two crabs from a single crevice and brought them back up to where I was standing. He handed them over to me to look after, a male crab and a female one. The male is called a *Collach* in Irish. I'd only just got hold of it when it spread his claws apart and then seized my thumb and index-finger. No matter what I did, I couldn't budge it. In my terror I started screaming for all I was worth. My father rushed over to me. He knew immediately what had happened and why I was crying. The claw of the male crab was clutching my fingers so tightly that my father had to tear the claw away from the crab. After that he was only able to loosen the claw by breaking it with a stone.

Well, my two fingers were damaged beyond use, and to make matters worse, it was the fingers of my right hand. My blood was all over the ground, and my fingers turned as black as coal. My *Page 31* father was pleased that I hadn't fainted, although I came very close to it. He twisted the lining from inside his hat and bound my fingers with it. He thought that my mother would be very cross with him for letting me go along with him, but she wasn't. It upset my sisters a lot when they saw the state I was in. My mother quickly put my hand in lukewarm water and washed it carefully. That helped a lot. She cleaned all the poison out of the wound and put a plaster on it. After that I was as happy as Larry again.

The grey woman came over, asking how I was. Even though she was a whining old gossip, she didn't want to see me lose my fingers. I am not able to speak about my life without mentioning the old hag because there was never a day in my early years that I didn't catch sight of her, one way or another. In fairness to her, she never hit any of us, but, like everyone else, I suppose, she had her own little failings, and maybe she had a good reason for complaining about us at times. May God bless her and all of us!

Anyway, my father had four crabs. He stuffed them in a bag and made off up the hill. He went some way up, looking for the most likely places. He was out for a good part of the day, but he didn't come home empty-handed.

In fact, he had a bag full of big, speckled scad, and when my mother took them out there was a whole heap of them on the table. She chose one of the bigger ones from the heap and handed it to me:

"Here, Tomás, my boy, take this over to the old hag."

I didn't argue with her, even though it wasn't a job I fancied doing at the time. However, I reflected that the old hag often visited my mother with a gift for her, however good or bad it might have been.

Off I went with the scad, which I presented to the old hag. Her eyes opened wide, wondering where I had got it. She had no idea as yet that my father had caught anything. The old hag and I were on friendly terms at this particular time, although at other times

Page 32 we were not. She started to be so friendly with me that you'd think I'd become a little god. Bald Tomás, the man of the house, was at home, as were both the daughter and son — in fact all of them were there. They had just finished their meal. That meal used to be called the evening meal, and the meal in the morning was the morning meal, for at that time there used to be only two meals per day.

"Have you anything to give him?" says Bald Tomás.

"Only things he already has," says she. "But I'll give him our daughter when he's a couple of years older."

Although she couldn't give me anything more precious to her than what had come from her own body, the fact is that I knew, even then, that that offer would do me more harm than good. The thought of speckled scad, the hag's chat and the pledge of the daughter depressed me greatly. Not surprising, considering what could actually happen in only another couple of years time.

The first inconvenience after overtures such as these was that I suddenly had to start courting, something that put the brakes on all the other activities that I really enjoyed doing. My job in the morning, and after school, was delivering messages, and I used to get this over quickly enough before I started on the courting lark. It went on like this, with other tasks as well, until I understood what was actually going on. I wasn't much more than fifteen years old at this time, and you might well say that it was a bit too early for anyone as young as me to be on the pull, but sure the old proverb gives the lie to whatever we might say or think.

Take a look at this verse:

On the Sunday, on the Sunday, it was bright and summery,
The daughter and the mother are discussing men, but she,
The gentle little darling said, 'oh mother let me be,
For I'll have to marry very soon or leap across the sea.'

Page 33 Then the mother says to her —

'Listen, ugly hussy, don't you moan or lose your head.'
'You haven't listened, mother; since I came of age to wed,
I am thirteen years or fourteen if the truth were only said,
And I'll have to marry very soon or take the boat instead.'

The mother had to find a lad for her without delay.

The new schoolmistress spent three or more years with us until the same thing happened to her as happened to her sister, that is, she got a proposal of marriage. Her family came from the district of Dingle. Their father was a stonemason, the best in the district at that time. She married a boy from the town, a nice man and well-mannered to boot.

One of those days when we were in school a boat came from Dunquin. There'd always be someone looking out for every boat that came in because there were bad people going around in groups at that time — drivers and bailiffs who tried to take whatever they could from you and then leave you to die from hunger. However, every one of that wicked lot died in the poorhouse soon after that — with nobody too distressed about their fate.

Well, my story isn't about that, because the one in the boat was actually a school inspector. When we heard that, we were uneasy. A lad positioned at the door kept a constant watch to see when the inspector would come into sight. A fine strapping girl saw him first; she sprang from the door with terror in her eyes. It wasn't long before he came striding into the building. A person here and a person there held their hands over their mouths. One of the biggest girls started laughing, and soon another joined in. The inspector had his head in the air looking at the wall, or up into the rafters and then at the pupils.

"Mary, Mother of God!" whispers the King to me, "he has four eyes."

"Yes, and they're lit up," says I.

"I never saw anyone like him before," says he.

Whenever he turned his head there'd be a gleam in his eyes. *Page 34* Finally, all the big ones in there burst out laughing, while the little ones were screeching with fear. The teacher nearly dropped with shame, and the inspector flew into a rage.

"There'll be murder today," says the King in a very low voice, "since I don't imagine anyone has ever seen a person with four eyes in his head before." This was the first person we young ones had ever seen wearing spectacles.

The inspector gave the schoolmistress a good tongue-lashing — and a shouting match ensued that none of us could understand — and with that he seized his travel-bag and stormed out the door, got on board the boat that was waiting for him, and was never seen on the Blaskets ever again. This madman left the school in the same way he came in, without asking anyone a question. And, I bet you, dear reader, that you've never read anything like that before, nor will ever again, as long as you live.

The poor schoolmistress had a fainting fit after he left. I had to look for a cup of pure water for her. Eileen sent me off to the nearest house. We were able to talk while the teacher had fainted.

"While she's out of it we'd better run off home," said the King, "for she'll surely kill us when she comes to."

"Yerra, you're not much of a soldier if you're frightened as easily as that. Take it easy; she'll treat us fairly," says I to him.

After about half an hour she came to. We all thought that she would beat us as long as our skin remained warm. But it often happens that things don't turn out as you might imagine and that's what happened in this case. She didn't beat us or even speak harshly to anyone. It wouldn't have been difficult for her to

Page 35 discipline one or two children who were misbehaving but she couldn't punish us all. From then on she used her common sense when dealing with us, something she wouldn't have been able to do unless she had the wisdom she had. The schoolmistress let us go home immediately, and she herself also left, as she needed to get home like everyone else.

The King was as interested in the four-eyed person as anybody else in the school, although he never said that the inspector must have come from the bowels of Hell, as the others said.

A few months after that another inspector arrived. He was a weedy little man, gaunt and sallow, but he had only two eyes. He got down to work immediately and questioned everyone sharply and thoroughly. I was in the King's class — there were eight of us altogether in it — and I suppose the inspector thought that he was a father-figure to us because he was so much taller than anybody else and because of his air of authority, which contrasted with our cringing before him. Although the King had a fine, elegant head, and the inspector thought that from it he would get the right answer to every question, it didn't turn out like that, because the little ones proved themselves to be his equal. The inspector was pleased when he was leaving. He gave a shilling to the best person in each class, and when the shilling was awarded to our class, it wasn't the King, but myself, who won it. My father was very grateful to me when I handed it over to him. He got a fine bit of tobacco thanks to the inspector — although if I had not performed so well in class, he would never have got it.

FOUR

*My first trip on the sea; Every strange thing I saw
on my journey; From house to house in Dingle;
The new shoes; After my return from Dingle:
'Who's this strange young fellow?!'*

After that we had holidays for a while. It was a fine uneventful year, and the big boats brought in a lot of fish. One day the three boats were full to the gunwales. As our house had a double share, our cottage was a sight to behold. I believe that was the first day I was no longer considered to be the family pet, because I, like the rest of them, was badly bruised from the heavy bag of fish I was carrying to the house. That day every man got a thousand fish — that meant two thousand for us. My father said that I brought home more than two thousand of them altogether. "As a reward, if the weather is fine, I shall take you to Dingle tomorrow with me," says he, "because the boat's going over to the mainland to buy salt." When I heard this I could have jumped for joy; I really thought I was in Heaven.

I wasn't the first person, however, to put his head out the door the following morning. It was Kate; being the biggest and the oldest of us all, she was my mother's house-help at that time. I took her seriously.

"What kind of a day is it, Kate?" says I to her.

"It's a lovely day," says she.

In one single bound I was over at the fireplace beside her.

"Oh Blessed Mary, Mother of God! what got you up so early; why are you so excited?" says she.

My father was the next one to wake up. After he had put on his new clothes he looked out the door and asked Kate to get out my new kit. Until then Kate didn't know what I was getting up to. *Page 38*

My father grabbed a rabbit-skin bag and off we went to the jetty. Everyone came down as soon as they were ready, until the whole boat crew was assembled. They lined up on each side of the boat and with a sudden push they launched it. There were oars and sails in the boat. They turned its stern to the land and its bow to the sea, as is told in the tales of yore.

Two sails were raised. A nice favorable wind took her eastwards through Dingle Bay. There was another young lad like myself in the boat. His name was Dermot; he was the son of one of my uncles. When the boat was east of Slea Head, Dermot turned as white as paper. The men knew what had caused this change in his complexion but I didn't, and I imagined he must be at death's door. His father came looking for him and told him that if he threw up he would feel better.

The boat was going along splendidly because there was more than enough wind that day. Pretty soon someone said that Dermot was vomiting. And he was, too, the poor chap; everything he'd had for breakfast he puked overboard, and a large flock of seagulls was trying to pick it up. I burst my sides laughing at the sight, but poor Dermot was crying.

One of my uncles was steering the boat, and I was asking him about every strange thing I saw. One of these curiosities was a large, slated house in the middle of a farm.

"Who lives in that house?" I ask him.

"Someone who isn't too well," says he. "Bess Rice — did you ever hear of her?"

"Yes, I often heard my father and Bald Tomás talking about her," says I.

When we came near the fine, broad harbour of Ventry we could see a lot of large, white buildings. My uncle told me about each one of them: the Catholic chapel, the Protestant church, the *Page 39* police station, the coastguard buildings, and everything else I was interested in.

My pal was recovering after everything in his belly had been snatched by the seagulls. His voice was squeaky and weak, and he still looked like death. He moved over to me, near the steersman — an uncle of his. "Is Dingle harbour far off?" says he to the captain.

"Upon my word, it's some distance yet, my good lad. You probably won't reach it alive because there's nothing left in your body but your guts; you're not like that other lad," says he.

The words were barely out of his mouth when the men noticed a heavy squall of wind, so they had to lower the stern sail. The bow sail only just stayed up as the sea foamed on all sides.

Pretty soon we reached the mouth of the harbour. It was so narrow that I didn't realise there was a harbour there until we were already halfway through, but after a while the harbour began to broaden out like a lake.

We reached the quay and I took a good look all around. I saw gentry standing on the pier, with chains around their waists. There were poor people with only half-decent clothing on them. There was a crippled person to be seen here and there, and a blind person with a guide. There were three large ships alongside the quay, laden with goods from overseas. There was yellow grain in one of them, wood in another and coal in the third ship.

Before long my father called to me saying that everything was ready and that the men were going up to the town. Off we went, myself and the young lad Dermot, and although there was little in his body after the trip, he preferred looking at the ships than coming in to eat. Everyone from the boat, young and old, made their way to a certain eating-house.

On the table there was bread and tea for us, and I assure you that we didn't talk much until we had stuffed ourselves. After paying the woman of the house, we all went out. The house where *Page 40* they were selling salt was our next port of call. Each man had his bag filled with two hundred-weight[7] of salt. The men left their

---

[7] About 100 kg

bags there until they were ready to return home with them. I followed my father into every house he went to. Dermot never left my side even though his father was right there along with us. The pocket in my grey breeches had plenty of money in it that day.

The Boat Prepared for Sailing

When the boat was ready to sail home, my father searched my pockets. They contained mainly copper coins, and there was quite a heap by the time he'd finished counting them.

"Upon my word, you have almost the price of a pair of shoes. You only need one more shilling," says he.

Who should be there at this very moment but my father's sister. She was often in Dingle, spending her time visiting places here and there.

"Well," says she, "in that case here's another shilling for you; put the shoes on him, since it's the first time he has ever visited Dingle."

When I heard my aunt saying this, my heart jumped for joy, for I knew that my father wouldn't go back on his word. And I was right.

"Come on, so. We'll be able to buy them up the road; it's not far from here," says he.

Off I went with him, all excited. I had no socks, but along with the shoes the woman in the shop gave me a pair, as well as some for my father to bring home. Then there was a great squeaking in my shoes! I felt like a real gentleman, and who would dare say that I wasn't — me in my polished shoes, my suit of grey sheep's wool, and the cap with two peaks on it!

Dermot had been happy until he saw the new shoes I was wearing, but there wasn't a peep out of him after that. His father was an old miser, for there was nothing stopping him from buying shoes for his own lad, but he was just too damn mean; he didn't have the same sort of generous nature that my father had.

That's why I'm writing this book in Gaelic because, as I have already mentioned, I would never allow the language to die out if I could help it.

Page 41 ### After We Returned from Dingle

When the boat reached the Island jetty, with its load of salt and food from Dingle, a lot of people were crowding around the bank of the jetty — as was the custom then and still is — looking to see if there was any news for them. They recognised everyone in the boat except for the young gent. Some said that 'the gent' must belong to a dignitary from the town, and that his family was probably sending him to spend a week on the Island. My sister Eileen was among them, and even she wasn't sure that it was me, on account of what looked like the dazzling light around my feet. For when I had left the house I'd been a lanky, clumsy, bare-footed creature. Kate and Nora were standing near the boat down at the water-edge.

When the first person came up, the people at the top immediately asked: to whom did the strange lad belong? Another young lad came up but his answer wasn't a bit polite.

"Are you all as blind as bats?" says he. "Don't you see that he's Tomás Donal?"

When the boat had been emptied and made secure, everyone made off home. My brother Paddy carried the two-hundred-weight bag of salt on his back. The salt in it would be used to preserve some of the fish that was still unsalted.

My mother thought that it was a fully-grown man coming when she heard me prancing along in my new shoes. I became a source of wonder on account of my new shoes, which I had obtained very early in life. In those days men and women would receive their first pair of shoes only on the day of their wedding. Wouldn't you have thought it very odd to see someone such as me in my new shoes, a neat and tidy gentleman, living in such a leaky shanty full of smoke!

A slab of yellow cake, and a saucepan of milk, was placed before the two lads who had been in Dingle. We didn't fancy fish that evening as we were tired of it. So Nora jumped to her feet, and brought in four eggs.

Page 42 "I thought", says my mother, "that there wasn't an egg in the house today."

"Yesterday, I found a hen's nest with eight eggs in it, up above in the roof," says Nora.

"It'd be a long time before you'd find a hen's nest — or a cock's — in the roof of a slated house," says Kate, precociously.

When I'd gobbled my chunk of yellow bread, swallowed my saucepan of milk and my couple of eggs, I went out. I was keen to run over to the old hag so that I could have some fun with her, for I was as quick-tongued as herself by that time. The poor woman welcomed me back from Dingle.

"May you live to wear out your shoes, and isn't it fine and early they got them for you," says she.

When I saw how polite she was to me, I put my hand in my pocket and gave her an apple, and one to everyone else in the house. I gave them sweets too — for my mother had told me to do so. The old hag jumped up while she was crunching the apple, just like a horse. She took half a rabbit out of the cooking pot and offered it to me.

"Perhaps you'd like that," says she, "since you're so manly."

"But I wouldn't be able to eat it all," says I.

"Give it to your mother then," says she.

I took the rabbit home and gave it to my mother. She gave me the hind quarter and I picked at it.

Night was drawing in, and I was getting sleepy so I went to bed. I flopped down immediately because I was worn out after my trip to the town on the mainland. It was well past school-time by the time I jumped out of bed. My mother told me that I'd almost passed away in my sleep. When I woke up the following day I was as lively as a trout. I got some water, thrust my head down into the bowl and washed the sleep from my eyes. Then the lot of us went off to school.

FIVE

The school closed again; Looking for crabs along with the King: we're two embarrassed nudes; Me, as a great yellow hunk; The sore finger; Bald Tomás with us every night; The boat from Gortadoo; The steamship and the army: the woman preparing to throw her child; What happened one day: The pension clerk; The 'burning ship'; The Wise Old Nora; The land held by the Earl

Page 43 The King was in his usual place, and as he had a rather large backside it must have left its imprint on the stool. He started whispering to me about Dingle. He himself had been there three times: once with his grandfather and twice with his father. I knew that he was sweet-talking me into giving him some of my sweets. But what kind of friend would I have been if I had ignored him? I gave him four sweets and he was extremely grateful.

When we were let out at mid-day, the King turns to me and says:

"Keep it under your hat but I hear the mistress will be leaving us soon."

"How do you know?"

"Oh, she received a letter the other day and she's to be married immediately."

"What sort of man is she going to marry?"

"A gentleman's coachman from somewhere or other," says he.

He was right, for she remained at the school for only one more week. Then, on the following Sunday, off she went. And so the school was closed once again.

It was around 1873 that the second schoolmistress left us. I was then sixteen years old. I had spent six years at school, but as yet I wasn't proficient in English, nor anything like it. A man once told me that he mastered Irish having studied it for only two years; before that his knowledge of Irish was minuscule. Why then do people say that it's a difficult language to learn? This proves that there isn't a language in the world that a person couldn't learn in two years. There are many Gaelic scholars in our country now, and some of them have only spent a year learning the language.

Page 44

Well, I'm wandering from the tale I want to tell. On Monday, from the time when the school was closed, the King bumped into me rather early in the morning. He had already had his breakfast, while I was just starting mine. I had a fine soft cake that had just been taken from the fire — and it's not often you see a harness on a cat, as the man used to say long ago about anything surprising. I had a chunk of butter with it, since we had a good milking cow, from which my mother made butter in a tin box. Well, I had a yellow scad and a fair amount of milk in a saucepan, and, more importantly, a fine set of teeth to grind my food. My mother asked the King if he'd care for a slice of buttered cake, but his stomach was too full, so he took only a couple of bites out of it. If he had been King in those days my mother would never have offered him a humble slice of yellow bread, but of course at that time he didn't have any such title.

In those days we were in the habit of going fishing on the rocks, where we often managed to catch a crab to use as bait. This wouldn't be the first day we had spent like this.

"You take care of yourselves out there looking for crabs," says my mother. "Not only is it ebb-tide but it's also neap-tide at the moment."

Out the door, and away we went, fishing for crabs, but we didn't seem to be having any luck that day.

"There's nothing in these small gulleys," says the King. "We'd better strip off and look under water, where we're sure to find a few," says he.

No sooner had he said that than we were both stripped naked, and off we went, diving under water and coming back to the surface. I myself went down into a hole about my own height, and when I put my foot into the gulley, I could feel that there was a crab down there. It was extremely hard for me to put my head down as deep as my feet, but it was even harder for me to resign myself to the fact that I wouldn't be able to catch the crab when it was so close.

Page 45 I bent down but the water prevented me from submerging properly and I wasn't able to stretch out to reach the crab.

I thrust my foot into the gulley again, because it was wide and spacious. And what do you know but I brought the crab up with my big toe. It was a large male crab, and usually, when there's one of them in a hole, there's a female crab not too far away from him. I put my foot down again and found the other one, but it was smaller than the first and it wasn't hard for me to bring it up to the surface. Now I had enough bait for the day.

The King was out of sight by this time, but in the place where we were looking for crabs there was a large freshwater spring just at the high-water line. This freshwater spring was used for washing clothes. When I reached it, the King was waiting for me over on the far side. There we were — two long-legged fellows with no clothes on. When we looked up, what did we see but three fine strapping young women staring at us.

The King was a lot more embarrassed than I was; he turned away from them and faced the sea, trying to cover himself so that they wouldn't be able to see him stark-naked. I myself remained standing up, just as I was when I came into this world. It was then that a thought struck me: why should I be intimidated in front of them, and not they themselves who are looking at me?

I covered a certain area of my body with my hands, and to spite them I stayed bolt upright without budging an inch. Two of them scurried away, but three[8] of them, the brave ones, remained. None of them had seen such a hunk of a sallow lad so brazen in

---

[8] Sic: the text seems unclear about the number of girls.

front of them before. One of the women wasn't too far away from me and what do you know but she spoke up and said:

"You ought to be good and dry by now!"

Because I was angry with her I replied that I was only dry on one side, but that I had to expose my backside for another while to the sun "and, since it doesn't seem to worry you to see me from this side, perhaps you won't mind either if I show you my backside too," says I.

"I'd say that every part of you must be well and truly dry this long while," says she, grinning.

"Sure, if I had your fat, smooth and tanned skin, it wouldn't take half the time," says I to her. *Page 46*

That was when she shrank away towards the other lot.

The King came back with his clothes hurriedly thrown on him.

"Have you nothing on yet?" says he.

"No. What's my hurry — haven't I got the sun keeping me warm," says I to him.

"Weren't you a bit embarrassed being stark-naked in front of those women?"

"And why should I have been? They weren't a bit embarrassed, although they should have been. I notice that you didn't show much courage when they appeared; it's a wonder they didn't chase you into the hills," says I to him.

This Amazon of a woman who was giving me all the lip was more interested in being wanton than being wed, as her behaviour clearly demonstrated.

Off we went along the rocks. He had to go back up to the village to get a line and some hooks, but it wasn't long before he was back. We set out west towards Dunleavy Point, which is named after the Blasket poet. The scad were biting well and we put an occasional good one behind us. Finally, when I was casting, what got caught in my finger but the hook. That put an end to my fishing. The King had to take his knife and cut the snood that connected the hook to the line. The hook was in my finger with the snood dangling from it. It wasn't too painful as the hook wasn't very deep.

We had forty scad, twenty for each of us. The King brought them home with him, and we shared them out at our house. Kate quickly used a razor to remove the hook from my finger.

The Sore Finger

The finger hurt me a lot, and it took me a while to get over it. Bald Tomás used to be in our place every night until it was time to go to bed.

Page 47

He was great company, so I didn't feel the sore finger half as much while he was talking and telling us about the hard life he had lived. And although my father was nearly as old as he was, my father wasn't half as good at story-telling, or at remembering things.

One night my father said to him: "Do you know why there was that falling-out between the parish of Dunquin and the parish of Ballyferriter, that lasted so long?"

"Oh," says Bald Tomás, "did you never hear the story about the Gortadoo boat?"

"Oh yes, I heard about it," replied my father, "but I've only a dim recollection of it now."

"There was a shipwreck north of Beginish and a boat from Dunquin went to it. They went on board and threw everything they wanted down into their own boat. Another boat set out from Gortadoo, a village in the parish of Ballyferriter. There were twenty-one men in this boat, all the top brass of the parish. They didn't stop until they reached the stricken ship. They got on board too, searching and grabbing at things picked up earlier by the Dunquin folk. In the end they threw down so much that they overloaded their boat, and the twenty-one heroes were lost without even one man surviving to tell the tale. The last pair, who stayed on board the ship throwing the stuff down, went down to the bottom of the sea with the ship, where they remain to this very day."

"Perhaps that pair are still alive in it," says I to Bald Tomás.

"Listen, you scallywag," says he, "that ship was ground into matchwood the same afternoon on Raven Rock."

"But how come the northern lot have hated the people of Dunquin ever since?" enquired my father.

"Yerra, me lad," says Tomás, "because they didn't take one of them out of the water, even though the poor devils were beseeching them to take them on board. They were even grasping at the blades of their oars, but instead of helping, the folks from Gortadoo just pulled the oars away from the Dunquin lads and left them to be swept away by the tide."

"And isn't it unbelievable that they didn't save at least some of them, even though their boat couldn't take the whole twenty-one men in addition to all those who were already in it," says my father. *Page 48*

"They couldn't take them all," says Bald Tomás. "What's more, they never intended to, because they attacked them while they were still alive, and took anything they needed or fancied from their boat, and they wouldn't let them near the ship from the time they came over."

"I suppose", says my father, "that the crews of the two boats were related — some of them, at any rate."

"Yes, indeed," says Tomás, "and some of them were closely related; this was very near to being a catastrophe for the Blasket boat. One man tried to rescue a relation of his who was holding on to the blade of an oar, but the captain stopped him, saying: 'If you bring in one man on board, then they'll all be trying to bring in their relatives, and the boat just won't be able to take them.' And so the twenty-one men who were in the boat from Gortadoo were lost, and the Dunquin boat came home with its crew safe and sound, bringing a lot of things taken from the other boat with them."

"I suppose the northern people hated them for that," says my father to Tomás.

"They did," says he. "There were sixteen widows in the Parish of Ballyferriter after that boat was lost."

"And", says my father, "I bet they were on the look-out at Mass and at the fairs for those who did it."

"Yerra, my lad," says Tomás, "didn't they come down from the north in the middle of the night, go into the houses and take away everything they found. And then they used to give the people of the house a terrible beating into the bargain. They killed a fine young lad, a son of a woman related to me over there at Mill Cove. The poor woman was very hard up and so she had nothing for them to take. And every market day in Dingle there used to be six or seven from Dunquin needing a priest after the day's fighting was over."

Page 49   "And what made the peace between them in the end?" says my father to him.

"I'll tell you," says Bald Tomás, "one of the mischief-maker's daughters married a Dunquin man. That was the beginning of the reconciliation between them, but it was a long time before that happened; in the meantime some of them had been left half dead on account of one another."

"God's blessing on the souls of the dead!" says my mother. "I never heard the true account of what happened until today."

It was nearing bedtime, and Tomás was getting ready to go home. Others also were coming back from the cottages they had been visiting.

My sore finger lasted a month. Believe me, it wasn't much fun for me, but I never noticed the pain while Tomás was telling stories. He used to be in with us every night during the winter; and every Sunday, whenever my father recited the family Rosary, Tomás used to recite it with us, and he was great at saying a full decade.

Tomás was always poor, so he had to send his son into service as a servant boy over in the Parish of Ballyferriter. There he spent five years herding cattle, without shoes or socks. Soon after the son left, one of the uncles sent fare-money from America for Tomás's daughter. It wasn't long before she left for the States where she spent five years. The son, who was in service, had to return home after that but the daughter used to send the odd pound over, which helped them out.

After the daughter left, the hag across the way was usually up out of bed very early every morning. She was often pining for her daughter being away, which was no wonder, for the daughter was all the old hag had, and she had lost all hope of ever seeing her again. When I heard her pining away I used to be very sorry for her.

The Steamship and the Army

Early one morning, when the hag was up early, what did she see at the mouth of the harbour near the White Strand but a steamship at anchor. It was full of men in black — that is, men dressed in black uniforms and head gear. This upset her, so she dashed over and knocked on our door.

"Oh, Donal," says she.

Page 50

"Well," says my father — he thought that there was something wrong with the son or with Bald Tomás — "what's the matter?"

"There's a large ship at anchor here below your house. It's full of men wearing black uniforms and tall hats," says she.

"Oh, that's right," says my father. "Something like that was bound to happen sooner or later. I'd say that by afternoon there'll be very few left with homes of their own on the island."

"God be with us!" says she, "there's nothing worse than being left without a roof over your head."

In a minute we were all up, and off we went together towards the jetty. When I reached the level place I got a job from the women who were gathered there. I was told to collect stones, and so was everyone else. No one stopped until there was a fair amount piled up. Eventually a woman said that they must have enough ammunition by now, and that before the whole lot of it was used up there'd be a different tale to tell.

"But perhaps," says another woman, "the bullets will kill us first."

"Yerra, bad luck to you! May you get killed or be murdered! Isn't it better for you to be dead than to be thrown into the ditch, and left without your cottage," says the other woman.

In from the ship came a big boat crammed full of men. As they came in close they were amazed when they saw the large crowd of women gathered at the edge of the jetty, although they imagined that there wouldn't be anyone around because they'd all be afraid. No wonder, since every man had a gun ready in his hand. But these women weren't a bit afraid of them.

The men got out, and the women surrounded them, each with a sharp rock in her hand. All the men from the boat were flabbergasted when they saw that the women were holding their ground, so they slowed their advance.

Page 51

Finally, they pushed the nose of the boat on to a rock, with two of them keeping their guns at the ready, in case anyone threatened them. As soon as the first man was out of the boat, a woman let fly with a stone boulder which nearly took the shins off him. He glanced upwards and cocked his gun directly at them; not a single woman stirred but all stood their ground above the jetty.

Before long another woman let loose a stone, and then several others, until they made the shore echo with the noise of their missiles. Instead of more men coming out of the boat, they had in fact to quickly get the man who was ashore back on their boat, and clear off out to sea in a hurry.

Two other big boats met them, and they proceeded to have a consultation. Then they came back to the jetty in a furious rage. They were particularly angry with the foolish woman who sent the boats back and prevented them from landing to do their business.

They quickly rammed the sterns of their boats onto the rock, and then put men ashore. As soon as they did, down came a shower of stones. One of their men was hit on the top of his head, and was laid out at their feet. It was a small lass that threw it, and so it was only a small stone. He'd have been a corpse if it'd been thrown by a stronger woman.

The captains ordered the men to return to the boats immediately, but they were slow about it, as they were trying to bring the half-dead man with them. The three boats full of armed men were bobbing around offshore, deciding what to do. After another consultation they tried to come in again, thinking that the women had used up all their ammunition. However, they now had another small heap of stones that had been gathered by the boys, and away they went again, hurling them down the slope.

Although the women were terrified that the armed men would open fire on them, they were no more afraid of them than the men were themselves.

There were five women on one side and by then there weren't *Page 52* enough stones to throw. One of the women was carrying a fine strong boy. She was furious and frustrated when she couldn't find something to throw. When she saw two policemen trying to climb up through the green slope below her, she cried: "The devil take me, I'll throw my own child at them!"

"Yerra, you fool," said the woman nearest to her, "don't lose your wits; hold on to your child, lass!"

She gave a short run to throw the child, but the other woman grabbed it. No sooner had she done so when a woman on the other side came and threw down a chunk of sod, which knocked the pair below right down the slope. The child that was to be thrown at them is over in America today, fit and strong still. Finally, the ship cleared off with its men later in the day, without taking as much as a red cent with them from the people of the Island.

When the word got out, all Ireland loved the tale about a steamship in the Great Blasket that was unable to collect rent or tax, even though there were armed men on board. That was the situation for a long while, and however great or small had been the rent and taxes claimed from the Island people up to that time, nothing was ever demanded from them after that.

For the next few years, nothing was seen until another similar ship moored below the houses. There were a few country folk in it and a few armed people. However, the Islanders had been tipped off that something like this was about to happen and that it'd be better to ignore them. The Island folk were advised to drive all their cows and sheep to the western end of the island.

And that's what they did. The lads drove the cows and sheep off as far as they could send them. In the ship was the Chief Collector of taxes along with some of his officials. They met with no opposition, but were given as much freedom to do whatever they needed to do. Off they went up the hill, with some of the Island people who had been selected for such an occasion.

Page 53 The Chief Collector went as far west as the old tower, but for all his searching he found nothing. He sent some others as far as the western half of the island where it was the same story: they found two ancient mules with no life in them, just skin and bones. Someone asked the Chief Collector whether he proposed to bring the two mules back with him.

"If we did, people would laugh at us," he replied.

They returned home as they arrived, without a cow, a horse or a sheep.

What Happened One Day

We had another day of fun on the Island which I didn't miss. Since what happened on that day made me laugh, I'll not rest easy until you also get a couple of laughs or more out of it.

Late one Sunday a large number of currachs were out at Mass. At about one o'clock a currach arrived. Everyone said it wasn't an Island currach, and shouldn't they ready themselves. Everyone kept a look-out because there had been talk of a dog-tax. When the currach reached the jetty there were strangers in it.

Off went everyone calling his own dog, and away they went out to the hills with some young fellows along with them. The only time you'd ever see any dogs was when a bugle horn was blown for them. No wonder everyone left, with four dogs in every house making a total of more than eighty dogs on the whole Island.

Well, when the men came ashore, the story went around that they were the pension clerk and two bank clerks. You never saw anything like the folk applying for the blind pension, running to take out the beds, and stretching out on them and pretending to be at their last gasp when the clerk saw them! There were some great strong men above the jetty, who only had just enough time to take their clothes and shoes off.

Page 54 At the first house the officials went to, a sick man was shown to them. When they got a look at him there was nothing to see but half an inch of the sickly, frail man's nose. When the clerk looked at him he saw that he had two hooves. He called to one of the other clerks.

"*See*," says he, in English. "*There's hooves on this one.*"

The other man looked.

"*By dad, he is the devil,*" says he. Everyone in the house screamed.

"*The people here can put every shape on themselves,*" says the pension clerk.

But the man with the hooves didn't uncover any part of his body — except his nose — from beneath the blankets.

Then they went to another house where there was a couple they were looking for. The pair of them were in a single bed. The clerk went closer to have a look at them, but there wasn't a bit of their face to be seen, nor any means of doing so because they were shivering with cold. They were the man and the woman of the house. The man's hooves could be seen — his shoes that were dirty from having been out on the previous day.

The clerk called to the other man:

"*There is two of them here. By dad, they have the bed of honour here too,*" says he.

It took half an hour before everyone in that house stopped chortling out loud and laughing. There wasn't one of them after that who didn't see the hooves on them.

"*Faith, they might have the horns too under all those blankets covering them,*" says a joker who was with them.

It's no wonder what's happening to the country with people here getting so adept at pulling a fast one on the Government.

The 'Burning' Ship

One cold winter's night Bald Tomás strode into our place, as he usually did. There was a good turf fire blazing away up the chimney, and because the house was fairly small, it was cosy inside, even though it was cold outside. The bald man had come in before I could manage to get out of the house.

The rest of them had gone out of the house around half an *Page 55* hour earlier. They had gone off coorjeeking.[9] This is an old custom, which is still practised widely today.

[9] Visiting other houses

"If you had any sense," says my mother to me, "you'd stay at home instead of going off to bitterly cold houses that don't have any fire or heat in them. If you stay here you'll have fine company with your father and Bald Tomás," says she.

It wasn't really what my mother said that changed my mind, but the fact was that I enjoyed listening to Tomás's story-telling, and I preferred to listen to him rather than venture out to the 'circus' outside.

The first thing the pair turned their attention to was the 'burning' ship.

"The day of the 'burning' boat was a tough one for the two of us, Tomás," says my father.

"It was indeed," replies Tomás. "The pair in our boat were nearly lost after they stopped."

"When the ship didn't stop," says my father, "it was obvious to us that something was propelling it. There was no fire to be seen on the ship, no sail or wind to drive it and yet we were unable to catch up."

"Look," says the bald man, "the people of this district didn't believe the person who'd been here a couple of months earlier when he said that we'd soon see ships coming with fire; ships without sails or oars."

"Most likely no one believed what he told them and they called him 'Tomás the Liar'," says my father.

"That's it, exactly," says Tomás, "and when they got close to it, the crew of the 'fire boat' said that there were many men on board the ship."

"That was the first steamship that ever went to Limerick; she went to Russell's, full of Indian meal," says my father.

"There were boats from Dunquin and from the parish of Ballyferriter going north, ahead of her," says Tomás. "It was just a week before St Patrick's Day," says he.

"Was it long after that when the fat bullocks arrived?" my father asked.

Page 56 "Exactly one year later, in the following spring, the week before St Patrick's Day," says he.

"Wasn't it amazing, the amount they brought ashore, all completely unharmed," says my father.

"No one knows how much was salvaged in all," says Tomás. "In Farran, in the Parish of Ballyferriter, they got twelve barrels of salt," says he.

"I think the people here got least of all," says my father.

"Yes," Tomás replied. "The reason for that was that the weather was too blustery, and they weren't able to go looking for salt. But bad as their equipment was, even those who salvaged the least amount had a lot of meat for themselves."

"I myself had a year's supply, and I was one of those who salvaged the least, because I didn't even manage to get any of the salt," says my father.

"I'd say that you had enough to pay for your rent, Donal," Bald Tomás smiles to my father.

"We had four barrels of food, full to the brim, salted and cured," says my father. "It was a great two years for potatoes, and fish too."

"Every man in our boat made thirty pounds out of it," says Tomás.

The Wise Old Nora
"Perhaps it was one of those years when the *Wise Old Nora* came," says my father.

"It was the following year," says Tomás. "Not one pound was made that year, because the scoundrels in that old ship made off with every fish that had been caught on the Island. I think it must have been a poor man's curse that fell on them," says he, "when the bottom dropped out of the boat at Edge Rock while it was on its way, full of fish, to Dingle."

"Oh, I'd say that everyone on the Island was cursing them," says my father.

"Indeed, and divine vengeance also fell upon them," says Tomás.

"How was that?" says my father. "We know that not one of them drowned when the bottom fell out of their old boat, so what was it that saved them?" says he.

Page 57

"There was a fine big, strong boat attached to it, and when the water gushed up over them, they all got into it," says Tomás.

"Then what was the other way that divine vengeance fell upon them, so?" enquires my father.

"Vengeance fell, it certainly did: forty persons escaped to this Island while the extreme violence was going on, and none of those who escaped died in his own bed, except for one man — Patrick FitzGerald, who lived out there in Coomeenoole," says Bald Tomás, "but every one of them ended up in the Poor House, because they were so poor. And it was a just end for them, for they themselves showed little pity for the poor, when they were in a position to do so. But thanks be to God, they're in the grave now and we're still alive."

The Land Held by the Earl

"John Hussey was the first honest man who came collecting rent after the bailiffs," says my father.

"Yes, he was a very straight person," says Bald Tomás. "From the first day he got the job he didn't take a penny more than what was due from any man."

"That's true," says my father, "but he often used to make life difficult for people who were working for him. He used to take boats full of people to collect seaweed and mussels for fertiliser, and other boats with people for sheep-shearing. The crew of these boats used to go without pay or food. All they'd be given would be a chunk of yellow bread three days old, with a mug of sour milk from which the cream had been removed several days earlier. All those who survived have good reason to be grateful for the rest of their lives that he didn't manage to drown any of them, and that they lived to tell the tale."

"Oh, may there be the curse of the twenty-four men on him!" continues Bald Tomás. "He nearly left the boat out that I was in, while we were going north with the tide. Our boat was loaded with black seaweed and we were making our way to the narrow bay. The tide was too high and the boat was too low in the water, but two strong men threw five or six bundles of the seaweed out into the sea," says he.

"He took the crews of our two boats to shear sheep on Inishvickillane," says my father. "It took three days for us to shear them all. The man who was in charge of the Island had salvaged a wreck and we had to take it east to Beldarg," says he.

Sure, I didn't notice the night passing with the two of them debating and chatting away.

SIX

*The former soldier as schoolmaster and his wife
with three legs; The inspector visits us; The
schoolmaster's fainting fit; Myself and the King act
as two teachers; Hunting rabbits with a ferret*

The New Schoolmaster

One fine Sunday a currach came in from the mainland with
strangers in it. No one knew who these new arrivals were until
the boat had reached the top of the jetty.

The man was a big, tall, tough and lean individual, with an
unhealthy appearance, who looked rather old as well. He was
married, and his wife and two children were with him. The wife
had three legs, a sound leg, a short leg and a wooden leg. One or
two persons let out a giggle, and another muttered:

"However crippled they are, their children look fine!"

"That's the will of God, my good man," answered another
man, who had a better understanding of his faith.

The man came from the parish of Ballyferriter, not far away,
and the woman's family was from Dunquin.

Eventually, they got to the schoolhouse, and made their home
there. The interior of the schoolhouse was partitioned to make a
room for the teachers to live in. The neighbours brought enough
fuel for them, and the new arrivals soon settled themselves in and
just got on with it.

The man was a former soldier who got a couple of bullet wounds while serving in the army. He had a pension of sixpence a day. He wasn't able to fasten his boots, or even bend over, because of a bullet lodged in his side. They were a crippled pair, though I wouldn't hold that against them.

The three-legged woman was a lot better off than her husband. *Page 60* With her third leg — her crutch — which helped her along at a fair pace, she could easily outrun any two-legged woman.

The school had been closed for nearly a year, but now it was opened again on the following Monday morning. Naturally, since there was a new teacher, no one was missing from school that day, and almost all the old people came along to see how the new master would perform!

School teachers were in short supply in those days, and the priest had difficulty finding one. But when he saw that the school had been without anyone for such a long time, he put this fellow in as a temporary replacement. The new man had never been to college nor was he much good at the primary school either. At any rate, the schooling started off on the Monday morning.

Right on time the King had been in his own seat before I arrived. He beckoned to me to come over and sit beside him, and so I did as he asked. Then he whispered to me:

"Look how pockmarked the teacher's skin is!"

"He's got a lot of little pockmarks," says I to him. My father had told me that these were smallpox scars, but at that time the King didn't know what smallpox was.

Most of the mob didn't learn much that day, for they weren't looking at books or papers, but were scrutinising the woman with three legs who appeared now and again. The teacher was a truly nice person, and we weren't as afraid of him as we would have been were he a bad-tempered man. So when all is said and done, the pupils used to be nice to him.

About every three months he used to go to the town, and he'd bring back a box of sweets and apples for the young ones at school. Whenever any child had to stay at home, he used to come to see how the child was, and he'd always have an apple or a sweet along for him, while he himself would mosey merrily along, munching a chunk of apple like a horse. Since the master was such a decent sort, the pupils rarely missed out on attending school.

Page 61

This was the last teacher the King and I had — and many of the rest of us too — for this one spent a good while with us. It was ill-health that drove him out in the end. He was heading for Cork, but he died on the way, somewhere near Tralee.

By the time he left, the King, and most of the others too, had picked up pretty well everything he had to teach them. In the end he wasn't able to teach me anything, so he decided that I should be doing some teaching myself, while he would go off to study on his own. I learnt from him for a while, but when this started happening too often, I got a bit fed up with it all.

One day when he told me what to do, he went out into the fresh air, but when he came back the job wasn't done. That annoyed him and he flew into something of a rage. To tell the truth, that was the first time we'd ever seen him behave like that. After that he resumed work without saying very much more. He was keeping his temper under control for fear that it would be himself who'd lose out if he were to continue.

The Inspector Comes

Although the teacher had a sallow complexion, you'd have thought it wasn't the same man when the inspector came in. His face had an animated look like someone who'd gone slightly crazy. Not that he wasn't always a bit crazy, whatever else you might say about him.

I personally didn't hold it against him when his appearance changed on seeing the inspector arrive. The kids at school shook in their boots when he came in. There were four eyes in his head that could let him see clearly everything that was in the schoolhouse, even when it was dark. No one was more fascinated by him than the King, although he had the same problem years later when he himself had to wear spectacles, and hadn't he the fine comely head to display them. From the inspector's thick sallow hide you'd think he had come from somewhere in China.

And then, with his frightening eyes, you'd have certainly thought that he was still in the army, and it was no wonder that pupils under his authority quaked with fear. But that's how it was, to be sure.

Page 62

All of us, big and small, spoke very little and we got on quietly with whatever work we were doing. It wasn't long before the master came to me with figures on his slate, and asked me to add them up as quickly as I could. That was no problem for me and I did it quickly. The inspector had actually given the problem to the master for him to solve but he wasn't able to do it.

As the master wasn't too healthy, the dreadful fright the inspector had given him suddenly made him very ill. All the same, the school was open every day after that. The master told me that he'd be eternally grateful to me if I'd teach the kids, and get the King to help me. The three-legged woman was a dressmaker; she came to my mother and asked her to urge me to go to school while the master was sick. "And, if there's a quilt or anything you need done, I'll do it for you," says she. The reason she did that was for fear that I might go on strike.

The King and I were teachers for a month, but — don't tell anyone — we weren't very successful at it, for either ill-luck, or the children's bad behaviour, prevented us from doing whatever we were able to do. There were fully-grown strong lads attending the Blasket school, and we were more interested in courting than doing any schoolwork. Anyway, a whole month was spent this way, without too much hassle or heartache, although nowadays it would be a rare month in this country when you could say that.

The master used to be in the habit of visiting certain houses that had a good fire in them, because he was always feeling cold. When the man of the house would come back from the beach, a chunk of coarse yellow cake would be set before him. He used to take it on his lap and make two halves out of it, and then he'd munch away at it, without any sauce. "Hunger is the best sauce," he used to say.

A short time after that the three-legged woman died. Her daughter and son are still living in these regions.

Page 63

The school was closed for another while, so the King and I spent our time together hunting up on the hill and down by the seacoast. I still had a tendency to be a pet, on account of me being the last of the brood; the King was tarred with the same brush, because he was the first of the brood. And I suppose for that reason we felt free to do whatever we pleased, more or less.

One morning he came early to see me.

"What brought you so early?" says my mother to him.

"I'm going hunting," says he. "The day's very fine. I'll make a quick dash over to Black Head, and perhaps we'll catch half a dozen rabbits," says he. "Where's Tomás? Still asleep, I suppose?"

"He is, indeed," says she.

"I'm here, my boy," says I, because I recognised his voice more easily than the voice of anyone else who came to our house.

"Get up quickly," says he, "and we'll go off hunting."

"But we've no decent hunting gear," says I.

"We have, my boy," says he. "I'll bring the ferret with me."

"But I'm afraid you won't be let have it," says I to him.

"I'll nick it from my grandfather," says he.

My mother gave me my breakfast and I didn't take long bolting it down. Whatever I couldn't gulp down, I had my fine mill of teeth willing and ready to grind it: a slice of cake made from coarse Indian meal, strong enough to satisfy a horse, some yellow scad, milk and water.

Off went the pair of us. He stuffed the ferret down his chest; we also had two good dogs. I had a spade on my shoulder and we quickly headed up the hill.

When we got near to some rabbits we came across a warren. (That's the name given to a place where there's a good number of them to be found together; a rabbit hole is the name of a place where you might find only two or three.)

The King pulled out his ferret, attached a string to her and let her into the hole. He spread a net over each hole in the warren, because some of them have up to seven openings. It wasn't long before a rabbit darted out, but the net caught it quickly and knocked it over, as there was a noose on it. He took it out of the net, and set the net ready again. No sooner had he done that when another one dashed out of a different hole. The ferret didn't come back up until she had driven the last of them out to us. Ferrets only return when they are unable to find anything to chase.

The ferret had driven out seven large plump rabbits to us from that hole; all of them were caught in the nets. Then off we went to another place. There the King let the ferret in to another opening and she remained inside for some time before anything came out. Finally, a big powerful rabbit darted out from the hole. The net caught it, but it pulled the post that was holding it, and off it went downhill, but the two dogs caught up with it.

In the late afternoon, and with the sun going down, the King said:

"We've done very well, but we won't be able to carry the rabbits home because we're so weak from hunger."

"I never saw a man as tough as you and yet always so liable to collapse from hunger. I'd bring them all home myself if we didn't have so many of them," says I.

"Oh, there won't be any more. We won't let the ferret go into another hole because she's tired, and when a ferret is tired it can be dangerous if left inside," says he.

We had caught a dozen and a half by then, a good lot, and were deciding to return home. I myself had a threadbare jacket. The jacket had a large inside pocket and in it I had a good chunk of bread. It wasn't I who had put it there but my mother. She said that the day was long and that young people have keen appetites, which was certainly true. I pulled it out, divided it in two and gave half to the King. At that time it wasn't so difficult to satisfy him as it is today, because he had no crown to wear in those days. The King gobbled the bread down with gusto. It tasted good, but there wasn't enough in it to fully satisfy his hunger. When he had chewed it all up, he felt stronger, so he put the ferret back to work again until we each had a dozen rabbits. Then we came home, with the wee star high above us.

Page 65

SEVEN

How our family split up in all directions like Mór's
piss; The law in action; Bald Tomás on the move
again; Red Joan; Six huntsmen on their way to
Belfast; My brother Paddy back home from America;
Pat Sheamus in Dingle: 'Good day, Mrs Atkins'; The
year of the tea; The driver from the North

Page 67 ***How Our Family Split Up, Going East and West, Like Mór's Piss***
Since I'm referring to Mór's pissing,[10] perhaps it's right that I
should tell everyone what I know about her. As Mór travelled
from the south to the north of the country trying to reach
Donaghadee, she came to Muisire Pass, where she had a fine view
to the north, south, east and west. Mór stopped and pissed at the
crossroads at Muisire Pass deciding to follow whichever road her
piss flowed the furthest, since she had no idea which way to go at
the time. But this didn't work out for her, because her piss flowed
the same distance along each road.

This is what she said:

Woe is me,
How long and wide can Ireland be,
This slender streamlet on it goes,

[10] In this edition Mór hasn't been mentioned. In an earlier version there was a
preliminary sentence: *"De réir a chéile bhí leagadh mhún Mhóire ag teacht ar an*
muirear againn." *"From then on, the family began to split up, just like Mór's piss*
flowed away."

Not far it flows …
I'd best be on my way, I should
Go home to my own cottage,
Ditching Donncha for good.

And that's what she did, too. She set off home, where she remained until she died and where she was buried about twenty yards from her own cottage.

Well, my story isn't about her.

My sister Kate got married and lived all her life in a small house Page 68 in the village. Her husband, a good hunter, provided well for her. I often used to hold him under the water with an oar whenever we needed crabs for bait. But one day I held him down too long — he was turning blue and was barely alive by the time he came back up to the surface, so he never trusted me ever again after that.

The house Kate went to was very much like the one she left. Similar to the old house, the new one used to have eggs in its roof too. Pat Sheamus was her husband's name. His father was Sheamus Senior; they were from the Guiheen family. Pat thought of going into the army before he was married, but his father would always say to him: "Paddy, my boy, the weight of the hill upon your shoulders," meaning that he wouldn't be able to manage it. When there were fights and quarrelling among the country people at the market and fair, this Sheamus Senior used to be a sort of fight-organiser. He came to the Island from the parish of Ballyferriter. Pat Sheamus and Kate were both good at doing rough work, but they weren't very practical people. There were hens' nests in the roof of their house and Kate had no trouble going up to look for them, which she preferred doing rather than collecting them from a coop.

I shall have to leave them there now, discussing and arguing away together, until my story brings me back to them again.

A year after Kate was married, my brother Paddy married a Dunquin girl, a weaver's daughter. They had two sons. When she passed away, the youngest was only three months old, and my poor mother had to set about raising him — and this after she'd already raised her own brood. Mary was still in America, and Nora and Eileen were at home. Mary didn't want to come home until the other two joined her over there, which, in the end, is what actually happened. Very soon afterwards Mary sent the fare over for them. And off they went a year later. When she saw that they could find their way around on their own over there, she herself began thinking about returning home, because her son was still living back on the Island. She needed to get justice for him, and for herself, and to sue the uncle who had dispossessed them both. She sailed over without delay and arrived at the Blaskets around the end of autumn with nearly a hundred pounds in her pocket.

Page 69 ### The Law in Action

Soon after Mary came home she started legal proceedings, and when she'd finished with the uncle, her husband's brother, he had the stuffing knocked out of him altogether. She herself got compensation, and the sum awarded to her son was lodged in the bank. It wasn't long before she decided to get married again, this time to a strong, stoutly-built hulk of a young man, owning nothing but the clothes on his back — and even they looked pretty ragged.

The two of them built a small house for themselves and they got on with their lives like everyone has to. The hulk was a naturally good hunter. Mary herself knew how to live frugally, like anyone did, anyone that is who ever had to spend time in America.

When Mary's son grew up he went off to the New World, and soon after that the bug bit my brother, Paddy, too. No one knew where he was until he was half-way across the sea. The two kids stayed with my mother. By then my father was fairly old, and they had no one to look after the cottage except the family pet — myself. I'd been a pet only for as long as I had been able to sit on everyone's knee. But look how soon we were all separated from one another. Gone was the joy, the fun, the carry-on we had before meals, at meals and after mealtimes. Now there was nothing but the voice of the old hag across the way, and the droning of Bald Tomás. But it was good that they were still there, as the man used to say to the old and decrepit.

Although Bald Tomás was a great storyteller, I didn't spend much time with him, but I used to put in the odd evening in his company when it got cold and stormy. That was because my mother would tell me to do so, and I never liked to disobey her. One night when I was at home Tomás got going. He'd always have some strange tale to recount.

"Donal," says he to my father, "did Red Joan ever get any money out of you?"

"Indeed she didn't," says my father.

Page 70

"I bet there aren't many on the Island that aren't out of pocket because of that woman," says Tomás.

"Is it true that she once invited you into her place?" enquires my father.

"Sure she did, two or three times," says he. "And of course, she cleaned out my uncle, Pat Senior. As soon as she'd done her business, she lightened his pocket by fifteen pounds."

"She had a lot of influence with the judges in Dingle," says my father, "which suited them very nicely."

"She took fifteen shillings off me on each of the three occasions I had a turn with her," says Tomás.

"You paid her well!" says my father.

"Even the King of Heaven couldn't afford her!" says he. "If she had carried on for another year at the same rate there wouldn't be anyone alive on the Island today," says Tomás.

"She was worse than any bailiff!" says my father.

"That one was worse than the devil himself!" says Bald Tomás. "Even if God didn't let her live too long, she, like the Fallen Angel himself, had free license to do as ever she pleased, be it for good or for evil," says he.

Red Joan

I've already mentioned this woman. She used to ruin men by taking them to court all the time. The men-folk were tormented by her constant accusations.

She'd been a widow since her husband had died while hunting. She had a bit of land, and a couple of children, a son and a daughter. When she had overcome her grief, she got the itch to get married again. Bald Tomás said there was no woman like her in all Kerry: she was robust, strong, well-formed with a good figure, and fair-skinned. "And," says he, "be it rain, hail or sunshine, she never took a cloak with her, for, whenever she needed to, she would just let down her great mop of hair and you've never seen such a golden sheen like that in Red Joan's hair."

Page 71

"Isn't it amazing that she didn't set about getting married again?" says my father.

"Yerra, she often tried — but her bad name preceded her before she could ever organise a marriage for herself. And everyone avoided her like the plague whenever they saw her coming," says he.

"Indeed, Tomás," says my mother, "what tricks did she get up to so that she could sue men whenever she wanted to?"

"Yerra, good lady," says Bald Tomás, "there was a lady who had authority over the islands at that time. She and Red Joan used secret signals between each other so that they could get up to whatever trickery they wanted," says he.

"Isn't it a great wonder that some man didn't strike her dead," says my mother, "rather than putting up with that from the likes of her," says she.

"Yerra, wouldn't that same lady put the noose around the neck of anyone who'd dare lay a finger on Red Joan," says Tomás. "Don't you see that no one could escape without having some kind of dealings with her?" says he. "One day Pat Senior was out there, eager to get to work on the bog, because he wasn't satisfied with what he'd already cut, when suddenly Joan appeared on the scene.

"'Get out of that hole,' says she. 'I think that you've already ripped a good enough portion of your rent out of that hill by now.'

"'I'll leave when I want to,' replied Pat.

"Without saying another word, Joan sprawled herself out in the bog.

"'See now if you'll leave it,' says she.

"Pat lifted the spade to strike her down with one fatal blow and leave her dead in the bog, but probably God restrained him," says Bald Tomás, "because he was a very powerful and bad-tempered man. But afterwards he often used to say to me that the only reason he had let her go was because of his young family who depended upon him and weren't yet able themselves to earn their own livelihood. 'I knew well that were I to do such a thing I'd soon be hanged for it,' he used to say.

"When she sat on Pat in the bog the first wise crack she made at him was: *Page 72*

'It's easy to see that you haven't much pep in you; it's obviously not a good time for that thingy of yours that goes in and out,' says she."

"It's a wonder she didn't hang every man in the West," says my mother, "if she was that type of woman."

"Yerra, my dear," says Tomás, "didn't she do all she could where she was, but she didn't get up to her tricks on the mainland. Did you hear what she did with Michael Junior's pig?" says he.

"I didn't, upon my soul," says my mother.

"When she got the pig, which had no ring in its nose, she took a shovel and was flailing it until she drove it into Michael who was inside the house, and she used the shovel to hack off every bit of flesh on it, every bit from its flank down. Then from his own doorway she shouted at him that if the pig's nose had no ring in it for another day he would have to eat it.

"'But,' replies Michael, 'it's not likely that the two of us will want to eat it alive. Haven't you already hacked off the best part of its meat with your shovel.'

"'Perhaps I'll put you somewhere that'll shut you up for a while, my boy,' says she.

"'Go to blazes,' says Michael, 'over my dead body; you'll not do to me what you did to the pig,' says he.

"A week later she had poor Michael in the courthouse, and she testified this, that and the other against him, and she'd have had him hanged if it weren't for all the people who spoke up on his behalf," says Bald Tomás.

"Mary, Mother of God!" says my mother, "how long was she carrying on like that for?"

"Four or five years," says he.

"And what made her give up?" asks my mother.

"Bad times fell upon her, because her friend, the lady, eventually stopped listening to her," says Bald Tomás.

Page 73 ### Six Hunters Go from the Island to Belfast

"Indeed, God's blessing on the souls of your dead!" says my mother to Bald Tomás. "Can you tell us anything about the hunters who went from these parts to Belfast?"

"That's an odd question to be asking me, and my own father in the very thick of it," says he.

"Go on out of that!" says she.

"Indeed he was," says Tomás. "He spent a fortnight away from home, absolutely miserable. I myself was small at that time, but I well remember that I could hardly recognise him when he came back."

"It's amazing that you found it difficult to recognise him after such a short time. You surely would have been able to had you been old enough," says my father.

"Upon my soul, I was ten years old, but the terrible ordeal had changed him so much that you'd have sworn that he wasn't the same man," says he.

"I suppose", says my father, "that they took the ferrets to Belfast with them."

"No, they didn't. They had only two ferrets, and they put them in the hole in a hollow by the creek from where the boat had taken them."

"I suppose they were dead by the time they came home," says my father.

"They were as dead as Henry the Eighth," says Tomás. "It's not altogether surprising since they'd been gone a fortnight and the poor ferrets didn't get a morsel to eat while they were away."

"Who did they belong to?" says my mother, who was still listening intently to the story.

"To Patrick Junior and Maurice Liam. They hadn't had them long after they brought them back from Killarney, and they paid fifteen shillings for each of them," says he.

"Indeed, Tomás," continues my mother, "were they far back in the hills when they saw the ship?"

"They were on Slievedonagh, and a lovely breezy morning it was. They had no clothes on them except flannel trousers and a knitted cap on their heads. The boat that took them was in Coosavaud, and not one of them knew that they wouldn't be going hunting until late that afternoon," says he. "And who should bump into them but Sheamus Senior, looking for sheep; his father being one of the hunters." *Page 74*

"Wasn't the captain of the vessel[11] a real scoundrel to pull out a gun on them as soon as they told him where he was," says my father.

"Of course, but it was worse than that," says Tomás, "because he wouldn't let them out of the boat to go home as soon as they told him he was in the Blasket Sound. He just raised his sails, but then, when the wind started blowing harder than usual, he lost control of his boat and it headed off to the north."

"O Blessed Virgin!" says my mother, "did he bring them all the way up to the North of Ireland?"

"He took them as far as he was going, and would have taken them even further if he had so wished," explained Bald Tomás.

"And then what did he do with them?" asks my father.

"Do: he brought them to an inn, and he privately told the woman of the house to keep them there for him until he returned or she'd hear about it. He ordered her to give them plenty of food and drink," says Tomás.

---

[11] There is a fuller and more comprehensive account of *An Seisear Fiagaithe* in *Seanchas Ón Oileán* where Tomás explains in more detail about how the hunters were kidnapped: "*Six hunters went to the hills and while they were there they noticed a vessel out at sea having difficulty reaching land. When the hunters went on board, the sails were suddenly raised and after they had told the captain of the boat that they were in the Blasket Sound, he took out a gun and threatened them. Then the vessel set off and didn't stop until it reached Belfast.*"

"I understand that one man slipped away from the others," says my father.

"That's what Sheamus Senior's father did, and no one who ever travelled through Ireland was more miserable than he, without shoes on his feet or clothes on his body. But hunger and cold overcame him, and terror as well for fear he might be arrested at any time," says Bald Tomás. "When the captain got himself ready, he brought them to court and they were convicted, because they had no English except for the little that Dunleavy's father could speak."

"And, Tomás, did they go to prison?" enquired my mother.

"They would have if it hadn't been for the gentleman who stood up for them. He had heard all the carry-on while he was passing by the courthouse, so he asked a lad standing in the doorway what was the reason for the row. The lad told him what it was all about, and where they were from, and how they reached that place, and how people were saying that these men were being convicted wrongfully.

"The gentleman got angry when he heard the tale and how it wasn't going too well for the men that were being convicted. The gentleman was a captain in the army who came from Kerry. He dashed in immediately and made them start the whole proceedings over again. The ship's captain and the army captain argued with each other, neither of them at a loss for words. In the end the ship's captain had to put forty pounds on the table and, in addition, the cost of the men's boat that he had lost on them — and that put him out of pocket another ten pounds."

"I suppose the first man had to walk all the way back from the north," says my mother.

"Yes, indeed, and so too did the five others who followed him, but it didn't worry them because they had a plan prepared. All the same, the hardship of the journey did really terrify the first man," says he.

"Indeed, I wonder whether they gave him any of the money they received when they got back?"

Page 75

"My family is not like that," says Bald Tomás. "They offered him every penny they had. However, he refused point-blank to take advantage of anyone; but all the same it was my father who put his hand into his pocket. The man who journeyed on his own was a poor man with a family, and when he was overwhelmed by fear the ordeal simply became too much for him.

"I often heard my father saying that every one of them would have done what he had done if it weren't for the fact they had decided their only real chance of escape was for them to stick together. Mind you, the captain himself would have been pleased if every one of them had pushed off. He originally told the woman of the house, in their presence, to keep them, but behind their backs he spoke differently to her, saying that if they did try to escape, to let them do so, because he didn't intend to do anything to them other than to deprive them of the payment that he owed them," explained Bald Tomás.

"But the eyes of everyone else were opened ever since then," says my father, "because after that no one ever asked where on earth they would eventually be when they got into harbour. Their undoing was to tell the stranger that he was in the Blasket Sound."

"Long life to you!" said my mother.

My Brother Paddy Back Home from America

Suddenly, without warning, Paddy walked in through the door one day, having been in America for only a year. He had nothing but the clothes on his back — and those didn't look too good on him either. I can only suppose that someone had extended a helping hand to him so that he could make the trip back home. We thought that he'd just take it easy for the rest of his life, but in this world things often don't work out as you might expect, and that was certainly how it was with Paddy. One spring he received an invitation to go to the States and to take his two children with him. He accepted the offer eagerly, taking his youngest boy and, indeed, almost carrying him in his arms until they reached their destination. The older boy was more robust and so he was able to look after himself. Paddy started providing for his two children

Page 76

and for himself, working hard every day. He spent ten years doing this. But even after that length of time he hadn't managed to save a single cent, although he never fell ill, or missed a day's work.

He was a tall, thin man, fond of his work, and he could easily do the work of two people. That's why he was never short of work in America for as long as he was there. While he was in the States, there would often be people out of work, but the boss used to hang on to the best man for whatever jobs were available — and that person would always be Paddy. When people here heard that, they were amazed.

There were three of our brood here and another three abroad. The two older ones were depending on me, the pet, at that time, when there were only three of us in our wee house. I was exactly twenty years old at that time and we were all getting on reasonably well together. I myself frequently drove to the market in Dingle, sometimes by land and other times across the length of the great Dingle Bay. Sometimes we used to have pigs, fish, sheep, or whatever on board, and occasionally other animals and wool. During my first trips I used to amaze the others by proudly pointing out the houses and telling them who lived there.

Page 77

Once I was there all day with my sister Kate's husband, Pat Sheamus. He was a man who couldn't hold a glass of whiskey, or a pint of porter, without gulping it down. He never got any real pleasure from a drink he'd buy himself, but he certainly enjoyed it when someone else would prod him in the back and invite him to have a drink.

The upshot of it all was that he was absolutely blotto with the drink that day. He went completely gaga. It ended up with him having about as much sense as he had when he first started crawling around the house after leaving the cradle. Well, unfortunately for me, I didn't manage to get away from him before he had become completely blotto, so I had no choice but to bite the bullet and take him along with me.

Around late afternoon we were in the Main Street. There was a crowd of people walking up and down, some of them coming up to meet us, and all who knew us greeting the men from the

Island. Then Pat Sheamus started speaking in an uncouth manner:

"Where has this pack of devils come from?" he kept on saying. "Aren't you a wild-looking bunch? Curses on the lot of you — all you lot can do is talk! There's no drink to be got from any one of you, and your poor relations from the Island here parched with the thirst!"

Without a word of a lie, he was telling the truth, but what good was that? The truth can be bitter sometimes, but Pat Sheamus was in no way embarrassed because he was so drunk. Often it is easier for a shameless person to go about his business when he is drunk. My heart, however, was in knots of embarrassment listening to his pointless blather, but what could I do but suffer in silence?

Occasionally a couple of policemen would come along and I'd *Page 78* have been glad if they'd caught him by the ear and taken him away and detained him until he'd returned to his senses. But whenever he'd see them coming, anyone would have sworn that he was a priest's sexton, he was so well-behaved — that is, until he'd see that they were well out of sight. Hardly would the policemen clear off before his hat would be flung in the air and he became the only show-off on the street. A man came up to give him a clout, but instead, Pat gave him a kiss, for heaven's sake!

Well, that was fine and not too bad, I suppose, but even when matters are bad at times, they can always get worse. And, however weird the day I'd spent so far with this rogue, the hardest part was still to come.

He put his hand in his pocket and took out his pipe, a clay pipe with nothing in it but chalk.

"Mary, Mother of God! I haven't a bit of tobacco," says he. "Let's go to that shop over there; there's surely some good tobacco to be had in that shop."

"Yerra, there'll be tobacco to be got in the shops right here; don't bother with that establishment," says I to him.

"Oh, even if I were over on the Island I'd be coming east for the good tobacco that is to be found in that shop," says he.

"But what's the name of this shop where you claim good tobacco can be found?" says I.

"Atkins, and it's over there," says he, pointing across the street.

There's no one on earth who'd say that there was a drop of drink in him all the time he was going on about the tobacco. Well, I knew that he wouldn't let me out from under his wing, so off we went across the street. The store was a branch of a foreign firm, where there was every sort of thing on sale. It was a fine ornate store with a statuesque woman on a chair sitting between the two counters on either side, facing the door. She had the appearance of a country woman.

When he went through the door the eejit took off his hat to greet the woman.

Page 79

"Good day to you, Mrs Atkins!" says he.

That quip caused the greatest fun there'd been in Dingle since the Famine. There wasn't a person from anywhere in there that didn't drop cold dead in stitches of laughter. So did the shop workers and bosses as well, hearing the talk of this silly man. If he'd given the slightest appearance of being drunk, no one would have bothered about whatever he had to say or do, but there wasn't the slightest sign that he had taken any drink at all.

Night was drawing in on us, and the others from the Island who were in the town were making for the road home. But there was no good pointing this out to my companion as he was more willing to go east than west. To tell the truth, it might have been the right direction for him to travel, for that was where the madhouse was; the only appropriate place for him that day.

When we left the shop the lights were being lit, and we hadn't gone far when he turned to me and said:

"I can't go on any further, Tomás."

"Yerra, what's wrong with you now?" says I.

"I'm perished with hunger, and I'm thirsty, too," says he.

"I didn't think that anyone ever had the two afflictions together!" says I.

"Well, I've got them now, so I have," says he.

I took him with me and we went looking for a place to eat. I thought that there might not have been enough food there for him, but there was. What he ate wouldn't have kept a rat going. He went to bed and no one knew whether he was alive or dead until ten the next morning.

The Year of the Tea

Three days after I'd been away from home on account of Pat Sheamus — Pat the sallow devil, may God forgive me for saying it! — there was a lot of wreckage floating around the Blaskets. There was every sort of wreckage, including wood and big boxes full to the brim. No one knew what sort of stuff was in them. When one or two of them were broken open, they took the boxes home after everything in them had been thrown out. Then, when *Page 80* the Islanders saw that the contents were of no use to them, they discarded them in preference for something else. When they didn't find anything useful in the contents they decided to take two or three of the boxes home with them.

At that time the women used to wear black flannel coats, which they dyed with black woad. They used red dye before the black, and would you believe it, one of the housewives, who had two coats to dye red, decided to dye them with the tea. (It was tea that had been in the boxes.) This was an excellent idea, because no red dye had previously penetrated so deeply. One woman showed her work to several other women as she was really proud to have done the job so perfectly.

"That great demon of a husband of mine didn't bring a grain of it home with him," said one shrew who saw the red-dyed coats, "and I've had two coats inside for three months and no red dye to colour them either. Just wait till I get my hands on him."

"For goodness sake, let him be," says the other woman to her.

This shrew hadn't been long home before her husband came from the hill with a big sack of turf.

"This has been a hell of a job, Joan; the fibres of my back are torn out of me!" says he. He thought that she'd have pity on him, of course, but the opposite happened.

"It serves you right if that load didn't put your thigh-bone out of place! For it'd be a very long time before you'd bring me a sack of anything that was worth more than it," complained Joan, her eyes blazing.

"Yerra, I don't know when I've ever not brought home any sack that might have been worthwhile," says he.

"Yerra, you demon, didn't you leave the tea behind! The tea for my coats that have been waiting to be dyed for the last three months."

"You're very angry, little woman." says he.

"It's no wonder I *am*, since that house over there has three large boxes full of tea, and I haven't a scrap of it I could throw to the hens," says she.

"Oh, you don't know what you have or what you want, for you're clean out of your wits," says the husband to her.

Page 81   "Oh, bad luck on you, I only wanted something that was right within your grasp and that everyone else around here has. And may my ear be cut off if the man who brought those boxes back doesn't get some benefit from them! Such an ornate box, jointed from the inside, as bright as a shilling, with lead around it; it couldn't possibly have contained bad stuff," says she.

Seán Senior was a nice easy-going man, but when she really got under his skin, he went for the shrew.

One day the following week, this shrew of a woman again visited the woman who had the undamaged boxes. But the latter had a new tale now about the tea and the benefit she was getting from it. She told the shrew that she had two greedy pigs that had been dying from hunger, but after she set about boiling the tea for them, and adding a handful of meal, they were out in the dungyard with their bellies in the air "and sure soon they'll be good and fat," says she.

"Indeed, bad cess to the man who didn't bring a grain of it home to me," says the shrew, "and us with two one-year-old pigs roaring at our hearth. They are only skin and bones, and on the point of eating their own piglets because they're so hungry."

"Yerra," says the other woman, "that's all water under the bridge now. It's easy to have hindsight, so there's no good in getting worked up over it."

When the scoundrel of a woman reached the house, she couldn't wait until Seán came back so that she could squabble with him again. She gave him a proper dressing down.

"Yerra," says Seán, "didn't many a person other than me throw it away?"

"Devil a one unless he was a fool like yourself," says she.

In the end she infuriated Seán so much that a neighbour had to come in to separate them.

The next day Seán picked himself up. He let on that he was going to Dingle to get meal for the pigs. He asked various people for some clothes. Then off he went and didn't stop until he reached the town. A relative paid for some of the *Page 82* expenses of the journey, and he has never returned home since then.

The Driver from the North

One night a very strong north-westerly wind started blowing unexpectedly. When I put my head out the door to go out night-visiting, I grimaced, as it was so cold. Shuddering, I crept back inside.

"Would you do something for me," says my mother, "leave off wandering tonight, it being so cold and wild. You'll have as much fun with old Bald Tomás as you'll get anywhere else."

"I'll do that, mother," says I to her, turning back inside towards the hearth.

My father never put a pipe in his mouth but the plume of smoke would only be in second place to the smoke billowing out from the fire.

"Don't you spend a lot more on that tobacco than the other two do?" says I to my father — the other two being old Tomás and my mother, who didn't have pipes.

"Indeed I do," says he. "I spend fifty-five shillings every year on this pipe of mine," says my father.

"Well, enough about that!" says I. "But can you explain to me who it was that hit the bailiff from the north with the rod, the day when the sheep were being rounded up on the shore?"

"I ought to tell you," says Bald Tomás, "since it was the rod in my hand that did the deed."

"May God bless you!" says my mother, interrupting me. "It's a long time since I heard how that day went, but I never heard who did it, or how it was done," says she.

Page 83

"Really?" says Bald Tomás. "A full month earlier the driver from the north was collecting rent, and I gave it to him, only, of course, because I happened to have it, and he was extremely thankful to get it. But, when all the sheep came to the shore that day, I had noted one among them, a beautiful wether that was as big as a cow. A rogue also spotted it in amongst all the rest of them. Most of the sheep were gathered up when this rogue of a man approached me whispering: 'Your big wether is tied up amongst the bailiff's sheep.'

"'You're mistaken,' says I to him, 'because my rent is already paid from the last day he was in the village, and that's only a month ago.'

"'You can go to the Devil; for I only paid him the rent yesterday,' says the man who was whispering to me, 'but your sheep is, all the same, tied up among the bailiff's sheep.'"

"But, Tomás — and I don't want to anticipate what you're about to say," says I to him, "what you heard must have made you livid."

"It put me into a furious rage, I can tell you, but I was most annoyed with the person who whispered this to me because I thought he was having a laugh at my expense," says Tomás.

"And what did you do then?" says I.

"I turned to where the sheep had been tied up, and took a big stick with me that had a thick end on it. When I reached the place I immediately saw my wether amongst them," says he.

"The man who whispered to you didn't lie then," says I to him.

"Indeed he didn't," says Bald Tomás.

"What did you do then?" asked my father.

"I bent down to free it quickly but, upon my soul, the monster of a bailiff was upon me before I had half freed it, and he told me firmly to stay away from that one. But I said it was mine and that I didn't want him to be tied up with the sheep, as there was no reason for it, and if I knew who had tied the wether up in the first place, there'd be no safe place for that man to hide.

Page 84

"'It was I who tied it,' says the bailiff, 'not that it's any of your business, and I'll oblige you not to untie it.' Then the bailiff grabbed me with his two hands to pull me away from the sheep."

"I suppose he knocked you upside down for saying that?" says I to Bald Tomás.

"Upon my soul, he did not," Tomás replied, "even though he was a tall, loud-mouthed thug."

"You were very angry, I'd say," says I to him again.

"I was never so furious in all my life," says he, "and when I happened to get the stick in my hands again I think that, with the first blow I gave the bailiff, I would have knocked out three boat crews, even if there were eight men in each boat. For I sent him sprawling, so that everyone there thought he was dead."

"It served him damn well right!" says my mother. I believe that was the first bad word I ever heard my mother saying, but it was the bailiff's evil deed against Tomás that provoked her.

When the bailiff came to, he went to tie up the wether again, but the second blow Tomás gave him left him almost dead.

"They didn't take many sheep with them that day, because their leader was completely knackered," says Tomás.

Then off they went to say the Rosary, and when it was over, Tomás had a good laugh.

EIGHT

The dream; Death of the seal: A hearty bite out of the calf of my leg; Trip to Inishvickillane looking for a chunk from a seal to put in the wound; The boat crew coming home in a gale: The splendid plan of Captain Dermot

The Dream

Tomás's loud blathering and the reciting of the family Rosary had my head in a spin that night. I'd just managed to doze off when I had a nightmare. I screamed out so loud that my mother had to get out of bed and come to me. I caused her a lot of trouble before I settled down. Eventually, I dropped off again, but I didn't have a proper rest because another rather unpleasant dream robbed me of any decent sleep.

This was my dream. I thought that I was on the strand and that a fine cow-seal encountered me at the high-water mark. As I had nothing to kill it, she got away from me. In the morning my mother told me that I let out three more screams in the middle of the night, which was probably when the seal went away.

The next morning I set out for the shore, and since it was the season for spreading fertiliser, I was down there good and early. Although I hadn't forgotten the dream, I didn't think that I'd see a seal while I was there. I had a fine new fork for collecting any bits of seaweed I'd come across. I turned away from the house and made for the beach.

When I reached the seaweed growing at the top of the beach, I leant against a small embankment. However, it wasn't bright enough to see anything from the top, and so I rushed downhill until I reached the beach itself.

Page 86

There was a little dry seaweed covering the whole of the high-tide mark, which I collected with my nice new fork. I was rather proud of having done so much useful work while everyone else was fast asleep. But it is my belief that that sort of pride doesn't last long.

I soon heard a horrible snort from behind me, like an eery snore, which scared the living daylights out of me. The morning was not yet very bright, and there was no one else around. With the daylight increasing I reflected that I'd be a miserable coward if I didn't go to investigate the source of the snorting since I had a good weapon in my hand. Just then I heard several more snorts. I turned quickly towards where I had heard the sound, and what did I see but a big, strong, mottled seal with its head in the air and the rest of its body stretched out in the sand. My heart gave a jump, but it wasn't for fear of the seal, because you're in no danger if you stay away from him and let him be. But what I feared was that I wouldn't be able to kill him. For at that time folk would much prefer a seal to a pig, however good the pig might happen to be.

It stretched out to sleep again. At this point I noticed that it was a cow-seal, so I became more courageous, for it's easier to kill seven of them than one fully-grown bull. She was at the high-water mark and it was low tide.

I got my fork ready while she was asleep. I kept the iron part in my hand and the handle in front of me, while I set about getting closer to it so as to give it a cracking good wallop. But as soon as she got my scent, she raised her head, and let out a loud, wild snort. Then rousing herself with terror in her eyes she left the nest she had made in the sand.

While she was making her way back to the sea I hit her seven times, one after the other. It didn't bother her a bit, because every blow of the handle was about as effective as me hitting her with

Page 87

this pen I'm holding. What's more, in doing so I managed to break
the fork in two. I hit her across the snout with the piece in my
hand, but she took it in her mouth and chewed it into
matchwood. The only thing I had then was a stalk of seaweed. I
beat her with it as hard as I could, but I wasn't doing any real
damage. However, I was succeeding in holding her back from the
water, which by then wasn't far from where she was.

In the end, when we were both exhausted, I managed to hit
her on the top of her head with a round beach-stone, and that
blow turned her belly-up. But it wasn't long before she recovered.
Finally, when I thought she was dead, though I was still pounding
her with my stump, what do you know but I went too close to her.
With a sudden pounce she took a bite out of the calf of my leg, as
much as her four front teeth could grasp. I didn't give up,
however, although the blood was pouring out of me, just as it was
from the seal.

Well, the seal had finally succumbed, but I, myself, was nearly
finished too. It could have been the end of my life, had I not kept
a careful eye on my badly-wounded leg that was gushing blood.
It was as though all my heart's blood was being shed.

I had to tear off the little waistcoat I had, twist it around the
leg and hold it in place with the cord around me. The tide was
rising, and the water was approaching the seal. I thought that,
after all my trouble, the sea would take the seal away from me
again, and still no one was coming to rescue me. By then it was
late morning, and all the time my concern was for my leg, which
was streaming blood.

Page 88
Finally, when I was getting very weak, I saw a man high up
above. It was an uncle of mine — Dermot of the Bees was his
nickname. He came down to me quickly. He was astonished,
saying that he'd never seen a dead seal as big as this one.

"I may have the seal, uncle, but my leg is useless," says I to him.

I had to show it to him, and he nearly collapsed when he saw
the ugly bite that had been taken out of it.

Pretty soon two men came, and we brought the seal up over
the high-tide mark and then went home. But by the time we'd

reached the houses, I'd almost lost one of my legs. My mother was out of her wits, and my father, too, when they saw the chunk that was taken from my leg. But since the person who had executed the kill did not escape unharmed, the prize of the great seal itself didn't bring a sense of satisfaction to any of them.

A lot of them went to strip the seal, with Dermot of the Bees in charge, being my mother's brother. My father didn't go; he wasn't himself on account of my leg, but he lent the donkey to Dermot to bring the seal home. He told him to give a slice to everyone who helped in stripping it.

Old women were coming in and out, enquiring about my leg, each one of them with her own remedy. The old hag from across the way soon came too. When she saw the leg, says she:

"Yerra, there's very little wrong with that leg."

Bald Tomás was stripping the seal, and the hag was sort of bragging since she knew that Tomás would be bringing home a fine piece of it. When she said that the wound wasn't serious, that meant a lot. I was grateful to her for saying that, greatly preferring her words to the rest of them saying that I'd lose the leg.

She said she'd seen a bite twice as big as mine that a seal had taken out of the leg of a man from Inishvickillane, and it didn't take more than a week to heal. My mother quickly asked her to say what had healed it.

"Yerra, Mary, Mother of God! I remember well," says she. *Page 89* "Wasn't I myself on the Island when it happened? Seán Maurice Liam was a young man on the Island at that time when a seal took a big chunk out of his leg. Maurice Liam, his father, killed another seal and took a fresh chunk out of it and fashioned it to fit Seán's wound. He applied it firmly, the same way you'd put a cork in a bottle. He tied a strip of cloth to bind it and hold it tight. Then he left it like that for seven days."

"And when it was taken off," says my mother, "how was it?"

"The hole was filled with natural flesh and the piece of the seal pushed to one side," says the hag.

"And how long was it after that before the skin grew back?" says my mother.

"The day the strip was taken off he went walking the island, without any covering on his leg, though it was open to the sun all through the day. And the skin was on it by evening," says the old hag.

I was absolutely delighted to hear the old hag talking like that. And, to give her her due, she never treated me badly, although she used to tease me when I was the family pet in grey pants. Perhaps I wasn't very big at the time. I imagine my mother would never have dreamt that one day I'd be seated at a window, scribbling down the things she once said and telling the world about it.

My mother looked out and saw Bald Tomás coming with a big piece of seal on his back. The top of the piece was hanging on his back. He was holding it from behind with his two hands so that the lower end of it was dangling just above his knees.

"Tomás is coming down, Eileen," says my mother to the hag — for Eileen was her name.

She jumped up suddenly and rushed out. When she saw Page 90 Tomás's fine load she burst out laughing. It wasn't a sarcastic laugh, because for a long time she'd had nothing but coarse salt as a sauce and now she had both fish and oil. They weren't the only ones who were living like that on the Island in those days; most of the Islanders lived in a similar manner.

When Eileen cleared off my father remarked,

"I suppose the hag's solution for the leg is to do it the way it was done on Inishvickillane."

"I reckon so," says my mother. "Because when Seán injured his leg, she happened to be over there at that time too."

No sooner had she spoken than Dermot came to the door with his donkey. No one had ever seen a donkey with such an enormous load on it. The seal had been cut into large pieces and there was nothing to be seen of the donkey's body but its two ears and its tail.

Potatoes were being boiled by this time. There was milk and fish to go with them, and my father said:

"Perhaps Dermot would eat some of the seal when it's ready."

"Oh, it's too fresh," says the other woman.

"But might there be another mouthful of salted fish to go with it?" enquired Dermot.

"There'll be plenty, my boy," says she.

Then, while we were eating —

"I'm afraid that this boy will lose a leg," says my mother, "because of that seal."

"He will not, to be sure," says Dermot, "since he succeeded in killing the seal. Now, if the seal had got away without being killed, his chances wouldn't have been good. There's no doubt that it is the same thing that injured the leg that will heal it, provided he eats enough of it," says he. And in what he said he wasn't too far off the mark, I thought.

Then my mother told my father about what Eileen said.

"That's how it was, indeed," says he, "but I don't know what it was that the old boy got to cure it."

"He put a piece of another seal in the gash," says my mother. *Page 91*

"It's possible, indeed," says he. "I'm telling you, if the mast is standing on *The Black Boar* — that was the name of his boat — then this time tomorrow evening there'll be a chunk of a different seal for your shinbone, young fellow!" declared Dermot of the Bees.

At the crack of dawn Dermot was at the door. He was let in.

"What kind of a day is it?" says my father to him.

"It's not bad, but not too good either," replies Dermot. "It'll be fine entirely when it has settled down a bit. Then I'll take the boat to the island over there; perhaps we might find all sorts of things there."

Every member of the boat's crew was up, talking about getting ready for the trip. He soon came back again, having grabbed a bite to eat.

"Come on out," says he to my father. "The beginning of the day is the best time for a journey like this."

My father put his head out the door.

"I'm afraid the day won't be too good; it doesn't look too fine in the west," says he.

"If that's the case," says my mother, "don't go there today. Perhaps tomorrow will be a better day."

Who should be at the door again but Dermot.

"In the name of all that's holy!" says he to my father, "what's keeping you? The boat'll be over at Inishvickillane while you lot are still humming and hawing here."

"He's afraid that the day won't stay fine," says my mother.

"The devil take it if *The Black Boar* doesn't speed west under sail today," says Dermot. "Show me your leg, young lad, before I set off."

I undid the binding cord, and removed the linseed meal that was like a poultice on it.

"I'd prefer a piece of seal on it," says he.

Page 92 *The Black Boar* left the Blasket landing-place with a crew of eight men: four oars, two sails, two masts and two gaffs. A hard, strong, north-east gale was blowing. It was a fine new boat, and its crew was as skilled a bunch of men as you'd ever find.

The two sails were raised quickly, and she was let out before the gale. A man followed her out past the hill with a lighted pipe in his mouth, and the boat was already in Inishvickillane before his pipe had been extinguished.

A man on the island thought she must be the wreck of a ship that had gone down. Or perhaps he wondered whether half its crew were dead, or whether she was a boat from this place. He was half up to his waist at the landing-place to meet them, as there was a big swell there. He immediately asked what brought them on such a day.

Dermot was the spokesman of the boat and he wasn't a bad choice, for he was a man who had balls and wasn't afraid to speak his mind. I believe that only people who are in charge like that deserve respect.

"I'll tell you exactly what brought us," says Dermot to the man from Inishvickillane, telling him the reason for our trip, "and we're not leaving the island without taking it with us, dead or alive."

"'Pon my soul," says the man from the Island, "I believe you have enough to do — more than anything you've ever done before."

A strong wind was beginning to blow, and I was in and out of the house. My leg wasn't painful but there was still the ugly chunk out of it, like what a horse would bite out of a turnip. When she heard the great gale around her my mother was jumping up and down, too, just like a hen laying an egg. After a while she said:

"I'm afraid the people in the boat are going to pay dearly for this day, because of your leg."

"Oh, but the weather isn't too bad at the moment," says I to her. *Page 93*

"All the same, it could be dangerous," says she.

However concerned I was about my leg, and the possibility that I'd end up with a wooden one, I was more worried for *The Black Boar* and its crew, especially as it was around November.

The man from the island took the crew to his house, which was decent of him. He gave them food, of course, every sort of food that was in his house. When they had eaten, he called for some of them to go with him to look for the seal. Four of them went; they looked in all the caves on the island but they failed to find a single seal.

They had to return home. Then Dermot was making a hullabaloo that the lad with the leg would die. The shepherd said that there was one more cave for which they would need twenty fathoms of rope to get down into.

"Have you any rope inside?" asks Dermot.

"I have, my boy," says he, "sixty fathoms of it. Such a thing is always necessary here in order to rescue sheep from off cliff ledges."

"Where's the rope?" asks Dermot. "We'll give it a try and if we fail we'll have to stop." He threw the rope over his back, and off he went out the door, the others along with him. He was let down on the rope, with a stick under his arm, and a knife in his mouth in order to kill the seal. He was let out until he was at the opening. The rope had to be pulled up and another man lowered to help. And it was the man from the island himself who was sent to help Dermot.

These two people risked their lives for me, and I owe them everything I have, and ever will have, as long as they live, until the day they are called to the Kingdom of the Saints. They found a seal and took it with them, although the men said that no open boat could make it home in the storm that was raging. Dermot said that if they raised the sails, the boat would go east in the same way as it had come west.

Page 94   Out they went onto the ocean. On the first tack Captain Dermot turned her towards Slea Head and then on his second attempt he brought the boat to his own jetty. Dermot didn't relax until he'd moulded a lump of the seal and placed it in my wounded leg. And in a week I was as well as I had ever been.

NINE

The hag's daughter back from America: her marriage; Mr Barrett: drink and dancing in the schoolhouse; The sunken ship; The dancing master; The King's marriage; The poet Dunleavy and 'The Black-Headed Sheep': Poor Tomás didn't put two loads of turf on the old donkey

The Old Hag's Daughter Back from America Page 95

One Sunday a boat came in from Dunquin. There was a fine lady in it. No one knew who she was until she came right up to them. And who should she be but the old hag's daughter, plastered with make-up.

They didn't stop shaking hands with her until you'd have thought their arms should have fallen off. She was wearing an ornate hat with a couple of feathers sticking out of it, and an ostentatious gold chain hung from her neck. She carried a parasol, and spoke with an accent, both in Irish and in English.

She had a couple of large trunks, full of all sorts of things. Best of all, though, she'd brought a purse of gold from the States: she'd been over there seven years and she'd become very astute at amassing money.

Of course no one knew who this good mare's foal was; in spite of the beautiful clothes that were on her, there was nothing inside them but a skeleton. She never had much of a figure, and after the seven years she'd spent in the country of blood, sweat and toil she was uglier than ever. Everyone followed her to her shack of a house. She had lots of bottles of whiskey, and as most of the old women had followed her it wasn't long before the old songs of Munster were in full swing and they were singing the praises of the person who had come bearing gifts for them. They spent the whole day without a bite to eat, for every time a woman sang there was toasting and drinking going on.

Page 96

It carried on like this until Shrovetide. Hardly had Shrovetide passed when news of the *Yank* was appearing in the papers — this, of course, was the work of her father, Bald Tomás, the prattler who knew everything about the stars and his locality. Since the old hag had previously tried to match me off with her daughter when we were small, it struck me that she'd begin the same carry-on again; and no wonder, the way things were with her now — I mean her being a rich woman and all — something that was very rare in those times.

Pretty soon the old hag started whispering to my mother, letting her know how much gold Mary, her daughter, had, and how she had a mind to go to live on a plot somewhere on the mainland. "But her father and I'd prefer her to be nearby," says she, "so if you find that agreeable, there's no one keeping her from your Tomás."

"Yerra, the situation is", says my mother to her, "that our lad is young, and I don't think there's any use suggesting anything like that to him. And what's more, I don't think he's too inclined to stay in this place. There probably won't be any of the brood left here except for him and his sister, so if it wasn't for the love he had for us, sure he'd be gone long ago."

"'Pon my soul, indeed," says the old hag, "he's mistaken if he thinks that! I'd say that he'd be over there for a long time before he'd meet with a girl as good as my daughter."

Early in Shrovetide Bald Tomás went off to the mainland and cultivated a flat piece of worthless land. There was only enough grass for a couple of cows, in a miserable place without any kind of shelter, but what else would you expect from a foolish, impractical man. He parted with a small sum of money as the owner wasn't asking very much for it.

When Bald Tomás had everything finally ready, he returned home and gave every house in the district an invitation to his daughter's wedding. The old hag didn't forget our family who were living directly opposite, and so I went to the wedding like everyone else.

In those days, unlike today, there used to be great feasting and merriment at every wedding. There was every sort of food and tasty nibbles to be had, along with a large crowd to eat it. There were eight barrels of stout there, and by morning there wasn't a drop left in any one of them. When everything was finished, we all returned home.

By the time we arrived back at the jetty in Dunquin, even the blacks[12] wouldn't have been able to leave it because of the tidal swell that was reaching up as far as the green grass in every cove and channel. We had to stay over there for twenty-one days altogether, if you please, and even the day when we got back wasn't anything to write home about. I doubt whether any of them had a good word to say about the wedding, they were so fed up in the end. The daughter of the old hag settled down there and had four children, all of whom are still living with her and her husband.

Page 97

When we arrived home, the island was full of wreckage. On the White Strand there were masses of beams of red deal and white deal, white boards, a piece of the ship, a bit of everything you might expect to find after a shipwreck; a chair, a stool, apples and so on. My father's boat took twelve beams; some people found more and others less.

The boat I was in, on its way from the mainland, ran into a fine beam in the Sound. We had to use one of the short sail ropes to tow it back, because there was no rope in the boat. After we

[12] Seán Ó Coileáin, having consulted Muiris Mhaidhc Léan Ó Guithín, a former Blasket Islander, confirmed that 'blaiceanna' means 'daoine dubha'. Apparently, Tomás would seem to have known of some folk tradition attributing preternatural powers to black people.

According to Harry Lush 'black gulls'; according to *Cnuasach Focal ón gCom* by Dáithí Ó Luimneacháin (*lch: 20*) 'black people'.

had brought it to the strand we turned towards the sea again and came across another two beams close together. One of them was about eighty feet long with a corresponding width. When eventually we'd dragged it in to the strand, people said that it was the finest beam anyone could ever remember.

We still hadn't had any food since we ate a couple of scrawny potatoes in Dunquin that morning. By now it was pitch-black night, and we had salvaged eight beams altogether. But it had been unprofitable work, since we only got thirty bob,[13] even for the big one. By the time of the Great War that same beam would have gone for something close to twenty pounds.

Mr Barrett

That was the year a gentleman came to the Island who provided every kind of entertainment. He had all sorts of food and drink, cold, hot and boiled. He had eight gallons of spirits and every other variety of drink you could imagine.

Page 98

No one would sing the first song because initially they were bashful. Then they saw a nice glass of spirits being given to the woman who eventually started singing. No one needed much inducement from then on; even those who hadn't sung a single song for many years, or who weren't able to, joined in. It was the same with the dancing, where there'd be a glass offered to any lilter as well.

The old men and women started dancing; if they hadn't, they wouldn't have got a beer for their bellies. I myself was only half as drunk as the old women. Young women were taking me out on the floor because I was a good dancer at that time. My father could dance, and he used to teach me before the dancing master came. That was why I used to be mildly drunk every single night of the week when I'd return home. If anyone got any rest then it certainly wasn't me, because I preferred to be out dancing, singing or lilting rather than sleeping; I was a bit of a cool character in those days.

[13] Thirty shillings, or £1.50

There were two boat crews from Cahersiveen that were fishing for lobster that year. They were living on Beginish in a small shanty, and there was a man from England with them. Even though the poor men used to be tired after the day's fishing, they'd still come over to the schoolhouse every night. One of them was the best dancer who had ever set foot on the floor. He received many glasses, and if you ask me, he was worth as much again. The same men were great at lilting, which I think can be as good as any musical instrument.

The drink didn't last the whole week — as Mr Barrett had expected. But he asked some men to take a boat to the nearest place and to bring the same amount back. He remembered that week as long as he lived, as did everyone else who experienced it. A couple of old women were singing together, and were mildly drunk. They didn't put their hearts into it, and they hadn't much voice either. As regards the men there, they were old and wise. I remember the poet Dunleavy was making great fun of the 'gentleman' and he was a dab hand at it too.

Page 99

Mr Barrett sent a lot of gifts to the Blasket after he returned home, including a pound of tobacco for the poet. The poet didn't let him down because he wrote a poem in praise of him after that.

The Sunken Ship

At that time there was a special tax on boats that went to Beginish looking for seaweed: it was a shilling a man, whether they brought back much or little. Large boats with a crew of eight men were charged eight shillings during the high season; that would apply to any single boatload as well as twenty of them.

The following season seaweed and every other fertiliser were scarce. The Dunquin boat was caught up with the law as were the people of this Island. One very fine day two or three boats from Dunquin happened to come in. They filled up their boats with seaweed. The tide was extremely strong, being very high then, and the wind was blowing in the opposite direction to the tide. One of the boats got held up, and as the sea rose it poured in over them, overturning their boat.

Three survived and two were lost; the boat, with its load of seaweed, went to the bottom of the sea. After that I don't believe that any boat went to Beginish looking for seaweed, and no tax was ever paid from then on. That is how misfortunes happened to us from time to time, as with the tithe and every other wretched affliction that used to be visited upon the poor.

A dancing master came on a visit for a while, and he gave lessons for a whole month, at four shillings a person. The place where he settled was in the old Soup monastery, and where there was a school during the Great Famine. It had a wooden floor, which made a great deal of noise, and that was the best part of it, at the beginning anyhow.

Page 100

On the first day those who were able to pay for lessons had to write down their names. It wasn't long before an occasional person came who wasn't a pupil, but the dance-instructor used to be teaching everyone who turned up, for he was a truly good person and he didn't like anyone to be left out, although he didn't always succeed too well.

My four shillings were in his pocket, and it wasn't long before I got my money's worth of dancing out of him. This was because the house where he was lodging was near where I lived, and he would give me some dancing lessons any time I dropped in to see him. It wasn't too long before I became a wonderful dancer. However, the crowd who had paid started to prevent anyone else from being taught, and the school soon broke up. That's the sort of begrudgery that's still destroying our country, and I'm afraid it'll continue to do so.

The King's Marriage

After the gentleman left the Island, the next Shrovetide an offer of marriage came to the King from Dunquin. He didn't have the title of King at that time. They didn't do too badly out of it; he got a couple of cows and a scrag of a woman who wasn't too shapely, although he himself was a fine man then.

At the wedding there was banqueting and feasting, of course. Folk who came from Dunquin were well able to consume a fair amount of both food and drink. On their journey home the boat capsized on them at the Blasket jetty. Two of them were inside underneath her. When they were rescued they were barely alive. Women who were nursing squeezed out their breast-milk and gave it to them with a spoon, so after about an hour they were as right as rain again.

There were four other marriages in Dunquin that same night, and the parish folk nearly killed each other. That was no wonder, considering the amount of drink flowing and that they had been insulting one another for years before that. Now they had the opportunity to do something about it. After the night's brawl six of them had to be sent to the hospital, and some of them didn't recover, if at all, for ages. One man was hit with a bottle, another with a stone. One person was struck with tongs — just as Owen Roe was — by the woman of the house; Owen died but this man lived.

Page 101

The Black-Headed Sheep

One day I wanted to go and cut a bit of turf. It was a very fine day and we didn't have much dry turf in store at the time.

I dashed out the door, with a nice spade all ready and sharp and, although I wasn't exactly like the Fenians of old, I had my own good qualities: I was nimble, quick and skilful.

I set off on the road up towards the hill. I was not panting, there were no cramps in my legs, or any twitch in my hand, or an ache in my heart. I reached a flat place where I thought there'd be a good supply of turf, either there or nearby, so that I wouldn't need to go searching for tussocks and therefore I'd be able to get a lot more work done.

As there were only the two old ones in the house, and no youngsters to bring my lunch out to me, I took a good chunk of coarse-meal bread with me, well-hardened, good and yellow, though it was white outside with flour, like whitewash on a house. I also had a pint bottle of fresh milk straight from the cow, and a good lump of butter about the size of a small potato. And although no one nowadays would consider these as anything special to eat, I was satisfied with them at that time because I had a good set of teeth to chew my food — unlike today, when most of my teeth are missing. But what I had set out to do that day was not what I ended up doing — often the thing we expect is not what actually happens.

Page 102 (That was a reference to The Black-Headed Sheep, but as they say, one conversation leads to another, and that's for sure.)

Pretty soon I was into my work, and keen to get on with it, when all of a sudden the poet Seán Dunleavy comes along, with a spade under his arm, intending to cut a foot of turf himself. And there were a good few others who also came to cut turf too, because it was a beautiful day, and most of the old turf had been burnt by then.

I don't think any poet was ever known to be keen on hard work, except when writing poetry, and that's how it was with Seán. I can vouch for what I say, because whenever I try to put a few verses together — which I often have done — I'm absolutely useless on the bog or in the field while I'm at it.

'Well,' says the poet to me, "isn't that a great job for you to be doing, out cutting turf — and on such a hot day too," whereupon he threw himself on a tussock. "Sit down awhile," says he. "The day is long and it'll be cooler in the afternoon."

I wasn't too pleased with his banter, but I felt awkward about not sitting down beside him. Of course I also realised that unless the poet were pleased with me he could easily write a satire about me, which wouldn't be helpful, especially as at this time I was a young man just starting out in life. So I sat down beside him, as I could see he wanted me to do something.

"Well", says the poet, "the first poem I ever wrote — perhaps you don't know it — was *The Black-Headed Sheep*. I had a good reason for writing it, since it came about as the result of an evil deed that was perpetrated against me."

And would you believe it, he started to recite every word of it, while stretched out on the flat of his back, with only a tussock of soft heather for his head. The heat of the sun, beating down from Page 103 the deep-blue clear sky over our heads, warmed the poet from head to toe.

I praised the song to the skies, even though, at the same time it was bitterly frustrating for me to have to listen to the poet droning on, and in so doing, keeping me from the important work that I'd intended to do that morning.

"The song will be lost," says he, "unless you record it. Have you a pencil in your pocket or a scrap of paper?" Isn't it true what they say, that the poor sinner who isn't lucky in the morning won't manage to improve his situation in the afternoon. And it was like this for poor Tomás O'Crohan, who didn't place two loads of turf on the old donkey that day, nor did he finish any of the great work he had planned when he started out. And that was one of the first times I ever felt the whole world was going against me, and from that time on, five days would go against me for every day that went my way.

Well, it wasn't for the good of the poet that I took pencil and paper out of my pocket, but for fear that he'd turn on me with the rough side of his tongue. So I began jotting down whatever came out of his mouth. I wasn't writing in Irish because I wasn't proficient at it then, and I was only so-so in English. I didn't enjoy doing this work one little bit. No wonder, for a man who had a great deal of work to get started on in the morning was now being obliged to put it to one side because of some pointless nonsense.

As the poet spoke, his mouth drooped, so that you'd have sworn he was Grey Murphy when he came before Cormac O'Connell.[14] I wrote down what I could recollect of the song, and another thing, if I didn't get an occasional word, the chief guide wasn't too far from me and he was only too willing to spend whatever time was required to explain every detail to me, even if his own ploughing team was standing idly by.

By the time the two of us had finished, the sun was setting over *Page 104* the hill and I was at my wit's end. After the poet had gone, the first thing I did was to go to the tussock where my lunch was, but the meal was fit for nothing. Even a horse couldn't have chewed

---

[14] This is a reference to the book *Cormac O'Connell* by Fr Patrick Dinneen (Dublin 1902) page 1, et seq, 75 seq.

the chunk of yellow bread, and as for the milk, it was like a rock in the bottle!

When all is said and done, I had great sympathy for the poet when he told me what condition he found the sheep in, and the trouble he had taken upon himself in trying to get it. He used to work as a migrant labourer, as far away as County Limerick, and his pay was very little at that time — merely a pittance. One year, when he was making his way home, he came upon a fair in Dingle. Along with everything else, there were sheep for sale at the fair. The poor fellow bought a fine sheep, and paid for it with the money he'd earned by the sweat of his brow. He took the sheep home, and there wasn't much change left in his pocket after he bought that sheep. He only had that one sheep and he loved it well.

The poet hadn't had her long before the sheep went missing, and although he soon heard that it was alive and not lost, at first he didn't believe it because, as he says in the song, "my own people are looking after it and there'll be no danger of me losing it at all." And as his relatives had it, he was certain that neither friend nor foe would dare slaughter his sheep in the manner in which he found it.

I think that I'll jot down two or three of the poet's verses here. It's a long time since I wrote it all down, but I think it'd be a novel thing to read it again. Whatever harm came to the poet's sheep, I have also suffered on its account, even though I wasn't born when the incident occurred.

Page 105 ### The Poet's Satire on the Pillagers
This is what I wrote down as he spoke:

> Last night when I was blissful,
> Stretched out on my right side,
> To my attention came a thought
> So upsetting[15] that I cried:

---

[15] 'Upsetting' seems to be a reasonable rendition of the puzzling word 'smaogaigh'.

They have gone and killed my sheep,
Close by me, in the line,
So their feasting might be marvellous,
And a-merrily they'd dine.

Startled, I stood anxiously,
I can't believe, hard as I try,
"My kin would keep it safe for me,
No reason for concern had I,"
But the gentle man recounted,
A man of fine repute,
"The thing that I have told you,
Is nothing but the truth."

Sorrow, shame, disgrace on you,
Oh thieving kin of ill-repute,
It's what your friends before you did,
A pitiable thing [you've done] forsooth:
The learned man who speaketh sense,
To whom five parishes hold fast,
Warns how the guilty, exiled hence,
Will out of God's domain be cast.

May not a plague beset this land,   *Page 106*
That doesn't take them in its grab,
May every day onto the strand,
A corpse be brought upon a slab,
And may my curse be doubled so,
Each moment of each day through time,
Their worst afflictions grow and grow
Albeit they are relatives of mine.

Were you to see a witless lamb,
Looking as he's wont to be,
In misery, a condemned man,
Held by the court in custody.

So that O'Connell[16] bright and free,
Brings aid to him from unjust laws,
As he considers him to be,
A hostage held without good cause.

If O'Connell knew what he was like,
He'd quickly build a gallows tree,
And place his head [for all to see],
On the top of a house, upon a spike.
And I promise [you] in sober mind,
That if he passes here again,
He'll not walk free or save his hind,
But he will certainly be slain.

My mind will not be satisfied,
Without a plague to make them sore,
And they prevented from henceforth
From pillaging [others] any more,
Page 107   *My curse on them is what I hiss,*
And the curse of God to follow this,
May they be swept away from life,
And none of them survive.

These were the first verses that the poet ever composed, and with
good reason. He thought up many others but not one of them
affected me as much as this one did. I lost three months' worth
of turf on account of him inflicting it upon my ears.

[16] Daniel O'Connell (1775–1847) often referred to as 'The Liberator'

TEN

The shoal of fish: spring mackerel; The hag approaching death; The priest to be fetched for her; A wake and a funeral; The young women: a little bit of fun out of them

S ince the poet had kept me from doing the great work I'd
planned, so that I hadn't managed to cut as much as a single sod of turf, I decided to do it another day. I didn't take any dinner with me that day because my mother told me that she'd send a young girl out to me with some hot food.

That's how it was. I bounded up the hill and caught up with two others who had the same idea. On our way to the mountain, one of them glanced back and what did he see but a shoal of fish down below us close to the island.

"The devil!" says he, "look at all the fish down there shoaling."

Off we went home as quickly as we could. We launched the boat, threw the nets into it, and didn't stop until we reached the shoal of fish, which was still on the surface just as it had been when we first saw it. We threw out the net and spent some time encircling them with it. We filled up our own boat with fish, and there was still enough left in the net to fill another boat. We had to send a man back to the island to fetch another boat to bring our catch ashore. I was the one selected to go back to gather a crew to man yet another boat, and I'm not bragging when I say

Page 109

that it wouldn't have been easy at that time for anyone to beat me in a race to the top of the hill.

Page 110 When I reached the house, there was barely a man to be found, for everyone was out and about doing whatever job he had to do.

This particular year on the Blasket there were only small boats and one seine-boat. I had to put one of them into working order; there were two older folk, who came along with me in order to crew it. Well, we managed it somehow together, as the day was very fine. When we reached the seine-boat we filled up the little boat with as much as it could carry. But it was a near thing, all the same, for the seiner wasn't yet empty and still held the full catch of another boat in it. So things were pretty tight and there were not enough men to man another boat.

The way we dealt with the problem was to send home the small boat when it was full, to unload the fish from it and to bring it back again. Four oars were thrown into it, with one man steering. She would be barely gone before she'd be back again, only to be pushed under the seine-net and filled to the brim once more. Then the two boats would go off home, laden down to the gunwale. They were spring-mackerel, every one of them the length of your arm. The old man said that never before had a finer pile of fish been seen in any single seine-net.

After that it was a real chore to have to wash and salt the eight thousand fish, there being no market for fresh fish at that time, and even less for such a coarse species. We were well and truly exhausted after the day's fishing, and slept like logs that night — you can rest assured about that!

Early in the morning there was a bang on the door. My mother opened it and was surprised to see the hag's son. He was rounding up people to bring the priest to his mother, who'd been very ill since midnight. My mother roused me out of a deep sleep.

I sat up quickly, and as failing to find her a priest was not an option, I dressed myself quickly while my mother heated a saucepan of hot milk. I gulped the milk down with a chunk of bread, and off I went.

Page 111

I was one of the first of the men to reach the jetty, but one after another the other men arrived until we were all assembled. It was a fine, soft morning but still dark. Off we went and didn't stop until we reached Dunquin, where the son of the sick woman, along with another lad, went off to find the priest in Ballyferriter.

The day was on the wane and we had still received no news. Finally and very late in the evening the priest arrived, but he knew nothing about the other two who had called on him earlier in the day. We launched the boat and set off with the priest for the Blasket.

We weren't far from the land when a bank of fog fell, so dense that you couldn't see enough to put a finger in your eye. We'd been rowing for a long time without catching any sight of land or even a house. We'd been working so long that we were worn out by now. We knew we were lost there, and as there was no use rowing pointlessly, we stopped completely. The priest asked us whether we had given up. We told him that we had, and that we would have reached the land by now if we hadn't gone astray. The priest began reading his missal and at that precise moment, one of the crew saw a rock or a stack, and off we went towards it, but alas, we were three miles off course.

Well, a sort of clearance appeared so that we managed to reach the harbour although it was evening by then. It wasn't long before the priest was back with us again, and it was dusk by the time we were on our way. When one of the men looked up, what did he see but two lads near the harbour, blood pouring from them because they were drunk and kept falling down. But the reason I remember this is because one of the two drunks was the son of the old hag who was lying at death's door. We eventually made it home, after a long day that had been no holiday for us, any more than the day when we caught the great haul of fish.

This is how a person's life ebbs away bit by bit, a good portion of it spent in useless pursuits. My week had gone by without getting any turf cut, which is what I started out to do in the first place, but at least, I suppose, I had acquired a fine quantity of fish.

The old hag died a few days later. That meant more work for me as I had to go into town to fetch the things needed for the wake.

Page 112

It's the custom for family members who fetch the priest to bring the wake things back with them. From then on, nothing happened without my being involved, because her son was always over at our front door asking for help. It wasn't difficult for him because our two doors faced each other, only a few yards apart. I didn't refuse him anything, of course. That was the end of the old hag from across the way and I assure you that I was never the poorer when she was alive, and if I was, it was never because of her.

Off we went; we had the big seiner, there were eight of us and four wooden oars. There were two men at three of the oars, with one man using an oar to steer. We reached Dunquin. The son collected a horse there and off we went on our journey. There were three men in the cart — two from the Island and the owner of the horse — and a woman along with them. It's an old custom for a woman to be present at every wake. Out of respect for the son I did not speak. I thought the horse would never reach its destination, but eventually it did.

There was a good wake for the old hag, as good as any they ever had. There was a pint of stout to be had and a glass of spirits. The weather was very fine on the day of her removal, but her ancestral place was a good distance away, in Ventry churchyard. There was a tavern in that parish, and it was the usual custom for the people following the funeral to have a drinking session there. Most of us went there too, that day. Some didn't go to the pub but set out for home, and it was very late when we got back. Others stayed in the parish until the following day and it was midday by the time they eventually reached home.

Well, that was over and done with. But the dead don't feed the living, and we all had to decide what most needed to be done. It was time for cutting turf, so every man was making for the hills as soon as he was ready. My own spade was constantly in the bog. *Page 113* I didn't mind what happened so long as I got the turf cut before the dry weather came, and so I was never really easy unless I had the handle of a spade firmly in my grasp.

I worked away like a dream throughout most of the day, and I had already done a fair bit of work when some young women from the Island approached me while they were driving the cows home.

The Young Women

When they came up to me one of them started pulling my ear. Another grabbed the spade out of my hands, while two others were waiting to put me on the flat of my back in the bog so that they could have a bit of fun with me. If one of them didn't think of a trick to play on me then another surely did.

It was just as well that my day's turf had been cut when I saw the first mop of hair coming into view. Most of the young women surrounding me were fairly wild, and although I was somewhat excited by them, they certainly put an end to my work that day. And it's no wonder — they were six young women ready to be wed, full of spirit, whatever food or drink they'd had. But kneading is easy when meal is available, and it was like that with them — chubby young ones, strong and earthy, as healthy as a sea-trout, not caring who might be food for their table; it was all the same to them.

However much they delayed me, they didn't anger or exasperate me. Indeed, it'd be a queer thing for me if they did: it was the passion of youth that was affecting them, and surely I too had the right to have the same spark of passion in me. I'm sure there was many a young man like me who would have preferred to have these young ones playing with him than to have all the turf on the mountains. The greatest worry I had was that the six of them would get together and pull my trousers down, but it didn't occur to them to do that.

A few days later, on the day I had planned to be the last day of work until the New Year, who should come my way but the same group of young women. They were again driving cows home, and up to their usual pranks. And of course they found me. *Page 114*

They came straight up to me, throwing missiles and playing all kinds of tricks. As I had just finished the turf-cutting I told myself that I'd spend the rest of the afternoon flirting with them. There wasn't one of the six, were I to wink at her, who wouldn't have been willing to have a snog with me. But whomever I had my eyes on at that time, it wasn't on any of those six. That didn't matter; it was no skin off my nose to have some fun with them, and that was exactly what I did.

The upshot of the matter was that the girls' clothes were soon in tatters, and however tired I had been, I had by now recovered, for the six kept attacking each other, and no sooner were they standing than they were upside down again, very often with parts of their body to be seen on which the sun had never shone until that day.

I've always remembered that afternoon, and I suppose I always will. As the man says: "Women are the sort that it's better to avoid," and that's how it was for me, because from that day on they persistently kept me from whatever I was meant to be doing.

ELEVEN

*Fashioning a new stone shelter; My nice puppy
runs away: my father getting him out of the hole;
Killing seals; My Uncle Dermot in danger of
drowning: me saving him*

I had the turf cut now and I was reasonably satisfied, but there *Page 115* was still a lot to do to it when it dried out and the dry weather was already starting to set in. So I decided to spend another day arranging a stone shelter so that I'd only need to throw the turf into it as soon as it was dry; otherwise there'd be another day's delay.

It was a dry day, with a strong, gusty wind, just right for the job in hand. After I got myself ready I went out to the hill. When I reached the top I stripped off to my shirt, for there was a good bit of shelter in the place where I had to do the work.

I started on my job in an old chimney that hadn't been touched for forty or sixty years, and I began clearing it and using the stones to build a new shelter. One day, after I'd spent a full three months working there, I had a puppy with me. I didn't realise what was happening until he had already slipped between my two legs and had run down into a hollow under a flagstone. He went so far down under the rock that I couldn't see any sign of him.

(I've already mentioned the young women, and my fear that I would not make much progress with my work for a long time because of them. And I was right because when I saw them

Page 116 huddled together that afternoon it struck me that I could do no better than to get one of them for myself, as I had plenty of time for it then.)

Well, my nice puppy had run away on me — and it was a very fine pup. What's more, he had a pleasing, famous name. We had looked to the Fianna of old Ireland to find one, and finally decided upon the name Oscar, the heroic son of Oisín. All the work of that day was put aside because of my pup; it soon put a stop to any plans I had about doing any of the work that I intended to do.

I began by bending down to peer in under the hollow beneath the stone and I managed to see about an inch of the tip of his tail. I then began calling him but that was no use, and I soon realised that he was stuck.

I was in a queer fix then. I hadn't built the new shelter, my puppy was missing and — much worse — I was afraid of my father's reaction because it was he who brought Oscar all the way from Dingle, carrying him in a creel on his back, a journey of eight miles.

I had a big fishhook in my pocket and some good cord, which I tied to the handle of the spade. I let it down into the hole as far as I could. The hook managed to get a grip of the pup at the top of his backside. I drew him towards me and he came out easily, with a plump rabbit in his mouth. The rabbit was dead and he had eaten one of its forelegs. When I took it from his mouth he gave a jump and went into the same hole. There wasn't a trace of him to be seen, so I wasn't very pleased with myself.

When I got home I wasn't in too good a mood. I took the rabbit over to hang it up. The food was ready, of course, and I went to the table.

"I suppose", says my mother, "it was the puppy that caught the rabbit for you."

"Yes," says I, "and he's paying for it."

"How's that?" says she. "Did he fall down the cliff or what?"

Page 117 "No, that's not what happened — he's down under the hollow rock." I told her how it all happened from the very start, and how

I got the little puppy out with the hook and how he immediately dashed back under the stone again, "into a place where he'll remain forever," I told her.

"Don't worry about that," says she.

My father didn't say anything during this conversation and so I thought that he was biding his time, and that I'd hear him giving out to me soon enough. I imagined that he'd get the idea that it was due to my carelessness that the puppy had run away on me.

Things often don't turn out the way one might suppose, and that's how it was for me and my father, because when he did finally speak, he spoke good sense.

Says he: "I doubt whether Oscar would go back again into the hole unless he'd detected another rabbit, or perhaps two or even three."

There's nothing a family likes to hear more than a kind word from a good father and mother, and that was how it was with me. However upset I was on leaving the hill, I'd felt even worse having to face my father and mother. But in fact they put my mind at ease, and everything remained that way until the following day.

If I ever did have a lie-in I didn't the next morning because of my concern for the dog, and so I was already sitting up at daybreak. I ate a couple of bites and about a quarter of a pint of milk. My mother noticed I was up early and asked me where I was going, when there was such a long day ahead of me. "You didn't see your father anywhere around?" she enquires.

"No," says I.

"Oh, it's a while since he got out of bed; perhaps he has gone up the hill," says she.

This seemed a likely possibility, so when I was ready I set off after him. I didn't stop hurrying until I arrived at the flat area where I'd been working the day before. The first thing I saw coming to meet me was Oscar. He was soon with me, and you'd think that it was half a year since he last saw me. I caught up with my father who was on the flat rock, having just freed Oscar; he *Page 118* had five big strong rabbits that had been taken out of the hole along with the puppy.

My father was a lot more skilful than me; he cut a small hole underneath the stone, where he expected the bottom of the hole to be, and when he put his hand in he found a rabbit, then some more, until he had five of the finest rabbits that were ever taken out of any single burrow. When he had a reasonable load he threw them on his back. Then I went off to build a new shelter.

I had thought that I'd be able to take a rest when the turf was cut and the shelter would be ready for storing it when it was dry, but it wasn't like that, my boy.

Ever since he'd been a young man, my father had always been a very early riser. He often used to say that no good ever came from a person on the flat of his back in his bed when the sun was shining; and, as well, that it was a bad thing for a man's health.

Well, whatever he said, I had determined that morning to treat myself to an extra nap until my next job. It wasn't long before I heard a man speaking at the hearth and asking whether Tomás was awake. My mother said that he wasn't.

"Why?" says she.

"The boat's going looking for seals," says he. The man speaking was an uncle of mine, one of my mother's brothers. I thought it was my father when he started to speak, but it wasn't, for my father had gone down to the strand.

I sat up suddenly and after I'd eaten a bite I shoved another bit into my pocket and headed off towards the boat. Every man was ready before me, with their gear all set for catching the seals. They had ropes for pulling seals out of the cave after they'd been caught, and a big, strong stick with a thick head for felling them. Off we went out of the harbour.

Another boat manned by early risers had gone out, but they had set out towards the Small Blaskets. They reached Inishvickillane, well-known for the great number of seals to be found in its caves.

Page 119   It's best to have calm weather and a nice ebb tide.

Well, like the wild Fenians of old, we put out 'the four tough, smooth, sturdy, white, broad-bladed oars', and we didn't slow up until we reached the mouth of the cave we were heading for.

The cave we wanted was at the west end of the Big Island. It was a dangerous cave, with a swell constantly around it. To get into that cave you had to swim quite a long way, and much of it has to be done sideways because the cave's narrow entrance is only wide enough for a seal.

When the boat stopped at the mouth of the cave, there was a strong suck-back of swell. Often the mouth of the cave would fill up completely so that you might have good reason to be concerned that a person might be left in there for ever, and needless to say, that left all of us speechless. The only young fellows in the boat were me and another lad, but chaps like us weren't yet skilled enough for this sort of work; only grown-up, older men would have had the necessary experience.

The spirit of the Gaels of long ago must have been wonderful. The captain of the boat spoke and said: "What on earth made us come here; is anyone prepared to have a crack at the cave?"

My uncle upped and answered him. "I'll go in myself, if someone else will come with me."

Another man answered: "I'll go along with you." He was a man who certainly needed a chunk of seal, seeing that he and his family had been on a starvation diet for most of his life. This same fellow had a large family, none of whom helped him in the slightest.

Well, the two of them got themselves ready. There was a rock bridge across the mouth of the cave, with water over its top and below its base. Two men had to go on to the bridge so as to help the other pair to go in. One of the men was a good swimmer but my uncle wasn't.

The swimmer went in first, with the end of the rope in his mouth. He had the cudgel under his armpit, a candle and matches in the cap on his head. It was no good going into the cave without *Page 120* a light, as it went too far in. My uncle entered after him, with another rope around his body. One of his hands held the rope around the swimmer; one end of it was tied to something inside the cave and the other end of it to the bridge so as to be constantly ready.

I and the other young man were out on the bridge to drag the seals out from the pair inside. The two inside lit a candle, and when they went to the back of the cave they found a shoal of seals there, small and big, male and female. The female is called a cow and the male is a bull. Some of them were absolutely impossible to catch; it's often like that.

The two inside prepared themselves for the extraordinary deed they had to do. Each of them had a little cudgel, with which they noisily bludgeoned the skulls of every one of the seals. That had to be done, as the one that remained quiet might manage to escape. A candle had been on a rock, and each man had, of course, kept his flannel shirt on while wading through the sea-water.

Well, when all the seals were dead, they still had another problem to face. Most of the seals were very heavy, the cave was very awkward, there were large stone boulders between them and the water, and the passage was extremely long.

There's no limit to a person's resourcefulness when it's needed, as the two of us proved when removing the heap of dead seals from such an awkward place. We brought each of the eight seals to the surface, and when we had done that, the swell ripped into the cave, so that the two of us had to hold on for dear life, on the bridge high up by the side of the wall.

When that was over, there came a lull, and the man inside would roar to pull the rope out.

Page 121 We thought that one of our crew was on the rope, but it was four of the large seals that were tied to it.

We had to drag the end of the rope to the boat to get it back again and into the cave. This rope was tied to the seal that remained stretched out in the cave, and the fellow with me on the bridge shouted to pull it in again, which they did very quickly. It wasn't long before the man inside yelled to pull it out again, with the swell raging all the while.

When we pulled the rope towards us, there were four other seals to be seen, although at the time we had imagined that it'd be one of the men on the other end. We had to do as much work as we did before, just to get the end of the rope to the boat and back again into the cave. After that was done the men were told to pull the rope back in and to waste no time in doing so. Very often we were actually forced off the bridge because of the huge swell that filled the cave.

It was the swimmer who went in first with the rope, leaving the other man to hold it; he would usually be inside the cave. A swimmer who took a long time in the fissure might not reach the bridge because of the strength of the swell. On finally reaching it, his flannel shirt was in shreds. My poor uncle, who was unable to swim, set off on the last rope. When he was just reaching the bridge, the rope suddenly snapped. As I was able to swim well at that time, I immediately jumped from the bridge into the cave. Catching hold of the broken rope, I dragged my uncle out, safe and sound.

Our large boat was heavily laden, with four cows, two bulls and two yearlings. There was a seal for everyone in the boat, a full barrel for every man. The general feeling at that time was that each barrel of seal-meat was as good as any barrel of pork.

The skins went for eight pounds, and a pound for the left-overs. It's strange how weird life is; people would turn their nose up at seal-meat today. The seal-fat used to be melted down for light, because there's plenty of oil to be found in them. Moreover, if you presented the skin to a gentleman today he'd hardly *Page 122* condescend to take it from you, and it's a long time since anyone made any use out of seal-flesh except to throw it to the dogs. Seals were, however, a great help to us in those times, both for their skin and their meat. You could get a pack of meal for a seal's skin at that time, and if you had any seal-meat in your house you could easily get its weight in pork anywhere you took it.

No one knows what is good for them to eat; the people who were eating those things were twice as healthy as the folk around now. The poor people out in the country used to say that they believed they'd have a heavenly life if they had the food that the people of Dingle had. But the truth of it is that the people who had 'good' food are in the grave long since, and the people of the famine are still alive and kicking.

TWELVE

*The Daly family from Inishvickillane; The girl
who used to be flirting with me; Us taking the pigs
to market; The foreign braces; Drink and songs in
the town: 'there's music going on'; 'It's life's best
day'; Two days and two nights on Inishvickillane;
Bidding farewell to the best fun-time I ever had*

One particular year — it was around 1878 — was good for potatoes, fish and fuel. And so, whenever that sort of year came along, it was easy for poor people to get some good work done. Usually, in a year like that, a lot of matchmaking was discussed. Around Christmas of that year there was a fat sheep hanging in every house in the Island, rabbits galore, and meat from the town too.

I don't think there used to be as much meat in any other country district as there was on the Island at that time. There were bottles of whiskey, too, some obtained as gifts and the rest had been bought. I remember a time when there was only one oven on the Island, which was kept going seven days of the week without its fire ever being let die out.

It was a custom among the Islanders to go from house to house on Christmas Eve until the drink ran out. At the end of the night everyone would be ready to go to Mass, provided the boats could be launched. It was often a struggle with the wind and the sea but God always came to the Islanders' aid. No bottle from Dunquin was drained without the Islanders knowing about it, and most of them used to be tipsy, or even very drunk, on their journey home.

I'd say that they aren't as sturdy today as they were at that time.   *Page 124*

In those days there used to be a shepherd called Maurice Daly living on Inishvickillane. He had a good life there — that is, after his family had grown up, although up till then he had a pretty poor time of it. Then there came a great demand, particularly from England, for the kind of fish called lobsters.[17] By then the shepherd's family had grown up and had their own boat.

At that time I often used to go over there in the evening, looking for fish. If we didn't catch fish to bring home with us we'd run the boat up onto the beach, since that's what the two old ones in the house told us to do.

People used to say that they were the best couple that ever settled on Inishvickillane and there was a special reason for things going well for them. They had five sons and five daughters, the finest family that any couple ever had for generations.

I was the only young man crewing the boat, and because of that I used to have great fun bantering with the young folk of Inishvickillane, and it wasn't long before one of them and I were great together — a grand lass she was, the finest singer around at that time. We were always being invited there during that season and a good time was always had by everyone. The year remained fine until Christmas.

The man on Inishvickillane had two fine pigs, and because they'd always been so good to us we promised them that we'd go out for the pigs the following week. There was no fair there at that time, except on Saturdays. Well, one fine day the Dalys had planned to bring the pigs over, and that morning it wasn't long before my old uncle strode in, that same uncle for whom I went into great danger to save in the seal hole when the rope snapped. (There was no one else on this Earth at that time I'd have risked my neck for that day, except for my father, although he had two other brothers, and they were also my uncles, of course.)

[17] In the original version Tomás explains that lobsters are shellfish.

Page 125 When my uncle blew in that morning —

"Yerra, what's your plan for today?" says I to him.

"Why, my boy; today's going to be a good day for us. I'm off for the pigs, and I don't think you'll need to be asked twice to come along," says my uncle.

"Yerra, why is this?" says my mother, butting in.

"Oh my God! if you only knew the half of it," says he. "Aren't all the young women on the island going crazy over him — there's some beautiful girls there too, and I think there's one of them there you fancy yourself! Come on, jump to it!"

As soon as I had dressed, without even having had a bite to eat, my uncle was already making his way out the door. I shot after him and dragged him back in. I knew that the poor man hadn't had a good breakfast that morning, because his family didn't help him and his life wasn't all that great at the time.

A wooden mug of fresh milk was put in front of each of us, with a wedge of bread and a plate of fish, and the two of us started munching it down quickly. Suddenly my uncle jumped up: "Well, I'll be damned; what I've eaten here will keep me going for three days," says he. "Well, no dawdling," says he, bounding out. I sped out after him and soon more of the crew came to join us.

We launched the boat, and no boat ever went as smoothly as this one did towards Inishvickillane. There was a good life to be had there, too, for this island was very prosperous: rabbits, dead sheep, birds, and all kinds of unusual things. There were four milk cows that provided just enough butter for the islanders. Boats arrived from all over the place during the summer, and sweet milk and sour milk used to be mixed together.

Page 126 We didn't stop until we reached the jetty, and the day was very pleasant for November. We reached the house, which was filled with warmth and good food. There was a generous spread prepared for us, with every sort of food and drink, anything at all you might desire. Four young women were sitting at the hearth that day, and they were as easy on the eye as any four women you might find in Ireland; full-bosomed, shapely, clear-skinned, with their hair yellow and gold. When you'd be with them you'd hardly notice day or night passing.

When we had enough to eat, the one I was continually flirting with went out the door, and beckoned to me to follow her. It wasn't long before I went after her without letting on. She wasn't far from the house.

There were hunting dogs on the island that were used for killing rabbits. The two of us went some distance from the house where she bent under a flat stone and drew out two rabbits, and they were two fine rabbits indeed — no joking! She picked out the two best from the couple of dozen they'd caught the day before.

"Now," she said, "give these to your mother, and when we go inside, tell them that the dogs have just now sniffed these out for you" — good thinking!

Although we weren't averse to each other before that, my feelings for her were even greater after this boldness she showed me. It crossed my mind that my mother would also think highly of her when I brought the rabbits home.

Well, while I think about it, with part of my life behind me and a good portion of it still to come, I ought to pray for those who are in the hereafter, since I should think about them as often as I did when they were alive. Only very few of them who were living then are still alive today. May every one of them be in Paradise with the Saints, and when we are all called, may the good Lord bring us there too.

While we were moving off from the house with the pigs, the *Page 127* woman of the house gave her husband a bottle of spirits to share between us. She was the woman who had the best reputation of her time, although, from what I knew of the two of them, I wouldn't praise her more than her husband. While he was pouring out the bottle the man whistled *Kate Maguire*. We left after swigging it down.

They didn't stop drinking until they were in the boat, along with the woman of the house, one of her daughters — the one Uncle Dermot was always trying to get me hitched to — and two fine one-year-old pigs.

Out into the open sea we went and up went the sails with a favourable wind that brought us to the Great Blasket jetty. They were put ashore that day so that the pigs from the Great Blasket should be with them the following day. There was no lack of food for the pigs that night.

The next day, after eating, everyone who had a pig or two got ready to set off for the mainland. I myself had a fine pig, and my uncle Dermot had one almost as good; he was the man who faced death in the seal cave. The pigs were put into the boat, along with another pig belonging to a local man. So in the boat there were pigs from Inishvickillane, a woman from that island and her daughter. It was a large boat, but with all of us in it, it was nearly full.

They were put ashore at Dunquin, and then the boat came back again. There were a couple of other boats with pigs out, too, and they went home as well. Off we went with the pigs, walking along the road, and about half-way, Dermot's pig gave up as the road was hurting her because she was very heavy and had bad feet.

Dermot was going to meet a friend at that time. "Look after the pigs," says he to me, "and the devil take me if I don't find something so that she doesn't have to walk the roads of Ireland."

I had to do this for him, even though my own pig could have walked to Tralee — no bother. Two women from Inishvickillane, with their own pigs, myself and the two other pigs, stayed near each other until he returned with a sturdy horse and a cart with *Page 128* rails on it. The owner of the horse was an uncle of my mother and Dermot.

We pushed Dermot's pig into the cart, which was the toughest job I ever did in all my life. The man who owned the horse, and my uncle, linked their hands together under the front part of the pig, and I had to lift its rear-end up over a hefty, tall horse. I wasn't doing too well until the young woman from Inishvickillane gave me a helping hand.

"Now put your own pig in," says Dermot to me.

"But my pig can walk okay," says I to him.

"It's better to have him in the cart," says he.

I had to do what he asked.

"When we reach home, you might very well tell your mother that I left you to walk the road," says he. "I'd gladly take four of them with me but there wouldn't be room; the two of you can ride on the side of the rail."

Dermot also said that the old woman and I should tag along too, because the cart would carry him, the young woman and the pigs.

I jumped in and caught hold of the other woman's hand, and away we went towards Dingle. On our arrival the woman of the Island wouldn't let the horse leave without first pouring a drink for the driver and myself.

"Shouldn't you wait until the horse has been rested?" says he to her.

"But don't you have plenty of time?" says she.

I took the pigs with me to a friend of mine in Middle Street. This friend enjoyed the best reputation for hospitality of anyone living in Dingle. He never threw anyone out of his house, or employed any force to do so.

The driver and I started back again when we had the pigs in and the horse had eaten. When we reached the pier-head on the other side of the town we saw the other pigs coming into sight and we waited until they arrived.

Then the old woman from Inishvickillane came over to us, and *Page 129* when she got up close to us Dermot said to her in a loud voice:

"Where shall we put these pigs, little woman?"

"Put them in with your own pigs," says she.

While she was saying that, Dermot gave one of them a lash of a stick and hurt it. It turned away from the other one and off it went down the quay towards the harbour. The man who owned the horse dashed in front of it, but the pig shot between his legs, lifted him up, and eventually threw him over on the flat of his back in such a way that the poor fellow fell into the water, with the pig following him soon after.

Dermot hooked the man, who was only barely in the water, and fished him out; the poor fellow was very embarrassed.

Meanwhile the pig headed on out to sea. My uncle ran towards me in a hurry.

"Mary, Mother of God! the pig has drowned on the poor woman," says he. "That's a terrible thing to happen to such a good woman."

I've already spoken of Dermot as though he were that Dermot, the great hero of the Fenians. I knew that he was only slagging me off about the pig and wasn't serious about me going into the water after it. And anyway, there wasn't as much as a boat or an oar in the harbour at that time, as they were all out at sea. But all the same, I didn't like the idea of the pig being lost.

By now the pig was facing the quay, so I snatched the stick out of my uncle's hand and down the quay I went. I stripped off my clothes and started swimming out from the top of the quay. I wasn't long at it when I heard Dermot speaking to me from above.

"Don't be an idiot and get tangled up with that pig, or it'll leave you out there," says he. That was something he didn't need to tell me, but I suppose the poor man was very worried about me.

Page 130 It wasn't long before I caught up with the pig and took the stick, which I'd been holding in my mouth, to give it a right smack across its rear end. It went a good perch-length[18] forward, and turned back towards the shore. I tried one thing after another until I got it into the slip, so that the horse-owner could catch hold of its two ears. It wasn't hard for him to hold her this time, unlike the last time when he was thrown upside down. Then I got out of the water and put my clothes on.

The pigs were put into a house at one side of the harbour and the horse-owner got a drink or two, and then drove off home. My uncle and I went to the friend who was looking after our pigs and he also gave us a drink.

"Come along," says I to my uncle, "and see if we can get a bite of food." I knew that he hadn't any money in his pocket.

The pub wasn't far from the house. The two of us drank our fill and then we went out again. We had another drink, and a

[18] About 5 metres

friend started bidding for the pig. He managed to do a quick deal with Dermot, and then they came over to me. The friend paid five pounds ten shillings for that pig. It wasn't long until he had my own pig, too, for six pounds.

We'd just done that when the young woman and the old woman from Inishvickillane came rushing through the door. I turned to the shopkeeper and asked him to give them whatever they wanted to drink, but the old woman said quickly that it'd be more correct if they bought a drink for me, because they wouldn't have a pig if I hadn't intervened.

"Mary, Mother of God!" says Dermot, "let him be; there's no fear that he'll buy a drink for us, and him with a clear six pounds for the pig he sold."

"Who bought it?" asked the other woman.

"The man of the house, and he bought mine too," says Dermot.

I gave Dermot half a pint of whiskey.

"Here," says I, "take that into the room, and bring the women along with you. I'll be with you shortly."

"But where are *you* off to?" says he.

"A short way down the street; I've got a small job to do there," says I.

Page 131

"Oh, Mary, Mother of God! if you do that it won't be any fun for us," says he.

"It'll only be a couple of minutes before I'll be back again."

"Off you go then," says he.

So I left him with the two women, and marched down the street. I went into the premises of a woman who was related to me and who ran a clothes shop.

"Yerra, you're welcome from the West," says she.

"May you yourself live to be a hundred, good woman!" was my answer.

It wasn't for her good qualities that I called her a good woman because I was well aware that she didn't deserve any praise on that account, but I said it out of good manners. She asked me about this and that, and all the time her eyes were darting around, wondering when I'd ask for whatever brought me there. As soon as I put my hand in my pocket her eyes sparkled in her head, and she kept glancing at the shop and at me.

I didn't have any braces at that time and my breeches were being held up by a cord around my waist. My old braces were in bits ever since that time we went to the island and I struggled with the pigs.

Well, while we were talking with one another, another woman came in. We exchanged greetings. She was a woman from the big town, a fine, imposing woman who wasn't related to the woman in the shop, and it was just as well for her that she wasn't.

"What brought you from the West today?" says she. "Did you have some pigs to sell?"

"Yes, I had, good woman."

"Oh, there's a good weather forecast for tomorrow," says she.

"I had only the one pig and I've already sold it to my friend Maurice O'Connor, and I have six pounds in my pocket on account of it."

Page 132   "Indeed, it must be a good pig," says she. "I never heard of such an amount being paid for a pig, unless it was a sow."

"I raised it for a year and so she had plenty of flesh on her."

"Oh, you're the real money-maker, God bless you!" says the scrawny one inside, with her eyes darting around at her goods.

"Please show me a pair of braces," says I to her.

I would have kept her guessing for a bit longer, not knowing whether or not I'd show my money, only I was afraid of my half pint disappearing, having left it in Dermot's care. Sure, I wouldn't have put it past him to finish it off for sheer devilment while I was away.

The shop woman didn't take long laying out the braces, because her bones were rusting from lack of business.

"These are a shilling a pair," says she.

While this was going on the other imposing-looking woman was politely watching and listening to us.

"These braces are foreign," says the shop woman, "and they're all the rage. They're good and they're cheap," says she.

I took hold of the pair of them in my hand and noticed their quality.

"Twelve pairs wouldn't have kept up my breeches yesterday when I was putting the big pig into the cart," says I to her.

"Oh, Mary, Mother of God!" says she.

"Show me your best ones. If these are your foreign goods, keep them until foreigners come to buy them," says I.

Another woman who had just come in roared with laughter when she saw how saucy I was with her, and the oaf of a shopkeeper blushed. She went back inside and brought out the old sort. I selected a pair of them, handed her a shilling and left.

When I reached Sunshine Dermot — for that's how he was known then — everyone who was in Goat Street was gathered around him; some were sitting on stools, others were standing, and the house was full. The other lot from the Island, along with their pigs, had arrived by this time, and drink was flowing copiously.

The old woman from the island was singing *Nothing Would* *Page 133* *Make Me Reveal Her Name,* and you wouldn't go looking for food while listening to her. And the young woman, her daughter, was even better than she was.

"This music would put a spell on you," says one man to me.

Everyone took lodgings that night. The next day pigs were plentiful, as were people from the countryside. After the day in the big town it was a time for drinking and companionship, with groups of people pairing off with other groups. Every family had relatives and were spending their money on each other. We and the pair from Inishvickillane went and sat with the person who'd bought our pigs. More people from the countryside were gathering around us, some of them related to us and others not.

Many of them spotted Daft Dermot and knew that they'd have some sport with him, and they did, too. The drink started flowing. The old woman from Inishvickillane brought the first half-pint with her, and a half-gallon of porter, because, being a generous woman, she wanted to give plenty of drink to the boatmen who brought the pigs over.

She shook the hand of fun-loving Dermot, and then approached me to shake my hand.

"After such a hard week, would you sing me a song to lift my spirits," says he.

I didn't want to refuse him because he might have slagged me off. The song I sang was *The Fertile Hill of the Dark Woman*, and I had to sing it from beginning to end. If there were two people who were better than me, there were three who were worse. The old woman sang the second song, and she was great at it. The young woman sang *The Bog Deal Board*, and she sang it perfectly. The drink went down fast, being poured until everyone had drunk their fill. There was plenty for everyone. The house was full, and people overflowed into the yard.

We hadn't been there long before I saw a sturdy man pushing his way through the people.

Page 134 "I beg your pardon, men," says he, and he didn't stop until he reached me. He shook my hand warmly.

"Well, I'll be damned; I was nearly going off home without hearing a single song from you," says he, pounding his fist on the table, and saying, "Half a pint of spirits here!"

"Yerra, indeed, would you ever sing us a song," says he.

He knew me well, and I him, because I'd often had to sing a song for him before. He was a great man for the drinking, too, and I mean serious drinking.

The half-pint came quickly. I had to knock it back and they wouldn't take no for an answer. Then the music began. I well remember the songs of that day. *Nothing Would Make Me Reveal Her Name* was the one I sang for him, knowing well that it was the strong man's favourite, because I'd often sung it for him before. After I had finished it, the big man handed out drink to everyone around him.

"I wonder", says he to me, "whether there's anyone else here who could sing a song."

"There is, my boy!" says I to him, and I pointed to the two women from Inishvickillane.

Neither of the women from Inishvickillane turned him down, and sure, didn't the two of them start singing a song together. As they were mother and daughter, it was no great wonder that they were great singers; hadn't one of them given birth to the other.

I don't think that the others present were as moved as I was, because it was certainly no problem for me to spend two days and nights without food or drink, listening to the voices of that pair.

When the song was finished, the big man shook the two women's hands heartily — and mine also, because I was the one who had directed him to the beguiling music. Then he pounded the table again and ordered another half-pint. At that time a half-pint cost a shilling, whereas today it's nine shillings.

He handed me the pot that was to be shared out. One person *Page 135* tasted it and two of them didn't take a drop of it. I saw Sunshine Dermot puffing away, having consumed a great deal of drink, and I realised that we'd have to spend another night in the town. No one was getting ready yet, and it was going to be a long journey home.

It wasn't too long before the big man turns to me and shakes my hand.

"I'd like another song out of you before we set off home," says he. "It'll probably be quite a while before we get to meet each other again."

Of course I didn't refuse him. I sang one song and then another. Then the women from Inishvickillane sang three or four, and so, by the time I realised we should be going home, I was in a drunken stupor.

In the end, it was late in the day, the wool-market time — that's the market that was always open the latest — and it was time for us to be making our way back home. But Dermot was going crazy, and had no thought about returning to his cottage, nor would he have had until Christmas, or until all the beer had run out.

I spoke with him angrily and told him that it was time for him to be heading back home after having already been away for two days and two nights. So what did he do but run towards me and give me a smacker of a kiss. I spoke to the woman from Inishvickillane and told her what I was thinking.

"Yerra, indeed," says she, 'it's been a great day for us, and we won't always have days like this one."

Now that I'm old I understand these things. And perhaps I shouldn't complain now about how I understood things at that time, because we were all young then.

I brought my uncle home, and it was full of children. Some of them hadn't had much to eat until the money we got for the pigs allowed us to provide something for them. The woman from Inishvickillane left only two stone of yellow meal with us. When I thought about this I gave up the idea of advising the likes of them. And that's how I played it from then on.

Page 136 I'd made sure my own cottage was full of food so that the old people wouldn't want for anything if I were away for a while. The roof wasn't leaking either, because the new roof was ready for the winter. So far every spring one hen's nest had been found in the roof, but the nests were always empty anyway. To make a long story short, I didn't think it worth my while to bother about them any more, and I wanted to take it easy.

Most people had cleared out of the pub by this time, but not the big man. The woman from Inishvickillane went and told him that she'd need a horse from the town to take her to Dunquin the next day.

"And if I'd got myself rural horses in the morning, my load would be home by now," says she.

"Do you have anything to be carried?" says he to me.

"I have a half-sack of meal," I replied.

"Dermot will probably have something, too," says he.

"He will, of course," says I. Dermot was witless by this time.

"I give you my word, I'll be here at eight o'clock tomorrow morning, if I'm still here amongst the living," says he.

He harnessed his horse and off he went down Main Street and I guess it didn't take him long to reach his own house. I went back into where the rake Dermot was. He was hardly able to stand. The woman from Inishvickillane followed me.

"Come," says I to him, "let's go home — have you no consideration for that fine hunk of a woman you left behind?"

"She's nothing to write home about," says he, "so we don't need to worry about her."

We got him on his feet and went to find somewhere to eat. There was good food, but we ate little of it. I went to bed, and fell asleep immediately. Late in the night my old uncle came to bed too, and slept like a corpse until morning. I drifted off again and by the time I woke up, morning was breaking and a new day had arrived.

I stayed awake then because I said to myself that it wouldn't be long before the horse-owner would come to collect us — that is, if he were a man of his word. I didn't think that he'd be with us as soon as he thought he would, but I hoped that he'd at least come sometime during the day, because he seemed to me to be a reliable sort.

Page 137

While I was thinking about this I heard the sound of a cart. I didn't think it'd be the big man as early as that, but I was wrong, because that's exactly who it was. He put his horse where he usually did and came over to us.

After breakfast he harnessed his horse while we packed everything into the cart, just as we'd done the day before. Dermot of the Bees still wasn't in great shape, but nevertheless the horse was ready and off we went out of the town where we had spent three days and three nights.

We had drunk our fill in the pubs, and now we were setting out for Dunquin. We soon arrived and it being a very fine day, a boat soon came out to fetch the woman from Inishvickillane. The horse-owner, having said farewell, gave us his blessing and set off for Ballyferriter, his own home town.

We rushed down to the boat immediately and sailed towards the Great Blasket. The Inishvickillane supplies were not unloaded from the boat. Dermot had intended to go back to Inishvickillane and stay a couple of days there. We'd bring our hunting gear with us, so that we could get ourselves a nice bundle of rabbits while we were there.

Although I didn't want to, there was no arguing with him on this occasion as I was so exhausted after all the goings-on in

Dingle. Furthermore, Dermot was married to a sister of the woman from Inishvickillane, and my mother was Dermot's sister, which meant that I was often spending time with them. In the past I'd liked being with them but now I was even keener since I'd started flirting with the young woman I'd met on the island. So we got ourselves ready, raised our sails and didn't stop till we finally reached the western island.

Page 138

We spent two days and nights on Inishvickillane. Every afternoon we returned with bundles of rabbits; at night we had songs aplenty until the early hours. Then we slept on until late morning. My uncle couldn't stop match-making, morning, noon and night. There was always a bit of devilment in him — there's no doubt about it. He never missed a thing that was going on between the two of us, whether we were aware of it or not.

On the morning of the third day the weather wasn't too good, but we made plans to set out for home. Each of us carried a full load to the boat, and everyone on the island followed us down to the water. There wasn't a peep out of them because they were sad about us leaving.

I don't need to say that whoever else might have been down in the dumps, I certainly was. That's no surprise, since I was bidding farewell to the best fun-time I'd ever had. Moreover I was also turning my back on the most pleasing young woman on the blessed earth at that time.

Well, we returned from the west, and the people at home were very envious of us. We had a load of fat rabbits, whereas those who had stayed at home only had their seaweed, turf and manure.

THIRTEEN

*Death of Bald Tomás; Christmas trip to Dingle; Sheep
and uproar; Pat Sheamus in custody; Boat crew
departed aimlessly; The stormy night: pelting rain
and wind; Favourable wind home the following day;
'Hair of the dog that bit you': Marriage arranged for
me; My uncle Liam and the fighting cocks*

W hen I returned home, Bald Tomás was at his last gasp, *Page 139*
and in need of the priest. At the end of the night there
was a knock on the door; my mother called me and
said that Paddy was enquiring whether I'd go looking for a priest
for his father, who was on his last breath.

It wouldn't have been right for me to leave him in the lurch as
it was I who had brought the priest to his mother. I learnt quickly
enough that some folk in this life always seem to get the raw deal.
Surely there were others around who were more closely related to
Tom than I was, but *they* weren't woken up that night.

I snatched a bite to eat and off I went out the door. Paddy and
the priest weren't long in getting back, as they made the trip
quickly. By the next day Bald Tomás was dead. Now two trips had
to be arranged; one for his wake and the other to bury him. That's
how I spent a whole month from the first day we brought the pigs
from Inishvickillane until the day we buried Bald Tomás in Ventry
cemetery.

Paddy was on the point of moving up the hill into another
small ruin of a house, opposite our house. He was married to a

great hunk of a woman; from her appearance she looked like someone who'd been born in the Orient.

It was now the beginning of December. All the fishing was over at this stage, so the Islanders set about manuring the land. We were at it from dawn to dusk, early and late, collecting seaweed with rakes. That was what we used to do together every year until 1 February, St Brigid's Day.

Page 140 ### The Christmas Trip

In those days it was the custom at Christmas time for islanders to go early to the town. I'd piled up a good heap of seaweed at the top of the strand, and as it was a dry, windy day I was keen to transport it on a good donkey I had. I looked up and saw a slip of a boy coming towards me. I guessed that he had a message for me, and indeed I was right.

"What brought you round here, my boy?" says I to him.

"Your mother sent me looking for you, to see whether you'd go to Dingle," says he, "because everyone around is going there."

I thanked him, and told him that I would go. "Please ask my mother to get my clothes ready for me — and I'll give you some sweets."

The boy dashed off again to where he'd come from. I set out on the road after him without hurrying too much, for I was in two minds about what to do, not having brought my manure up to the field. Furthermore, since everyone on the Island was getting supplies in for Christmas, I thought that it'd be easier for me to make the trip along with the rest of them, rather than going there later on, all on my own.

When I got home, I was overjoyed to see the donkey, which had been harnessed by the old man.

"Where's the seaweed?" says he.

"At Clashmore," says I to him.

When I got myself ready I dashed off; every man on the Island was at the top of the jetty, wearing new clothes. One man had a couple of sheep, one a few baskets of fish, and another had a bundle of wool. Each of them headed for his boat and set off for the quay at Dingle Bay.

My three uncles were also going on the boat to Dingle with my sister Kate's husband, Pat Sheamus. Even though they were close friends of mine I wasn't too chuffed to be in their company, since I'd already had my fill of Pat Sheamus when I'd been transporting pigs with him and my uncle Dermot only a few days earlier.

Page 141

I was standing at the top of the jetty when Dermot came along, carrying a creel of fish down to the water.

"Are you going to Dingle?" says he to me.

"I was thinking about it," says I.

"If so, why not get yourself ready," says he. "Have you fish or something to bring with you?"

"I had fifty pollock that I could have taken with me, but I haven't a moment to collect them now. Is everyone waiting for me?" says I to him.

"Be off with you at once and get the fish; the boat will wait for you, my boy," says he.

As I've already said, Dermot was better than all the others. I was never too keen on the rest of them, even though I was related to the lot of them.

I leapt up at once and got my fish ready. I had two ropes. Another boy brought one of the bundles of fish to me, and I had the whole job done in half an hour. The boat was afloat and everything was ready to go.

"Mary, Mother of God!" says Dermot, "you weren't long."

The bundles were lifted into the boat and off we went to Dingle.

At that time there always used to be women at the quay who were called hucksters. They earned their living selling and buying fish. When everything was out of the boat, and the boat pulled ashore, the women rushed over and bought fifty pollock from me for fifty shillings.

"Mary, Mother of God!" says Dermot, "it didn't take you long to get the price of a drink from the women."

"Yes, my boy," says a cheerful woman who was with us, "and you'll also get a drink. I'll come along with you."

As Dermot loved a drop, he went along with me to the same

Page 142 house. The women paid me every penny, and when I got the money I asked what they'd have.

"Ah, you'll have a drink on us first," says this woman again.

That was how it was. She called for drink and paid for it immediately. The second drink was, of course, on me, the man who was making money. The third was on Dermot, since they'd also bought fish from him.

By this time I'd had three drinks, and so had Dermot. Because his behaviour was always a bit cracked, you'd think he'd been drinking for three months. Then we went off down to the slip where the boat was, but as yet not moored. We'd hardly got there when my uncle Tomás called to me to accompany him again as he still had two sheep to be sold.

"I'll go," says I.

"Mary, Mother of God!" says Dermot, "you may as well moor the boat. It's getting late and you lot will all be to-ing and fro-ing until morning, by which time the tide will probably have swept it away."

"May the Man Above have mercy on your soul!" says Tomás. "You certainly made sure you'd finished your own business before you worried about the boat. Hold on to it now or say goodbye to it for ever, you rascal!"

As I've written before, an ill wind blew in my direction ever since the day the poet and his songs prevented me from cutting my turf, and the young women suddenly attacked me. This was borne out when my uncle referred to me as a rascal in front of my other uncle. I realised then that the day would be no holiday for me. It was also clear to me that I wouldn't have a moment to myself, especially as one of their men who was a right rascal and never had much sense anyway, had taken a drop of beer. And I was right, for Tomás immediately received a cowardly punch in his ear-hole.

That blow knocked the hero Tomás off his feet, over the sheep and onto the flat of his back. But when he got to his feet again he went for Dermot, and if it hadn't been for the fish-women who were around at the time, Dermot would have been sent into the next world — and me after him, no doubt.

I'd put my life on the line for Dermot to save him, as I had done previously in the seal cave, but of course I had managed to survive on that occasion.

Page 143

When the battle was over, the first thing I did was to call the women across to give them another small drop. In my opinion, these women could go for days without food; all they needed to survive was ale. Dermot had scarpered off to you-can-guess-where by now, and that was alright by me. The women tugged at my clothes to get me to have another drink on them, but I was loath to scrounge any more off them that same day. I had another reason, however: I knew that all that rumpus wouldn't go down too well with my relations, for we had no business acting like mad things, especially at this holy time. For wasn't it in honour of a sacred festival that we'd made the journey in the first place?

I left the house with this thought in mind. Down the street I saw Tomás, with two lanky butchers trying to take his sheep off him by offering him some ludicrously small sum.

I increased my pace, and when I reached my uncle he was all the colours of the rainbow. Their antics upset me greatly and the two rogues didn't seem to recognise me at all as they didn't even know whether I was from that part of the country or not. My uncle had a fresh rope around his sheep, and in trying to prevent the pair nicking it, the rope had cut his hand.

The butchers didn't know the meaning of bad luck till they had met me; they thought that I was some kind of country hick who had just blown in, and that perhaps I'd be on their side.

"Let go the rope and give it to me," I told my uncle, and he didn't need to be asked twice.

"Defend me and the sheep now, and surely, if you're as strong as you look, these two gangly devils won't give you any trouble."

I think that never before had I been as angry as I was at that very moment.

Tomás let fly with his foot, and the youth jumped to one side. The kick struck one of the sheep and killed it stone dead.

Page 144 There was a knife in my pocket and I got to work and drew its blood. My uncle wasn't too happy now, with one of his sheep unsold, and the other dead. Moreover, a shilling was more important to my uncle than a pound to the other pair. When the father of the youths found out what they had done, he gave my uncle the same price for the dead sheep as for the live one.

I left my uncle and the man who bought the sheep and set out east along the main street, meeting a few men going about their business. They had to do this very quickly, because they were in a hurry to get home again while the day still remained fine.

I hadn't as yet seen Liam or Pat Sheamus, my sister Kate's husband. I bumped into Liam in Maurice Bawn's pub — he was a true Irishman and a friend. He had sold two packs of wool, and had consumed a good deal of drink.

"Come over and have a drop of this stuff," says he to me.

He was gulping down black porter, like a cow drinking water.

"Give him a glass of whiskey," says he; "I don't think he likes that devilish black stuff."

The man behind the bar did as he asked. There were five other men around Liam by now, talking together and drinking. I heard more talk outside and made for the door to see what was going on. What did I see but two policemen taking a man into custody. Then, looking more closely, who should it be but Pat Sheamus himself. I went back in and told our friend, the man in the shop.

"There's no getting him out, anyhow, until ten o'clock tonight," says he.

All joking aside and no word of a lie, I was frantic when I heard this because our boat crew was legless by now, while the crew of the other boat was ready to return home and the evening was beautiful for the journey.

Page 145 I thank God today, as I thanked Him on that day, that I hadn't done what I had been planning to do, namely, to sit down and drink my fill. I know that if I had done that I'd have been as laid back about life as the others were.

The boat we came in had returned home, and the crew of my own boat had all gone their separate ways. The three brothers were sodden with the drink, and one of them was in custody. There had been two others but I hadn't seen them for quite a while. One of them was the husband of an aunt of mine — Kerry was his nickname, but he was christened Patrick Kearney — and the other was a lad from the same family who was along with them.

I turned towards the harbour quay just as the other boat was being cast off from the slip, bidding farewell to Dingle. They had taken a fair amount of drink, for this was their Christmas stock-up, and drink is available in all the shops at these times. They said their goodbyes to me, and I bade them farewell. The evening was beautiful then, although the sky didn't look too promising.

When I turned away from the quay, whom should I see but Kerry with a load of carded wool on his back.

"Where did you get that wool?" says I to him.

"From Toorgeen Mill, east of here," says he.

"The other boat has gone off home," says I to him.

"It has, has it?" says he. "If it has, indeed it won't reach home with the kind of weather that's on its way. I suppose you've gathered all your things together."

"I have not, nor have I bought even sixpence-worth of anything," says I to him.

"There's lots of time yet," says he. "There's plenty of time between now and ten o'clock."

"It seems to me that you're as shameless as the others," says I to him; "the other boat's gone home, we're still here, and perhaps it'll be another week before we'll be able to leave."

"We'll be home as quickly as them," says he. "Let's go in here and have a quick drop, then we'll get all our things together and we'll be ready to sail back first thing after Mass tomorrow."

When I heard this, I changed my mind. And why? — because *Page 146* this man was speaking good sense, in stark contrast with the other eejits of his crew, who were totally blotto by now.

We went in. He quickly knocked back a drink. The other lad was beside him all the time. We bought some things there, the three of us, and when we were finished the shopkeeper gave us a free drink. Then we set out in an easterly direction, and who should be coming towards us but the man who'd been arrested, Pat Sheamus.

"Hello," says he. Kerry returned the greeting. Pat's speech was still slurred. It was Maurice Bawn who had had him released from custody.

I hadn't yet seen the three rakes. So I left the three others, and I didn't stop until I reached my friend Maurice Bawn's house, where they were usually to be found. The three of them were right there in front of me, so loud and boisterous that they could well have woken the dead. They were so befuddled with the drink that they barely knew who I was until I spoke.

"Is that yourself?" says crazed Dermot.

"It's me," says I to him. "Are you in any better shape than you were when I left you earlier?"

"I am, my boy. Isn't it a great feeling to have your *bladder*[19] full," says he. "Have you seen Kerry or the other lad since morning?"

"I have, and he isn't in the shape you're in," says I to him.

"Be the holy, that lazy-bones was never anything like me," says he.

"Is the crew of the other boat ready yet?" says Tomás.

"Sure they're nearly halfway home by now," says I to him.

When Dermot hears this, he sticks his head out the door, looks up for a while into the sky at all the stars, and then, turning back, says:

"Mary, Mother of God! young man, that's a boat that'll never reach the harbour, because the sky is beginning to look very ominous."

Page 147   I was concerned when I heard this same conclusion from two different sources, both of whom I considered to be good judges of the sea, i.e. Kerry and Dermot. I left the house where they were, and went off to the shops where I wanted to spend a crown[20] or a

---

[19] 'Bladder' is in English.

[20] A crown was 5 shillings, or one-quarter of a pound sterling.

halfcrown. Shopkeepers always have high expectations around holiday time that people will spend a shilling or two in their shops. I hunted around until I got what I wanted in one of them.

May God forgive me, this was the reason I had made this trip: and had it been a fine morning ahead of us I'd have gone back down the road and left them to stew in their own juice. I knew damn well that it wouldn't be easy to persuade them to do anything sensible as long as they had money in their pockets.

When I'd done my shopping, I made for the pub, for I hadn't had a bite to eat since I'd left my own house, and neither had any of the others. When the food was ready I ate it, and by then it was already getting dark.

I went out again, and the lights were coming on. I went to a friend's house, and all my other friends were there waiting for me — the three uncles, Pat Sheamus, Kerry and the lad. Each of them had a small, white, open bag. Maurice Bawn, the shopkeeper, stripped to the waist, was measuring out tea, sugar and anything else they wanted. The bags were filled; a stone of flour, or a stone and a half, and two stone for the boss. Supplies were hard to come by in those days, so they made sure they got everything they needed while they were there.

Then the shopkeeper said it that it would be soon New Year's Eve, and enquired what sort of drink they'd like. Each person asked for whatever he wanted, and, because it was the last house they were visiting that night, they all drank a toast to the house, and then everyone returned to their lodgings for the night.

One of the men snatched a bite to eat, and two others didn't. Kerry and the lad were in the one bed with me, and we had barely stretched out when the night suddenly got wild, with pelting rain and wind.

"Do you hear this, my good lad?" said Kerry to me. "How far *Page 148* do you suppose the boat is on its way by this time?"

"Near Ventry Harbour," says I to him.

"If it has reached there, they've no need to worry," says he.

The night was becoming more stormy and wild, and although I didn't let on to them, I was terribly worried about the boat. And no wonder, as some of my relations were in it. And another thing, even if none of my relations had been in it, shouldn't a person be concerned about the welfare of their neighbours?

It wasn't very long before the house was shaking with the noise of the storm. It was so bad that the three of us didn't get a wink of sleep until morning. Then there came a lull, and the wind started blowing in towards the land, that is to say in the right direction — a wind that would bring us from Dingle quay to the Blasket harbour.

I jumped out of bed and dashed into the street. I looked north, south, east and west; the sky had calmed after the turmoil. Meanwhile the drunkards in the inn hadn't noticed that the night had been stormy; neither had they yet realised that it was day.

I dashed in again to my bed where half my clothes were still lying. I was in such a rush that I forgot even to kneel down to give thanks to God for having saved me from the storm and for having so graciously brought us the light of that blessed day.

"The day is fine," says I to Kerry.

By this time the people of the house were waking up, and some of them were heading off for first Mass. Kerry and the lad were the first to come down, and Kerry told me to wake the others — for wasn't it about time for them to be getting ready since the day was fine, and favourable for the journey home.

I told him that whoever was going to call them, it wasn't me; I'd seen enough of them yesterday, and I didn't want to spend today doing the same. As far as I was concerned they could blooming well wake themselves up.

Page 149 While the two of us were talking like this, who should come down the stairs but Pat Sheamus.

"Hello, boys," says he.

"Hello," says the man of the house.

"What kind of a day is it?"

"Fine to go home, my boy," says the man of the house.

Pat went back upstairs to call the others and it wasn't long before we were all gathered together. Dermot asked the woman of the house if she'd get everything ready on the table while we were at Mass, so that the sails could be hoisted on *The Black Boar* as soon as we had had something to eat.

Everyone got ready for Mass and when it was over we had our breakfast and off we went. We dropped into a friend's house. He provided us with a horse to take everything down to the quay. We pushed the boat down and shoved everything on board. When everything was in order, 'the boat's stern to the land, her bow to the sea, her sails raised,' off we sailed with a fine following breeze.

It didn't take *The Black Boar* long to bring us to Ventry Bay. As we were going across the harbour, one man glanced towards the land —

"There's another boat coming towards us," says he.

"Where might she be going?" says Dermot, who was steering the boat.

I looked closely at it and quickly recognised the sails.

"That's the boat that left Dingle last night," says I.

"Indeed it is," says Kerry.

The Black Boar was brought up into the wind until the other boat came alongside, and it was indeed the same boat. They told us what had happened to them, and what remained of the goods that hadn't been washed overboard. If they hadn't reached the harbour before the storm, none of them would have lived to tell the tale.

We let the two boats out together under their four sails. We *Page 150* had a fair wind all the way to the Blasket harbour. Every woman, child and baby was there waiting for us. All the stuff we'd bought was taken home, and for the next couple of days we had great stories to tell about our visit to the town.

I had five bottles of spirits, four of which had been given to me by various people, and one that I had bought myself; indeed at half-a-crown a bottle it was cheap at the price. There were raisins, candles and plenty of sweets that the two boat crews had picked up in Dingle. There was plenty of fuel that year too, potatoes and tasty morsels of fish.

I well remember when there was only one oven on this Island for cooking soup; this belonged to the schoolmaster, but this particular year there were three or four of them, and they were all in use. The next day my mother had one of the ovens, and it was working like nobody's business, as there was only one week left till Christmas, and there was plenty to be done — four loaves were needed for each house.

We had just baked our loaves when crazy uncle Dermot rushed in. He had just been down to the strand.

"My soul to the devil! my trousers are falling off me. I haven't had a scrap to eat or a drop to drink since I left Dingle," says he.

I felt sorry for him and went to a box I had. I brought out a bottle and a cup, filled it to the brim and handed it to him; he gulped it down without drawing a breath.

"Indeed, may God grant that I repay you some day!"

"Boil up some water," says I to my mother, "and make a drop of tea for him, and give him a chunk of the loaf. He was completely sozzled from all the drinking in town."

"Oh, for goodness sake, leave me alone; I'll be as right as rain as soon as I have that cup of tea," says he.

Page 151   Oh Blessed Virgin! wasn't it a wonderful cup of tea I had that day, as was the cup I gave to my crazy uncle. And although I had often enjoyed a drop of the hard stuff with my people before, I never enjoyed anything as much as that cup of tea, or indeed any other cup of tea I have ever drunk since then.

The drop went quickly through every part of his body, because he was as thin as an eel in those days. I wouldn't have done myself any favours if I'd given him whiskey earlier in the day, for there's no doubt that the whole day would have been ruined on me. And in the event I wouldn't have been the only one to lose out; everyone else would have had to endure his goings-on too. With all his jabbering, I wouldn't have been at all surprised if someone had suggested that my crazy uncle ought to be tied up or put in a madhouse.

When I put my head round the door, there was a boy looking for him, whimpering.

"What's wrong, Shawneen?" says I to him.

"I want my Dad," says he.

"Oh, come inside, me boy. He's in here and in great form, because he's expecting to get married again. He seems to think that your mother probably wants to leave him; she's wised up to him, and with good reason, I'm afraid."

I said all that to the boy to cheer him up, because of all the people I'd ever seen I pitied him the most, and today was no different. I took the boy by the hand and brought him straight to his father.

"Is this boy yours?" says I to the rake.

He looked at him.

"He's mine, and he's not mine," says he.

"We're as much in the dark as we ever were," says I to him again.

"Yerra, man, don't you see that he doesn't look like me. He wouldn't be that fat and sallow if he took after me," says he, "but he gets it from that ugly eejit of a mother of his."

"I think," says my mother to him, "that none of them takes after you; the whole lot of them take after their mother."

"Divil a one of them. Sure, not one of my kids looks like me," says the joker, Dermot.

When we'd finished enjoying ourselves, I stood up and gave a slice of the loaf to the boy, told him to go home, and said that his father would be staying here for a bit longer, on into the late afternoon. *Page 152*

No sooner had I sent the boy away when a woman burst through the door, and who should it be but my sister Kate. Her arrival was a great surprise to my mother because Kate didn't visit unless it was something serious. My mother was afraid that there might be something wrong with one of the children. Something that's rare is always surprising and as Kate only visited us occasionally I asked: "What has brought you so late visiting us?"

"Pat Sheamus isn't feeling too good since he left Dingle. He hasn't had a bite to eat yet," says she. "I've come to get a drop of whiskey for him."

"Didn't he bring a drop with him when he came home?" asked my mother.

"Indeed not; he didn't bring anything with him," says she.

"You wouldn't expect that fellow to bring anything with him," says Dermot, trying to stir things up. "No one behaved like him in Dingle," says he, "from when he left the house until he returned home."

"Indeed it's hard to beat the proverb," says I to Dermot, "'It's the madman that takes pride in his own sanity.' What applies to Pat Sheamus goes for you too."

Kate was in a hurry, so I went for a bottle. She had brought a small jug the size of an eggshell, as she didn't want to appear to be asking for too much. But I got a noggin bottle and filled it. She took it, thanked us profusely and ran out.

The bottle I had in my hand was Dermot's, and it was the same bottle I'd taken a cupful from a moment earlier. All I had to do now was to give it back to him.

"Oh, may he make mincemeat out of me if I touch a drop of it! I've had more than my fill of it already," says he.

I put a glass in my father's hand and told him to hold it for me. He left about half a glass in it. My mother only tasted it and that was enough for her. I had a glass of it myself. It was the first glass I'd tasted since I left Dingle. I filled the glass again and handed it to Dermot the playboy.

Page 153

"Oh," says he, "after all I've promised!"

"Yerra, of course, what are you getting worked up about, you fool?" says I to him. "Sure, it's just a turn of phrase."

He glanced at me —

"Mary, Mother of God! I suppose you're right," says he as he swigs the drink down.

He stayed with us until it was time to go to bed, and although he didn't stop gabbing all the time, he never seemed to get hoarse. Until he drank this last glass my mother had known nothing about the risk I'd taken saving Dermot's life in the seal cave. The first thing she did when she heard was to go down on her knees and give thanks to God for bringing the pair of us out safely. My father didn't pay much heed to all of this, because he'd often done something similar himself. He was a great swimmer, but in my case I was in greater danger, as I had so little room to manoeuvre in the cave.

When we had eaten, I dashed out and went looking for Pat Sheamus. I told myself that I'd have a little bit of sport out of him, as I hadn't the slightest sympathy for him and his little weakness. He was near the fire, with a jacket thrown over his shoulders, a pipe in his mouth and nothing left in it but ashes. I asked him whether he was getting any better.

"I am, but I would never have been if it hadn't been for that wee drop," says he.

"It looks to me as if your pipe is empty."

"It is, and I've nothing to put in it, Tomás O'Crohan, my boy. I blame it on the bad glass of whiskey I drank that day when we went to Dingle."

"Perhaps you've a few more glasses of the same stuff inside you today," says I.

"Oh, I'd already drunk five glasses when they arrested me," replies Pat.

Then I left Pat, who had just arrived home from Dingle, the rotten devil — and no better word to describe him — a man who had brought nothing to his children but poverty — along with his failing health to boot. And he didn't look as if he was going to be any better tomorrow — or the day after, for that matter. *Page 154*

When I returned home, Mr Gasbag met me, still nattering away ten to the dozen and not a bother on him. Words never failed him; he had the appetite of a horse, and he was 'on the pig's back', as he'd say himself, after having taken the wee drop. My mother was still fussing about, fixing the fire and getting everything ready for bedtime.

"By the Mother of God!" says Dermot to her, "you ought to find a strapping young woman for that son of yours, instead of you having to run about like that all the time yourself."

"It's not me that's stopping him," says she. "I'd be happy enough if he were married in the morning, but I don't think it's as easy as that to find the right woman."

"Yerra, may the devil take you! aren't there five Daly women back on Inishvickillane crazy about him, and all of them longing to know which one of them he's going to choose. The finest five daughters that anyone has ever seen, may God prosper them all." Even though Dermot had been gabbing away the whole night, his voice was still as clear and as fresh as that of a man just ready to start talking. I never knew his throat ever to get dry or rusty.

When I saw the rake in the early afternoon, I suspected that he wouldn't leave until he'd started on something like this, because all year there had been a lot of gossip throughout the district about who would get married and who wouldn't. And another thing, I sort of knew, from the time of the porpoises, that he and the old woman of Inishvickillane were hatching intrigues together, and no doubt he'd promised her that he'd start things rolling, and this was exactly what he was up to.

I didn't mind him talking about this because I expected this kind of conversation would be going on. Truth to tell, it was a subject close to my own heart too at that time.

"But", says my mother, starting up the discussion again, "sure he's still plenty young, and will be for some time yet."

Page 155 "Is he old enough now?" enquires the rake.

"He'll be twenty-two, three days before next Christmas," says she.

"Yerra, little woman, wasn't I barely twenty when I got hitched to that ugly rag over there, and she isn't much of a catch, is she?"

"I think", says I, answering him, "that she's far better than you by a long shot. It's yourself who's useless, away from home all the time, and it's been ages since you brought anything decent home for the poor woman, you miserable waster!"

"Yerra, I pity you, you silly ass!" says mad Dermot. "If you think I'm wasteful that's nothing compared to how threatening I can be."

"Mary, Mother of God! would you ever push off and leave me alone," says I to him. "Don't you feel any need to go to your own cottage tonight, or indeed to be in your own bed? Aren't you at all worried that someone might run off with that sallow wench of yours? And another thing, aren't there plenty of young lads around the place who'd easily take a fancy to her if there was any hint at all that your affections for her had cooled."

"Oh," says he, with a big grin, "there's little danger of that happening in this life, or in the life to come."

I slipped out then with a box of potatoes for the donkey, and a sheaf of oats for the cow and its calf. My father usually did this himself, but he had been distracted by the goings-on of crazy Dermot. So, as I was already going out, he asked me to do this for him.

When I came back in, Dermot was standing in the middle of the house, assuring the old couple that a young woman's help around the place would be very handy for them. As far as Dermot was concerned there was nothing wrong with this daughter of the Daly family, and that it was a girl such as her that would be most suitable for them. Although he seemed quite open and frank, he was also looking after his own interests, I suppose. Firstly, the Daly family would be eternally grateful to him for marrying off their daughter, and secondly, if we took the daughter, he'd get the whole house for himself, of course, because the old woman of the house was his sister. And I'm guessing that the young girl he was suggesting wouldn't be against the match either. This wasn't the *Page 156* first time, or indeed the last, that someone pretended to act innocently on behalf of another person's interests out of having some hidden ulterior motive of their own, as Dermot was doing on this occasion.

I had to take him by the shoulder and send him out the door. He turned back in again and said, as he dashed out through the door:

"I have a big wether to kill on Christmas Night, and you'll get half of it from me."

Then it was high time for bed.

When I put my head out in the morning, I saw a man with an empty creel on his back, motionless in the middle of the road. I went in and spent a while inside and when I looked out again, the man with the creel was still there, without a move out of him.

He was some distance away from me but I could still clearly recognise who it was — my uncle Liam, looking like a complete fool. All I could see were two cocks fighting, both of them half dead.

"I suppose you're keeping a keen eye on those two cocks?" says I to him.

"I've been watching them this long while, and that's the reason I haven't collected any seaweed today," says Liam.

"Getting the seaweed can't have been that important to you," says I to him, "if it only took two fighting cocks to keep you from your work."

"I'd never have been able to get back to work until I found out which of them had won," says he.

By now one of them was dead and so Liam set off. I myself went home. I didn't get much sleep, however, as I was waiting to see if Liam would be delayed in getting back. But it wasn't long before I saw him on his way, returning to the very same spot where I'd left him.

"Oh, divil a bit of the seaweed was left for me!" says he.

FOURTEEN

Dermot and the wether; A little drop for Christmas;
God's holy night; Christmas Day; A hurling match on
White Strand: Dermot missing; New Year's Eve: on
the go again; My uncle Tomás's dislocated kneecap:
'Good on you!'; Swigging back bottles and singing
songs; Women squabbling over eggs; My last trip to
Inishvickillane: music, dance and song; Youth is
beautiful; Some hunting and returning home

O n the morning of Christmas Eve I had my four uncorked Page 157 bottles of whiskey. I was quite certain that there weren't another four bottles to be found anywhere else on the Island at that time.

"I suppose", says I to my mother, "I'd better go and find a sheep, whatever's left of them out there."

"Don't go," says she. "Leave it to that windbag Dermot. We'll soon find out if he can live up to all his talk. If he kills that big sheep, there'll be enough for both houses, but I'm afraid he's more talk than action."

She had much less confidence in him than I had. I expected that he would manage to kill the big sheep and keep his word. All that day the story spread from mouth to mouth that Dermot of the Bees killed the wonderful sheep, and that a couple of people were bringing it to the house. When I heard that story, I promise you I had no doubt that I'd be eating at least half of it — or close to it, at any rate.

Dermot was a skilled butcher because he often had to kill a sheep for his brothers when they lived with him in the same house, there being a huge household of brothers to feed at that time. They had a fine herd of sheep, and this joker would often butcher a good one for the family without anyone having to tell him to do so.

While I was taking a stroll late that evening to see whether the cows were on their way home, whom should I see coming towards the house but the rake, with half a big sheep on his back. Dermot split it so exactly that half of its head was attached to half of its body. When he went in, he dropped the load.

Page 158

"Here's your joint, little woman, for New Year's Eve," says he.

"May we all live in prosperity and joy until this time next year!" says she. "And here was I thinking you wouldn't keep your word."

I came in while this was going on. I glanced at the gift, and it wasn't a present to be laughed at.

"Yerra, good on you, uncle!" says I to him. "You're a man of your word, and let no one say otherwise."

"Oh, didn't I tell you that I'd do as much," says he. "And sure, if it hadn't been for you I wouldn't have been alive today to kill it. May it be in God's honour that I killed this sheep today in order to share it with yourself. Don't you know that I'll never ever forget what happened in the seal cave. Wasn't it great the way the rope caught your foot, and the way you swam along, holding it in your mouth."

Well, I turned away from him and went to my chest. Then, taking out a bottle I came back to him.

"Now, you've certainly earned a drop of this today, if ever you have, Dermot."

"Mary, Mother of God! where did you get it at all?" says he.

"You haven't seen much of this stuff yet, of course. Did you get any booze from your relatives?" says I to him.

"Divil a bit! Only a drop from my old friend, Maurice Bawn," says he.

Well, I filled a glass and a half for him, for that was the amount I had in my tumbler.

"Oh King of the Angels!" says he, "don't you know that my old frame isn't able to swallow that much drink all in one go after the day's grind," says he.

"This is a little drop for Christmas, and you must have another *Page 159* small swig, so that the sweat the sheep knocked out of you will be replaced," says I to him.

"Oh, Blessed Virgin!" says he, taking hold of the glass, and pretty soon all of it was gone. "I hope to God that we'll have a good Christmas, and Shrovetide afterwards," he exclaimed, jumping up and rushing out the door. I myself jumped up after him, and brought him back.

"Yerra, aren't you in a dreadful hurry!" says I to him.

"Oh," says he, "tonight is different from any other night; I have no right to neglect my own little ones on Christmas Eve."

I'd never have thought that he was so pious, because he was usually rough-spoken, and whenever he got angry he'd use language that would shame the devil himself. But what he said that evening made me respect him all the more, because he said it so poignantly, and as well as even a beggar might have done.

I made him sit down in spite of that and gave him another swig or two. Then I grabbed him by the hand and led him out the door.

Soon it was time to get the lights lit up for 'God's holy night'. Were you to go round the whole town that evening, you'd have seen everywhere faces peering out of lighted windows. For there was every kind of light lit that night, so much so that you would have thought that the whole place was part of some holy site, this grassy stretch of land, out in the middle of the great sea.

There were parties going on in every house that night. As long as drink was available, people were drinking. You might hear some old guy singing a song he hadn't sung for a year, or a woman who'd be reciting verses.

I didn't feel like spending the whole night at home and so I slipped out for a while. I headed out for Pat Sheamus's place, since he still wasn't feeling too great. I knew that he didn't have a drop *Page 160* to drink, and so I grabbed a half pint of whiskey and went straight to his house. I was given a hearty welcome when I arrived. He was a man with whom you could have a good time, but he was a bit down in the dumps because he had nothing left to drink. He'd had a couple of bottles but he'd drunk them by now as he'd already been bingeing.

I put my hand in my pocket, and I poured him a half pint.

"Bottoms up," says I to him. "That'll cost you a song."

"You'll get no song out of him", says Kate to me, "once he gets that half-pint down."

"I'll only drink half of it, and I'll sing a song as well."

He took a good swig of the drink, and it wasn't one song he sang but seven.

Christmas Day

It's been my experience that people take Mass-going on Christmas Day more seriously than on any other day of the year. But that Christmas Day was too wild and stormy. Whenever the weather was like that, the whole community used to organise a match, and everyone took part.

Two men were chosen as captains for each team. Then the captains picked teams from the men who were left on the strand until all the men had been selected.

In those days we used hurley sticks and balls.[21] We used to play on the White Strand, without stockings or boots. Whenever the ball was knocked out to sea, one of us would dash out to get it, sometimes up to our necks in water. During the twelve days of Christmas there wasn't a man on the Island who was able to drive a cow to the hills due to backache or aching bones. Two men had their feet badly bruised, and another was lame for a whole month afterwards.

That day Dermot and Tomás, my two uncles, were playing on opposite sides. I was on Dermot's team, which was where I preferred to be, because if I played against him I was never at my best, or anything near it. That day we won three matches, one after

[21] As opposed to 'sliotair'

the other. Both teams were going hell for leather, each trying to win before the day was out. However, the other team didn't manage to win a game that day. As we made our way home, Dermot sighed — "It's a shame we didn't let you win one match today!"

While Dermot was saying this, his brother Tomás was going up the path just ahead of him. He turned around and clouted him in his earhole. He sent him flying down the strand, where he left him lying close to death.

"You old devil, it was nothing that you did or didn't do that caused our defeat!" says his brother, Tomás.

I was beside him when he fell, but he didn't fall very far — only the height of a couple of men. The place where he fell was very rough, but he hadn't been hit too hard. However, he wasn't able to speak for an hour after being struck, and by this time Tomás had gone home, having left nothing behind him that day but the ill effects of his own bad behaviour.

The attack on Dermot upset me greatly, because I had more respect for the dust on Dermot's feet than I had for the head of the one who had hit him. Soon Dermot's voice was getting stronger, but even so, he wasn't yet himself, since the first thing he said was: "'Pon my word, that brother of mine'll need a priest by the time I've finished with him!"

He was helped back on his feet, and was soon back to his normal self, but his forehead was badly scratched.

We set off home, but were barely able to make it. No one on the Blasket ever did any work during the twelve days of Christmas; all they did was to recover themselves for the matches they were playing during those days.

New Year's Day *Page 162*

We weren't up to much after the great match of Christmas Day. Everyone was half banjaxed — with painful legs and aching bones. But we had a week of quiet relaxation right up to New Year's Day. Anyone who had broken their hurley was busy replacing it.

Most of the hurleys that were used on the beach came from the parish of Ventry. They were made of furze and were curved at the end. The furze was flexible, and bent in the sand. The ball was made of stocking thread, which had been woven with hemp thread. Whenever the ball hit the ankles of a player, it would send him flying onto the flat of his back. In all probability he wouldn't be able to walk on that leg for the rest of the day.

However good a player I may have been, I was a bit clumsy with my hurley, and I happened to be out on the wing this time. I belted the ball for all I was worth and who should be in its path but my uncle Tomás, and where did the ball hit him but on his kneecap, dislocating it.

"Good on you!" says Dermot; these were the first words I heard, and they were so loud that they must have been heard all the way back at home. All who were on the beach gathered round the 'dead' man, for a person might as well be dead if he were crippled.

Dermot thought that he wasn't too badly hurt. But when he saw that the situation was worse than he had first imagined, all his joking and banter stopped. Tomás had to be helped home, and Dermot was fully aware of this.

After we had brought Tomás home we went straight down to the beach again, because it was the first day of the New Year and I suppose it was one of the worst days that ever was. The stars had just appeared in the sky while we were coming home that evening, tired, sore and exhausted.

While I was making my way to my own house, who should be coming up the path behind me but Dermot, and you wouldn't have given tuppence for him after all the harrowing experiences endured that day. I waited until he was right beside me.

Page 163 "I've still got a bit of business for you," says I to him. He couldn't have cared less what the business was as he walked alongside me.

My mother mentioned Tomás's leg to him. He really had received a nasty blow, and he wouldn't be able to walk on it next year. The kneecap is a tricky business, and it might well be the case that it'd never be right again.

"He will make a good cripple!" says Dermot.

"Is that all the sympathy you have for him?" says she.

"It's only a week since he beat the hell out of me on the beach, for no good reason at all," says he. "But I do feel for his children."

When they had finished chatting about all this, I darted over to a box where I had stored some beer and took out a good big bottle which hadn't yet been opened. Dermot thought he had landed up in heaven when he saw the full bottle of booze, and in addition to that, cooking on the fire, a big hunk of mutton, which he himself had given us. It had never been in my nature to refuse hospitality to anyone who asked for it, and Dermot was like that too. Actually, Dermot's gift of mutton was much more to my liking than all the whiskey in the five bottles.

I got a big glass and filled it right to the brim. He didn't refuse it because he had no excuse to do so. When he had put it in the place that had need of it, he said:

"The devil take me! I'd be dead and buried today if it hadn't been for what you brought along with you. But I suppose that it was the will of God."

"But I got most of the drink as a present," says I to him.

"The devil take the lot of them! Wasn't I bringing food to many's the person before you were even born, and it was little I ever received for my trouble," says he.

"I suppose they felt you were nearing your end and that there was no point in trying to induce you to go anywhere as they wouldn't be likely to be getting anything more out of you," says I to him.

"May God give them nowt, the pack of rogues!" says he. "For I got sweet damn all from them."

I had crazy Dermot eating out of my hand by now. He'd *Page 164* become quite talkative after taking the wee drop, so I decided to pay a visit to Pat Sheamus. Pat was usually a man full of foolish prattle, and a bit naïve, but he hadn't been feeling himself since the unfortunate event that occurred on the day when he was in Dingle. But he still played hurley with the same great zeal every day, although he wasn't much good at it now. Yes, indeed, it was an entirely different story before that fateful day in Dingle, when Pat was one of the best players we had.

I was thinking that it wouldn't be long before I'd be having a drink with Pat, and getting a bit of fun out of him. So I grabbed the bottle and darted out. I was keen to share it with Pat, because he was always more than willing to share any of his own drink with me.

After being there for a while, I said:

"There is no story-telling or reciting of poems going on in this house tonight. Surely we should be celebrating on New Year's Eve?"

"The man of the house isn't too feisty yet," says Kate.

"I suppose he didn't get enough to drink yet," says I; "if he'd drunk another lot of spirits there'd probably be a bit more chat out of him."

"Are you joking, Tomás O'Crohan?" says Pat. "Can't you see our old bones are contorted with pain by now!"

I thought I'd never hear those words coming from his lips, and realising that it wouldn't be too long before it was time to eat, I made a grab for the cup that was hanging on the dresser and took it over to Pat. I filled it up with drink and handed it to him. He drank it with relish, and it wasn't long before he started singing *Bawb na Grave*.[22] One song followed another, and pretty soon I heard the sound of footsteps approaching. I thought it might be my father calling me home to eat, but who was it but Dermot.

"Your food is ready," says he to me.

There was a boy along with him to call Dermot home too. Whatever the boy said, Dermot wasn't too keen on going home. He simply sat down on a three-legged stool.

Page 165 "I suppose", says he to Pat, "you wouldn't know any verse of *Susheen Bawn*;[23] it's a long time since I've heard it."

"Yerra, go on with you out of that," says I to him, "didn't a boy call you to dinner over an hour ago, and here you are still looking for a song."

[22] Báb na gCraobh
[23] Súisín Bán

"God be my witness, if he starts singing, I'll stay until daybreak tomorrow," says the joker Dermot. "If it's all the same to you, I'll stay here and you go off and have your food."

Since Dermot wouldn't agree to come with me to eat his dinner, I went off and left him with Pat, who was singing the song. The two of them hadn't a care in the world, but by the time I got home the potatoes were pretty well stone-cold.

"You took your time about coming home!" says my mother. "Didn't the rake call you?"

"He did indeed, and the hound was faster than the messenger," says I, "because he himself is still there and I've arrived home."

"Oh, Mary, Mother of God! isn't it the useless creature he is!" says she.

Well, even if the potatoes had gone stone-cold, the meat — a slice of mutton — was hot and good. When I had eaten my fill, I wanted to go back to where the fun was. I thought that I mightn't have an opportunity like this for another year. When this thought struck me, I told my mother that I was going back again to Pat Sheamus's house, and that if I were late returning, not to worry about me, "because, if Dermot doesn't leave, I'll probably stay there too. Put the latch on the door but don't bolt it."

Anyway, I went to the chest where I kept my booze, and took another bottle with me. It was the third bottle, and it was still more than half full. This was one of those very special evenings for me. I gave a glass of whiskey to my father, although he didn't drink much of it. I gave another glass to my mother, but she only sipped at it, and I had the third glass myself.

"I don't know," says I to the old couple, "should I bring the whole bottle to Kate's house?" *Page 166*

I was checking them out, because even if they were to say no to me, I would have brought it along with me anyway — on the quiet — but they didn't. I wanted to hear what my father had to say to me, because he'd never complain unless he thought someone was completely out of order. So this is what he said:

"You often find people drinking together, even with people they don't get on with at all. Of course, that's not how it is with your sister and uncle, so wouldn't it be a sorry business if you didn't bring something along with you tonight to have a drink with them."

I stuffed the bottle into my pocket and dashed out the door. I wouldn't have been happy bringing it along with me if the old couple had been against the idea. When I went outside, I could hear, some distance from the house, Dermot carrying on, as per usual.

When I went into the house Dermot was standing there as large as life and in excellent voice.

"Hey there, how's it going? Good to see you," says he.

"Have you not gone home yet?" says I.

"Divil a bit of it!" says he. "There are plenty of relatives, praise be to God! all around. I'm making myself at home with many of them. I've eaten my food here, my boy, and along with it, I've had my fair share of the drink too."

"Has there been any singing going on?"

"We've sung five songs already, and now there'll be more, since you've rejoined us. It'll be a night to remember. Sure, none of us knows who'll be here the next time there's a gathering like this."

"How about Pat there singing a song for you?"

"Yerra, I'm sure Pat wouldn't mind one little bit if he got some help."

"What kind of help would he be needing?"

"Yerra, a drop of the herb that puts life in everyone. Didn't you hear that verse from long ago?"

"I didn't; if you know it, let's have it," says I.

Page 167

'Twas just what the doctor had ordered,
Drinking porter and this stuff's so cheap,
It banishes gloom and restores us,
For it makes our lives merry and sweet.
The old woman who lay in the corner,
A whole year on her blanket in pain,
When she drank a half-pint of the 'bould' stuff,
Sure she tossed her blanket away!

The whole gathering was ill at ease at first until this merry verse was sung, then everybody loosened up a bit. I took out my bottle, and my uncle thought that it was a jewel from heaven in my hand. At first they thought I was joking, and that there was nothing in the bottle, until I took a mug and poured out a drop for my uncle. He put it under his nose, and then, as he drank it, you would have thought that both his heart and his liver were smiling at you.

"You'll have to sing a song now, Dermot," says I to him.

I offered Pat a drop of the hard stuff, and he didn't say no. I let them have the whole bottle, so that I could have some fun with them that evening.

"I suppose", says Dermot, "that it's God who inspired him to bring all the bottles along. Upon my word, I'd be a heap of dust on the ground by now if it weren't for all this fine drink I've consumed!"

"Sing a song, Pat," says I to him, and he quickly sang *Eamon Vagoynie*.[24] I liked it a lot since Pat wasn't too bad a singer at all when he had a clear throat and after he had taken a swig of the hard stuff.

Dermot sang *Long Sallow Red Legs*.[25] Then he jumped up and said:

"The Blessing of God on the souls of the dead! Would you mind singing *The Quilt* for me, Tomás? I haven't heard that one sung since the last time the poet Dunleavy recited it."

I didn't require much coaxing, although *The Quilt* was a tough one for me — eighteen verses in all. That's all I sang and I didn't need to do any more as the dawn was already brightening.

"Oh King of Glory! May He be praised for ever! How did he get it together?" says Dermot. *Page 168*

Day was breaking as we went our separate ways. Dermot, the rake, setting off for his own house, exclaims: "May God grant that no harm befalls you throughout the coming year." Then he set off

---

[24] Éamann Mhágáine: traditional Irish folksong about unrequited love
[25] *Cosa Buí Arda Dearga*: traditional Irish folksong

eastwards, and I went west. When I got home I fell asleep, and it was dinner time before I woke.

After my dinner, I stuck my head out, and I saw one of our donkeys approaching the house. My father told me to take her south for the rest of the day, where she would be sheltered from the cold north wind.

I immediately did as my father asked, and it suited me because I had a dozen sheep of my own in the vicinity, and I wanted to have a look at them too. Off I went, and while I was going up the embankment directly opposite the houses I heard a row going on. I prodded the donkey some more so that I would get nearer to the commotion and to whomever was making it.

I first saw a shrew of a woman, with a mop of red hair on her head, standing outside a semi-detached cottage. She was going crazy, working herself up into a frenzy. I understood from what she was saying that hens' eggs were the cause of the dispute.

"And, you old devil," says she, "you're not satisfied collecting eggs from your own roof but you have to go taking them from mine too."

I was amazed that the person she was talking to didn't answer her back, but very soon the woman of the other house came to the door, and peered warily until she had managed to get behind the other woman. Then giving a sudden leap and grabbing her neighbour's red hair, she immediately dragged her to the ground.

Well, I didn't blame her for doing that as the red-haired woman deserved to be taken down a peg or two. But she wasn't satisfied *Page 169* even after pulling out tufts of her neighbour's curly red hair, throwing them on the dungyard and digging her knees into her belly. But to make matters worse, the red-haired woman was pregnant. So what would you suggest I should have done in this situation? There wasn't a soul to be seen except the two young women, shouting and screaming. If I'd had a witness to back me up, I wouldn't have hesitated to intervene, even if one of them were dead. But if I were to try anything on my own, and their husbands turned up, they would have certainly got together to put me away for a stretch; and sure, isn't that the way it has always been?

Well, even if I was aware of the risk, I couldn't look at someone killing another person and not do anything about it — that would have been shameful. So out of fear of God I had to try to do something. I rushed in and pulled the attacking woman's claws out of her neighbour's hair. The dark-haired woman on the attack was absolutely livid. But isn't it amazing how crafty people can be — because if she hadn't sneaked up, the red-haired woman would have ripped her apart. I carried the red-haired woman into her house and gave her a drink of water, but she still wasn't able to talk. When she recovered I couldn't understand her, although it was only Gaelic she was speaking.

Before I left the red-haired woman's house, who should come in but my mother.

"Mary, Mother of God! is it here you are, and the donkey already at home," says she.

"Is the donkey alive?" says I.

"He is, indeed," says she. "What did you think had happened to him?"

"I had to let him wander off home as I didn't want to have two dead women on my hands," says I to my mother.

The red-haired woman laughed. "Oh, we put on a good show for you," says she. "But even so, I suppose it must have been God who sent you to us." By this time her voice had become weak, even after saying as little as she did.

I went to see the dark-haired woman before I set off home, and upon my word, there she was, coming at me. "For two pins, I'd give you a clout of this," says she — with a shovel in her hand — *Page 170* "why didn't you let me teach that one a good lesson when I had her at my mercy? If she'd had me on the ground she'd have done me in quickly enough. After all, isn't she a red-head, my boy!"

"But I suppose she has seen her best days: her fine head of hair is in a mess now and she's hardly able to speak, and it'll take her some time to recover," says I to her.

"And no harm either," replies the dark-haired woman.

That same day the men had gone to the hills for turf, taking their cows with them. I realised that the best thing for me to do would be to head off home, because I'd had enough trouble already that day, and I'd no idea how things might develop when their husbands turned up. I set off, keeping an ear open in order to hear if there was any quarrelling between the men after they had heard what the women had to say. However, there wasn't a peep out of them, because women's temperament isn't the same as men's. Those women were two of the worst shrews that ever walked the roads of Ireland.

That afternoon was raw and stormy, and my father said to me:

"You'd better make tracks and head up to the cows, since that's all the cattle you have."

"I'll do as you say," says I.

I threw my jacket over my shoulders and headed out to the hill. When I reached the grazing ground where the cows were, there were people gathered there already. Amongst them was the poet, with a stick in his hand, because he had a cow at this time whose like wasn't to be found at a fair: a sleek, jet-black cow that used to produce over one hundred litres every year when she was in good form. She had a fine body as well.

"Well", I thought, "the poet won't hold up today's work as he did the other day when he met me." We hadn't met each other since the time he had delayed my turf-cutting.

"Do you know any bit of *The Donkey's Song*?" says he to me.

"I know part of it, but not all of it," says I to him.

Page 171 "Have you some paper in your pocket? If so, take it out — and your pen," says he. "Now's the time for it, because everything I've ever written will soon go to the grave with me unless you jot it down."

I didn't much like this idea, because I didn't want to be sitting on a tussock on a cold raw afternoon. But, if I hadn't done what he had asked, it wouldn't have taken him long to concoct a verse about 'yours truly' that might well have done me a lot of harm. All of us who were there threw ourselves down beside a ditch, and my boy started up on his song. Here's a verse as an example; a verse that is as fine as anything else you might find in any book or on any page:

My mind is troubled every day,
Since I received a communiqué,
From the army offering forty pounds,
To which I've not replied.
The reason that I so delay,
Is that I must seek good advice,
Perhaps I should accept their pay,
For there, from peril, none can hide.

I promise you, dear reader, that by the time I had a dozen verses jotted down, and my whole afternoon wasted on me, I wouldn't have been too upset if he'd already passed away from this world. And whoever has to endure writing down this poet's work in future, may it not be me. It was pitch black night by the time we'd finished.

All of us went off home. The cows were already back long before we arrived home.

"Yerra," says my mother, "what kept you so long on such a cold and stormy night, long after the cows have returned home?"

I told her what had happened.

"Indeed, the poet doesn't have much sense, to be keeping you all hours on top of that hill. Your food has gone cold on you now," says she to me.

I bolted down a dozen fairly cold potatoes, with a drop of hot *Page 172* milk and hot fish to go with them. After eating all that, I made my way out again. There were certain houses in the local area where the young boys and girls used to get together until all hours of the night. To give this house its due, and the young people who used to be meeting one another there, I am proud to say that, over the twenty-seven years I hung out in that place, nothing untoward ever happened between them.

We spent the evening there with one another in high spirits until long into the night. I came home and went to sleep, or perhaps had forty winks. When I woke I heard a fierce knocking on the door. Because I was awake, I sat up with a jolt and opened the door. A man stuck his head in and, because it was so dark, I didn't know who it was until he spoke.

"Put your clothes on; it's a lovely day," said the voice. Then I knew who it was — it was the gasbag Dermot. "Have some food and we'll set out for Inishvickillane. We'll spend a couple of days over there. We'll catch some rabbits and seals, and perhaps some of those women will tag along with us," says he. "Come on! No dawdling, now."

I'd heard many suggestions odder than that one, because it wasn't unheard of for me to spend a week amongst the young women over there, as one of them was dearer to me at that time than any other woman in Ireland.

Off I went and got myself ready. When I reached the jetty they were all there waiting for me. The day was very fine and off we went until we reached the western island. There was a large family on it at this time, all grown up, and everyone who was on Inishvickillane came down to the jetty. You would have thought that the island was Tír na nÓg[26] that day.

By the time we got to the house, everything was there ready waiting for us, because they could see the boat coming. Dermot was so merry at the time that he threw his hat off and sat down at the table. You would have thought that he'd arrived in Paradise.

Page 173
When we had eaten, we set off hunting, with all the boys and girls from Inishvickillane tagging along with us. It was a beautiful day; rabbits were darting off with dogs after them. The dogs would catch one while two others would escape. To tell the truth, I myself spent the whole afternoon with the young women, and it showed — as my hunting wasn't up to much.

There had been six of us altogether in the boat — four of us all facing each other. There was no one with me now except for a boy and a girl from Inishvickillane, and when they had caught a dozen rabbits for me, they said:

"Let's go to the house. You've got enough for today; we'll catch another fine bundle for you tomorrow."

---

[26] i.e. 'The Land of Youth' — a land free from old age, pain or sorrow where the legendary hero Oisín spent 300 years with the beautiful Niamh.

I did as they asked; I didn't mind because I was pretty sure that Dermot wouldn't be upset with me. We had eaten our food when the other three came in with a fine catch. They were served food, and they had a keen appetite for it, because hunting or fishing can do that to you. When our bellies were full, we lay down on the bracken that was all over the floor.

No sooner had we done so than Dermot came in with Kerry (Kerry was his hunting partner that day). Kerry was carrying so many rabbits that all we could see of him was his two eyes. And you wouldn't have believed that it was the same bright and cheery Dermot at all, because he was so filthy dirty from rummaging around in every hole and dragging out rabbits that had been chased by Kerry's ferret.

"Good on you, old uncle!" says I to him; "upon my soul, 'tis you who's the hunter and not myself; I only caught a dozen since this morning." He cocked his head at me while I was saying this.

"Oh, Mary, Mother of God! my dear lad, I knew that very few rabbits would fall to you when I saw you this morning in the company of the young women," says he.

"He only caught a dozen," says one of the lads, who wanted to have a bit of fun at my expense.

"My goodness, it's a good thing he managed to catch a dozen, my boy. Now, if he'd only had one of those fine-bodied sisters of yours along with him!" Dermot was still washing himself, before coming to the table for his food. *Page 174*

Rather than all the rabbits on Inishvickillane that day, today I'd much prefer to have the fine set of strong teeth that Dermot had when he sat down to eat his food. Even on the other side of the door you'd have heard every crunch his teeth made on the bones of a sheep or a rabbit.

"Sing a song or something for me", says he, "while I'm eating."

"I might do a dance when you've had your meal," says I to him.

"Stop codding around," says he. "Sing *Saint Patrick's Day.*"

I couldn't refuse him, of course, and besides I knew that somebody had to get the ball rolling because the night might well and truly have been over before anyone decided to start singing.

There were, of course, other good singers there, Kerry for one and my uncle Tomás being another.

I started singing my song slowly, gently and softly. I'd made myself comfortable, stretching out on the flat of my back in the warm dry bracken, with only my head to be seen. Dermot finished eating as I came to the end of my song.

"Indeed, well done, my dear lad!" says he, leaving the table and shaking my hand vigorously.

He turned to the other end of the room where the woman of the house and her five daughters were sitting. As I've already mentioned, there wasn't a mother or any five daughters in any house in Ireland who could equal or surpass their beauty.

Youth is beautiful; there is nothing as fine as it. At that moment I thought that there surely wasn't a lord or an earl in the Page 175 whole country of Ireland who was as contented as I was. I hadn't a worry in the world, lying on the flat of my back in a bed of sorts — a kind of green, rushy bank, as described in the tale of Dermot and Gráinne.[27] Here I was, amongst a fine company of people on a sea island, with a group of young women across the room from me. As I listened to their sweet voices, each more beautiful than the other, I couldn't tell whether they were from this world, or heaven, or from the land of the fairies.

By now the woman of the house had started smoking. After she'd filled her pipe she gave it to Dermot. (He would smoke huge amounts out of other people's pipes, but no one ever smoked out of his because he didn't own one.) He didn't sit on the ground but was organising the singers. When everyone had sung a song, he got the dancing going.

"You've been quiet for a good while there," says he to me. "Hop up there and do a bit of dancing for me. Pull out one of those fine-rounded young women over there. Let someone sing for them," says the rake.

---

[27] Tale from the Fenian Cycle of Irish mythology, it concerns a love triangle between the great warrior Finn MacCoole, the beautiful princess Gráinne, and her paramour Dermot O'Dyna.

It was no good refusing him, because he would have become upset and the whole evening would have been spoilt. The woman of the house began lilting and there was no better woman for it. I hopped up, of course, and called out to the eldest son of the household, because he was grown up at this time. We did a reel.

"You sure can move those legs!" says the rake.

We went on like that until it was nearly day, then everyone went off to snatch forty winks. The day was brightening in the east before any of us woke. Dermot was the first of us to notice the sunrise, waking us, one after the other, with a nudge of his foot. None of us wanted to set off until we'd eaten something. There was no sign that the women were willing to help Dermot, and he wasn't too pleased about that. He set a fire himself, and gave me a bucket to fetch water, but on sticking my head out the door, I saw that the ground was white with hoar frost.

When I returned with the water, I told Dermot that the ground was covered with hoar frost, and that no one would be able to venture out because of the weather.

"But", the rake replied, "you won't notice the cold when your *Page 176* belly is full, and you have two of your young women on each side of you and another one in front of you."

The fire was roaring up the chimney, with a cauldron of water boiling away above it, waiting for a morsel to be put into it. But the women weren't awake yet.

"There's no point in both of us doing it," says I to him; "would you not go and wake the women?"

He didn't pay much attention to me because he'd have preferred to enter the gates of hell than to disturb them while they were sleeping. If he were to do such a thing the women might very well hold it against him, and perhaps everyone on Inishvickillane would hate him for it.

I again urged Dermot to go to where all the women were asleep and to wake them. For if he didn't go, he'd get very little hunting done that day. He listened to what I said and set off to where they were. He called the older woman, who immediately said that she was getting dressed.

The two of them put a dozen fat rabbits, and a quarter of a sheep, into the cauldron; it was the most wonderful cauldron that ever there was. Afterwards the rake became more relaxed than he had been up until then. And if he had been in the halls of Paradise that day, instead of on this sea island, he couldn't have been happier.

I had to go out for another bucket of water while the other men were telling each other stories until breakfast was ready. The man of the house was already up and about. However, we hadn't seen him as he had gone to fetch the cattle, and hadn't yet returned.

The food was brought out and we soon got stuck into it — yellow bread, a bit on the hard side, but we all had a rugged set of teeth to grind it. There was no tea or sugar, as people hadn't heard of such things in those days. But when everyone had eaten their fill, one man lit his pipe, another started whistling, and a third began lilting. None of them had the slightest intention of leaving that cosy place.

Page 177 "Out you go, the lot of you, you pack of devils!" says Dermot.

Out they went, as if he'd set a pack of hounds on them. They left as they'd arrived the day before, in twos and threes. I chose to stay with the young folk, as I had the previous day.

Before I left, the man of the house came home. He had taken care of his cattle, and had walked the whole island. He'd caught six rabbits, and was bringing them home, along with his dogs.

"The devil!" says Michael, his eldest son. "Leave those rabbits with Tomás," — he meant me. "Dermot was giving out that, because of us, he had only managed to catch very few rabbits yesterday. He said that he suspected we had just spent the whole day messing around together."

"Oh," says the man of the house, "if that's the way it is, take these rabbits of mine, and that will at least be a good start for you. And who knows, you might do as well as them, yourselves," says he. Then he turned to his children and asked: "What made Tomás go off hunting when he'd come to see you?"

He was served a plate of mutton and rabbit, a mug of milk, along with all the sorts of things we had in those days, and he started to munch it down merrily. I don't think it'd be an exaggeration to say that there wasn't another man in Munster who was so easy to get on with, so big-hearted, and so hospitable as Maurice Daly Senior. I was about to leave when he said:

"Don't go anywhere until I've eaten this, and then I'll go along with you. We'll get another half dozen rabbits for you. There's a small dog here that'll chase them out of the holes."

Out the door we went, and it was about time too. I knew that the rake wouldn't be too pleased with me if I skived off from hunting for a second day running. Daly gave us the big dog, and he kept the small one for himself. He told us to go one way, and said that he'd go the other. And then he pointed to a flat piece of land where we could meet up later.

And that's how it was with us, the two lads and me and two of the buxom lasses along with us. With a spade in my hand, off we went. It wasn't long before we saw a man approaching us, and *Page 178* when he came up we saw that it was none other than Kerry, half out of his mind.

"It must have been something pretty important to have brought you this way," says I to him.

"Yes," says he; "the ferret stayed in the first burrow we put it in this morning, and we still haven't got a rabbit."

"What are you planning to do about it?" says I.

"Well, I want to see whether Daly has a crowbar, and to ask him if he'd bring it along so that we could try to break open the burrow," says Kerry.

"But Daly isn't at home, and I don't know whether he has a crowbar," says I to him.

"There is a crowbar up there alright," says one of the lads. And off he went to the house to fetch it.

"Mary, Mother of God!" says the wise guy, "perhaps there won't be so much guff out of Dermot tonight about the hunting, like we had to endure all yesterday evening."

"They won't catch a single rabbit," says I to him.

When the young folk and I arrived at our destination, we met up with Daly. We had a dozen rabbits and Daly had half a dozen. We tied them all together on one rope which made a fairly decent bundle of them. While we were doing this, Kerry arrived back from the house, with a crowbar on his shoulder. He was heading towards the burrow where the ferret had got stuck.

"It'd be better if you'd come along with me; perhaps you'd be better at getting it out, because you know more about things like this," says Kerry to Daly.

"I'll come along," says he, and off went the two of them.

As soon as Kerry was out of sight I called the young women who were some distance away from me, playing by themselves, and they came quickly. They took hold of the bundle and put it on my back, and off we went to the house.

The woman of the house welcomed me back, and said that it was good that I had come so early. In her opinion I'd done enough for one day, what with the ferret being stuck in the burrow, and Page 179 it refusing to come out for Dermot and Kerry. I added to the bundle the half dozen rabbits that the man of the house had given me in the morning, and it was a fine bundle now. I hung it up, and started dancing with one of the buxom lasses. The two of us did a single reel, and the woman of the house played for us. I don't know whether anyone had ever danced as well in that house. I don't think they had, or will ever again. That's how the spirit of youth was in the Blaskets at that time, my friends, although it's very different nowadays.

After that we went out, me, two lads and five of the young women, down to the edge of the jetty, the loveliest place where anyone has ever stood, a spot where everyone who arrived at the island ate their food.

It wasn't too long before one of the girls said that it would be a nice place to do a foursome reel. Straightaway the wise guy ups and says: "We'll surely do it," and asked one of the sisters, Joan, to start singing. There was one good thing about Joan — she didn't have to be asked twice. Another good thing about her was that no one could sing better than her.

The four of us went at it, and performed it beautifully, on the flat place they call Goolalockaboy.[28] Then another young lad stood up and did another dance, followed by his brother, who got up and danced with him. And indeed, they did so delightfully. After that everyone there sang songs, until the day was well spent, and eventually we had to make our way back to the house.

I reckoned that the hunting party would have been at the house by now, but I was mistaken, for they weren't. There wasn't even any news of them. The woman of the house said that she had just sent two small boys out with food for them.

After we'd finished dancing, the food was ready, and we ate our fill. There was a fat hen on the table the likes of which has never been seen since.

"Now, eat as much as you want," says the woman of the house, *Page 180* "before the other lot arrive," and she put a chicken on a plate for the dancers. "But I shall keep a quarter of it for myself as I was the one doing most of the singing for you lot," says she; she was a jovial, good-hearted woman.

When our bellies were full, I asked the lads whether they knew of any rabbit warren where the ferret might be.

"Mary, Mother of God! We certainly do," was the reply.

"Would one of you go there with me?" says I to them.

"Indeed, let the two of them go with you," says their mother, butting in; "what else have they to do?"

I jumped up and grabbed my hunting spade. We didn't stop until we reached the flat place where the men were. They'd done great work; their clothes were covered with clay and dirt, and each one of them was unrecognisable, except Daly, who hadn't soiled his hands because he was just standing by, telling them what to do. Dermot was down in the hole with only his two feet showing.

The rake came out of the hole, and catching his breath, welcomed me. Although you might often think he was half-crazy, this was more of a charm-offensive than anything else.

---

[28] Guala an Loic Bhuí

"'Pon my word we'll catch nothing today, my boy," says he to me, "since the ferret has let us down."

"Sometimes I think you're a bit too much of an old gasbag," says I to him.

I stopped a while, admiring the great work they'd done, and looking around to see whether there was any other way to get into the hole they were making. After a short while I saw Daly's small dog scratching and getting a sniff of something. I still had the spade in my hand, and I went over to the little dog. I dug away at where the dog was homing in on, and went on until I hit a rock. When I removed it, there was a hole underneath it.

Page 181

I put my hand as far down as it went, and I found a rabbit. I put my hand down again, and I got another rabbit. At the third attempt I got the ferret. The boys let out a great cheer.

"The devil take it! the ferret has been found!" says the pair of them together.

Kerry thought that the boys were joking until they brought the ferret out. I went on pulling rabbits out of the hole until I had a dozen of them. Dermot arrived, and stood over me.

"Indeed, I'm in debt to you forever!" says he. "Kerry would be without a ferret for the rest of his days if you hadn't come. Let's head back to the house."

"Let's," says I, and off we went. When we came to the house the other two members of the boat crew were already there, their backs covered with rabbits. We spent a merry night together. On the following two days we did some more hunting, and then we went home.

FIFTEEN

*Shrovetide, 1878; Choosing the girl: 'There's no
accounting for tastes'; Two marriages being
arranged for me; The two of us married: Tomás
Crohan and Mary Keane; A big year for fish from
then on; O'Niall's Castle: the song I sang at my own
wedding; The funeral of Sheamus Senior*

Shrovetide, 1878
Page 183

The next morning, while breakfast was being prepared, we made
a quick visit to Inishvickillane. Then we returned to the house,
and when the food had been eaten, everyone assembled by the
boat. As the weather was deteriorating and it was getting late, we
hurried up, as we had a lot of rabbits to carry.

The woman from Inishvickillane and her two daughters were
coming over to stay on this Island till after Shrovetide. She didn't
know whether one of her daughters was going to get married, or
whether the other daughter would find a husband either, as it
wouldn't be easy for a suitor to make his way out to Inishvickillane.

The woman from Inishvickillane stayed a week on the Great
Blasket. When anybody was going into town, she went along with
her two daughters, so that they would be out and about. There
are many who'd like a good wife and who wouldn't expect much
of a dowry. Anyway, even people who were reasonably wealthy at
that time weren't bothering much about dowries.

Shrovetide was early that year and of course the Islanders had
to get to work earlier than the people on the mainland, so a young

couple were launched out without much delay. I suppose that a dowry mustn't have been important to people anyway, since neither party ever received such a thing.

When this group reached the priest's house for the marriage, the girl wasn't to be found, dead or alive, although there were a lot of people out looking for her, just for the fun of it.

Page 184 A man from Dunquin who went to the north to another wedding told them that he met the bride going west. A horse and a rider were sent off to catch up with her, but when they arrived at Dunquin they found that she had set sail for the Blaskets in a fishing boat.

She hadn't been long home when she sailed out again with the man she preferred to the man she was meant to wed. No one bothered following them because all the fun had gone out of it by then. And she herself couldn't have cared less since no one was out to kill her. So she was let do her own thing. Mind you, looking at the two men you would never have thought that there was a smidgeon of difference between them. Yet just look at the lengths this girl went to in order to get the man she wanted.

The boy she turned down didn't let his oars go adrift, as they say. My dear reader, you could never imagine how far he went to find a replacement bride, but don't worry, as long as I have this pen in my hand I'll give you all details about this saga. To begin with, I have it on good authority that he first went off to the big town of Tralee, the main city of Kerry.

This boy used to live in Dunquin, the same town where I used to stay with some of my relations. We chanced upon one another after the 'joke-wedding', as it was called. What's more, I was closely related to the girl, and I wouldn't be the one to blame her for what she did, because 'life is only worth living when you have the freedom to choose', as someone said long ago, and there's a great deal of truth in that saying.

Before we managed to get home, the beauty from Tralee was in Dunquin. On the following morning the young man knocked on the door where I was staying.

"Would you mind going to Ballyferriter with me?" says he.

"Why on earth do you think I'd mind?"

"For one thing, you've just been there and, for another, because your relative and I didn't get it together," says he.

"But I suppose you'd be happy if you caught this other one you're after," says I to him.

"Indeed, maybe you're right, but I haven't caught her yet!" says he. *Page 185*

"When will you be setting off to the north?" I enquired.

"In about an hour," was his reply.

"I'll go along with you then, my boy."

"God bless you," says he.

"Has the young woman reached the parish yet?" I asked.

"She has, indeed — she arrived there yesterday," says he.

When we reached Ballyferriter (that's the town where priests are in permanent residence) there were a lot of people milling around. But that's how it is every year during Shrovetide. The thirsty man, the trickster, the comedian, and so on — they were all there. When a couple from the Blasket were getting married, their own people accompanied them, in order to congratulate them after the wedding.

That's when I met this young woman, and I can tell you — even if she were from Ireland's capital she'd be the belle of the ball. After chapel, the pub was the next port of call, where there was drinking, dancing, singing and all sorts of codology going on to pass the time. When it was getting on for ten, people started to disperse slowly, one by one.

One day two wedding parties got together. They had drink and everything else with them — enough for the whole Island. Everyone was in high spirits, and fun and amusement was had by the whole town in the two houses. The woman from Inishvickillane and her two daughters, who had been at the weddings, were there too, and with all their singing and dancing they certainly earned anything they consumed.

The young woman from Tralee was a wonderful woman, as fine and as good as you'd find at any fair. When I started to write this book I set out to present an accurate account about myself and about everyone else. Although this young woman was brought from Tralee, she didn't come from there originally. Her poor mother, a widow, who lived in a shack in the parish of Dunquin, had been a maid-servant in Tralee, and there was certainly nothing shameful about that.

Page 186   I doubt whether as many Gaelic songs were ever sung at any wedding as were sung at these two. The singing didn't stop in either of the two houses until the late morning of the following day, when the girl from Tralee sang one or two songs in English. They had to put more soap on the table for the father-in-law of the Tralee woman before he could dance on it, as there had been quite a few people up on the table before him. He was an amazing dancer, but since he'd had a few drops too many, he fell off after only a short performance. Undaunted, he picked himself up and finished the step on the floor, as smartly and as stylishly as ever was seen.

On the Blaskets it has always been the tradition — and still is — that anything one lot did, another lot copied. This particular year was one when people got married, and for seven years after that no one got married at all. It's bizarre, perhaps, but that's how it was. I'm only referring here to this particular year, because after the incidents with the Tralee girl and the other lassie running off home from the priest's house, the people thought that no other marriage would take place. But that wasn't to be the case, because not a girl nor a boy remained unmarried by the time this Shrovetide was over.

As I was going off to go to bed one evening, quite late, who should come in but Dermot the gasbag, as noisy as ever. In a loud voice he explained to the old pair just how difficult it might be for them to go on another year, or even two, without any help around the house. "And I have a suggestion about the finest girl that ever broke bread, and she's the best in every other respect too," says he.

They didn't stop the discussion when I came in, and it kept up for a long time, until everyone inside was in agreement, so to speak. Even so, no final decision had been made, since not all those who needed to be consulted were there. Be that as it may, when the rake went out he was on cloud nine, because he was under the impression that the matter had been settled.

There was another couple ready to be launched. Day after day was passing, Shrovetide was nearly upon us, and Dermot thought that there would be a message for him at any moment, but he didn't hear a word.

My sister Mary, who'd been in America, had come home and *Page 187* was married again, heard that Dermot, the rake, had been in our house, organising a marriage-match, so she came to check it out. She was told what had been decided but she wasn't too pleased with the decision. She warned the old pair that Tomás would be obliged to provide assistance to all the girl's relatives on Inishvickillane. For whoever might refuse to help them, he, as their son-in-law, would have no choice but to do so.

She herself had in mind a well-educated girl with relatives in the township, who could help us whenever necessary. She began to explain this to us, like a priest reading the litany, until there was no fight left in us.

She'd always been very fond of her first husband's family, and it was his brother's daughter she had in mind for us. She was held in great esteem by everyone and it was justly earned. Mary's first husband was Martin O'Cahon, and the girl was the daughter of his brother. She was a sister of the present King of the Blasket, though he didn't have the title of King at that time, or for a long time afterwards. (My sister who made the bargain was buried yesterday, on 4 December 1923, at the age of eighty. May her soul rest in Paradise!)

A week later the two of us, Tomás O'Crohan and Mary Keane, were married, in the last week of Shrovetide, 1878.

There hadn't been such a wonderful day like it before in Ballyferriter, which was where the priest lived. There were four pubs there, and we spent time in each pub until late in the day. There were four fiddlers there, one in each pub, encouraging the men to come in, and another who wasn't in any of the pubs but was out in the main street. Indeed, he didn't earn less than the others either, because there was a good crowd gathered outside as well.

Page 188 Eventually we had to leave Ballyferriter, just when things were really hotting up, as there was a rough sea ahead and a lot of us had to get back to the Island. It was a very fine night and there were many people outdoors. In those days there were big boats around, capable of carrying large numbers of people.

Many of the mainlanders — relatives of ours — followed us. There were songs a-plenty, dancing and every sort of amusement going on, plus loads of food and drink until late the next morning. Then, after the people of the mainland had left, Shrovetide was over.

People said that it had been fifteen years since so many had got married in the one year. Work and business carried on as usual for the rest of the year. It was a great year for fish from then onwards. There were no mackerel or lobsters, but fish were being caught during the day by the big boats, seine-boats and every other kind of boat. The country farmers were paying eight to ten shillings per hundred fish.

At the time there were seven seine-boats in Dunquin, and two fine new big boats on the Blasket. Although the outsiders and the home crowd were very closely related to one another, there used to be perpetual bickering between them over the fish.

One fine day, all the boats, both the island boats and the mainland boats, were around the North Island. There were shoals of fish aplenty there, and it was difficult for two Island boats to keep up with seven of the Dunquin boats. There would have been no profit if there hadn't been an understanding that the boats would take their rightful turns. Two boats would always have to be tied to a seiner every time it was launched. One boat would put out the net and the other would look after it. In other words, its job was to keep the first boat out of trouble, because if there were fish in the net, and the tide was strong, the boat might well be dragged onto the rocks by the weight of the fish.

We got the fish to change direction and, although the tide was roaring, our two boats managed to get away safely, just as the net was no longer in danger of being caught on the rock. There were enough fish in the net to fill one of the boats. That left the Dunquin crowd stunned, and the captain of our boat warned them that they had better take their turn or he would take it as soon as the seiner was ready. But rather than let the Island boats *Page 189* have a second turn, the boat from Dunquin put its own seiner out. No sooner was it out than the current drove them up onto the rocks, with a jagged, projecting reef below them and a strong swell of a spring tide dragging them in.

It wasn't long before the boat that was tied to her was let loose and off she went through the Sound to the north. No other Dunquin boat followed her, because they were afraid that the Sound was too dangerous to go through.

"'Pon my soul!" says the captain of our boat to the Island boats, "the boat from Coom is in trouble, so get your oars ready, lads, and we'll go out and rescue her."

Straightaway, our two boats went off northwards through the Sound, with the sky raging above us, and the swell of the sea beneath us. Our two boats took only a few moments to get through it, and as we came in sight of the other boat we could see that she hadn't yet gone under. But she was close to it, with sea-water pouring into the boat as the crew bailed furiously, trying to prevent her from going under.

The seine-net was still in the sea, as the boat hadn't been overturned. Our captain told us to haul the seine-net into our boat until the other boat had been bailed out. And that's what we did.

There was a full load of fish distributed between the two boats. We had to attach a rope in order to tow the two boats through the Sound up northwards. Our captain kept at the Dunquin people to let go of their boat, and he also urged the other boat he had rescued to do the same.

Page 190 **O'Neill's Castle or The Dark Mountain Lass**

> Farewell to where I was before; where tonight I cannot be,
> To that loving boy who ever wooed me gently on his knee,
> If I told ye my story, would ye tell what I've confessed,
> Oh my bright love thou art leaving, and sorely I'm distressed.
>
> Thou hast promised me a child, my love, a child to be our own,
> And afterwards together that we'd build ourselves a home,
> Thou hast promised me continually until I gave my heart,
> But I am sick since then, my love, for we must live apart.
>
> This grief, my dear, is endless, it's high and deep,
> My tears have filled my two wee shoes, because I weep.
> My reason's fled, for love of thee, I cry,
> And if thou weddest the dark mountain lass, I'll surely die.
>
> My garden's overgrown — thou dost not mind,
> With branches laden down with fruits of every kind,
> Birds won't celebrate their song; and harps won't play,
> Since for the Castle of O'Neill my love leaves me today.
>
> May I not die until I'm rid of this catastrophe,
> Until my cattle and my sheep are under roof near thee,
> And I'll not fast on Fridays, till the day that I am blessed,
> To lay my weary head upon thy snow-white breast.
>
> They say that I am lucky, like all fine women are,
> And, if it's true I'm sure that thou won't mind, my love.
> Nine days, nine different times, eleven weeks or so,
> I've harvested sloe-berries at my true love's home.

Page 191

> My bright love and my dearest, this summer come with me,
> To glens so fair and islands where the sun sets beautifully,
> A dowry rich with sheep and goats upon thee I shall shower,
> So hold my hand, and let us stand, until the midnight hour.

Let's go to find the priest whose house is in the north,
Where we shall slumber peacefully to birdsong from above,
Never have I met a love who could beguile me more,
Oh sweeter than the cuckoo are the lips that I adore.

This is the song that I sang at my own wedding, and that was all I sang. I knew well how to deliver it, and I also sang the tune perfectly. Until it was finished you might have thought that everyone in the house had been struck dumb. Everyone was bewitched by the song and the way it had been sung.

I said to myself that I would record it here since I was jotting everything down, and because I myself would never object to a book that had a half-dozen fine songs in it. If I had my way, I'd have included half a dozen fine songs here and there in these writings. However, I have no choice in the matter, and I have to do as I'm instructed by my esteemed editor.

I was no more than a month married when all the good men of the Island were nearly drowned at the time that Sheamus Senior — the father of Pat Sheamus — was buried. The boats had barely made it across the Sound between Beginish and the mainland when a terrible storm hit them and didn't leave a feather or a hair on them. So they had to stay out until the afternoon of the following day, when the weather wasn't too good either.

SIXTEEN

Cutting turf; The poet: 'stop a while; the day is long'; Fishing; The currach and the arrival of lobster pots; Home Rule on the Great Blasket!; Selling fish at Cahersiveen; The three women and the torn waistcoat; Joking and dissension; Another trip to Cahersiveen, looking for the boat; Valentia Island; Glanleam and the old Knight

Cutting Turf

Whenever I had to do any important work, I had terrible trouble getting any turf cut, especially while the poet was alive and was still able to come to the hill. By now he'd become wretchedly old, though he was still looking after his black cow.

One day I was just about to get started on the south face of the Island. I was basking in the heat of the sun, planning to do some cutting, when I heard a familiar voice behind me. It couldn't have startled me more than if I'd heard a ghost from beyond the grave, and may God forgive me, there was nobody in this world I wanted to see less than the poet just at that moment. It wasn't because I disliked the man but because he was always keeping me from my work.

"Yerra, stop awhile; the day is long," says the poet. This time he'd come up the hill from the north, where he had spotted me. "Do you see those rocks in the south? Those are the Skelligs. My father fought a battle on them."

"How did that come about?" I enquired. And though I may not have known the answer to that question when I asked, I certainly knew all the details afterwards, because I couldn't get away from the poet until he had related the whole story as he lay on the flat of his back in the sun.

"*Corraí* is the name given to the fledglings of the gannets when *Page 194* they're fully mature and fattened up. The gannets all breed on the smallest of the Skelligs, and the only thing to be seen there is the young birds covering it. There used to be a boat with twelve men in it keeping an eye on the rock; it was sent out by the owner of the land, and they were paid well," explained the poet.

"One night a big boat sailed out from Dunquin. There were eight men in it, and they didn't let up until they reached the rock at dawn. They jumped up and hurriedly started filling the boat, and it wasn't difficult for them to get what they were after because each of the young birds was as heavy as a fat goose.

"Then the captain stopped them, and said that the boat was full enough as it was. He told them to come back to the boat so that they could make their way home. They did so immediately. On leaving the rock, their boat loaded with the fat of the land, they were keen to be on their way home.

"When they came round from behind the back of the rock to set out into the bay, what did they see in front of them but the patrol-boat, which they hadn't spotted previously. The patrol-boat immediately came up alongside their boat, and told them to hand the birds over at once. They told the Dunquin crew that they'd be arrested, and that they shouldn't be too surprised if they were all to end up with a noose around their neck.

"But the men of Dunquin didn't hand the birds over. When they didn't, one of the men from the patrol-boat jumped on board and tied a rope to the bow. Then, with all their strength, they set about towing the boat away, intending to confiscate the birds and arrest the men.

"After about a quarter of a mile, one of the men in the boat carrying the birds jumped up, took an axe, and cut the tow rope. This infuriated the patrolmen. They turned back to the boat *Page 195* carrying the birds, and some of them got into it. Then they all started battering one another with sticks, axes and any other tools lying around in the boat, until they'd hacked flesh and blood off one another.

"The boat carrying the birds won the battle, although there were twelve patrol-boat men against the eight from Dunquin. The eight from Dunquin left the other crew unable to move a limb or a foot. They jumped into the boat and patched up the holes in the fabric. Then they towed the other boat out into the bay to leave them to their fate. There was a widow's son in the patrol-boat who hadn't lifted a foot or a hand to fight them, and he said to them:

'Shame on the whole lot of you, sending me to my death, when I didn't lift a hand against any one of your crew,' says he.

"The captain replied: 'If a sail were put on your boat, do you think you could reach the shore?'

"He said that he could. Two got into the boat, rigged up the sail for him and pointed the boat towards land. While this was being done, the two lads who rigged up the sail said to get a move on as two men in the boat were only barely alive by now. The Dunquin boat, still fully laden, reached its own harbour, damaged and badly cut up."

"And", says I to the poet, "have you any idea what happened to the patrol-boat?"

"Yes: the man who had the sail put up for him reached dry land. Two were dead, and the others were sent to hospital. There was no more bird-hunting after that, and since then the rock has been mostly ignored. Nobody's eating the birds these days anyway," says the poet.

He related the whole event vividly and calmly. Then he said, jumping up and setting off up the hill:

"Perhaps we should dig a bit of turf now; it'll soon be dinner time."

Page 196 When I stood up, the sun was hardly to be seen. The best part of the day had been wasted and I still hadn't cut my three loads of turf. Where was all the great work that I had intended to do when I left the house that morning? Another thought then struck me — could it be that the poet had deliberately targeted me so as to waste my time, because I never saw him relentlessly badgering anyone else on the Island?

This idea convinced me that I should ignore him the next time he approached me, and then perhaps he would leave me alone. But I never did so, I'm glad to say.

Fishing

At this time there were no currachs on the Island, or the tackle for them. The only boats were big ones that needed a crew of eight men. Each of them had a large heavy seine-net, with stones tied to its base to make it sink, and corks on the upper ropes to keep the net afloat. The idea of this was to prevent the netting getting tangled when it was thrown out of the boat. Both the older folk and the younger lads used to have small boats for line-fishing. They were often full of the kind of fish that could only be caught this way.

A while after this, someone said that there were two people from the Island at a fair-day in Dingle, both of them drunk, and that they had bought a currach from somebody. And it was true, for it wasn't too long until a currach arrived at the Blasket. At the time, it was considered to be one of the wonders of the world. The women whose men were in it started wailing softly and sweetly when they saw the kind of cockleshell it was. Two young boys went up to the women and said:

"Yerra, keep your hair on; won't the two of us do the business just as well for you, even if your men get drowned?"

Never before did the boys get such a tongue-lashing as they got from the two wailing women, who found the boys' remark completely insensitive to say the least.

I wasn't too far from the women at the time, and the boys' *Page 197* remark gave me a good laugh — two lads ready to take on the two wailing women as soon as their husbands were gone! Since then I've had a lot of fun with those same two lads.

A couple of days later I made a trip to the hill to fetch a load of turf, and what should I see below me but a currach, looking as though it was full of objects being thrown into the sea. I pressed on and brought down my load of turf.

When I arrived home, I recounted what I'd seen but no one believed me. How could a currach be there when there were none of them on the coast; and what's more, what good could they possibly achieve by throwing things into the sea?

Well, nothing happened until that afternoon, when the currach came around the Gob from the south, with four men in it. They made their way up to the Island jetty and then began looking for lodgings. They had a little bit of food and some goodies in a white bag. They were from Dingle, and were well known of course, so they easily found somewhere to stay. That was when Tomás O'Crohan was finally believed, and since then nobody has ever doubted my integrity, because the incredible thing that I related that day turned out to be true; the things I saw them throwing into the sea were lobster pots.

They stayed in Pat Sheamus's house. They had their own food, and they only spent a week each time they came, because they had to bring their catch home. At that time the Blasket people knew no more about lobster pots than a bank clerk would. It wasn't long before there were four currachs from Dingle fishing lobsters around the Blasket in this way. The people from Dingle got hundreds of pounds worth of lobster from around the Great Blasket coast before the Islanders themselves learnt how to make money out of this kind of fishing. It used to be a pound a dozen for them, and indeed it wasn't hard to get a dozen.

Page 198

When the people found out about lobsters, the two who had a currach put pots into her, and they took a young lad with them. For a whole year they had the only currach fishing for lobsters, and they made good money. The following year, all the crews were off trying to get currachs. It wasn't easy to find them, because very few of them were being made, and it cost from eight to ten pounds for a new one.

Like everybody else I went off trying to get one, and Pat Sheamus came along with me. We took another fine fellow with us, and I got a currach easily, newly-made by one of my relatives, and it cost me eight pounds. We had to go off again to get stuff in order to make the pots, and we had a great deal of hassle before we could even start fishing. We spent the season with the other two men and we had good weather. Each of us had ten pounds left after we'd bought the currach. The folk in Dingle were buying lobsters at that time, and some of us used to keep them for our own enjoyment. They were an excellent catch, since seine-fishing had petered out by this time.

There were about a dozen currachs fishing for lobster around the Island when news of this reached Great Britain. A British company sent two tank-boats to investigate the situation. These boats had ready-to-use fishing tackle on board. This was very handy for the fishermen; a shilling was paid for each dozen lobster and the use of the tackle was free.

Pat Sheamus and I were well and truly caught up in it, day and night, and although we never went to any island to fish for them, we always used to catch as much as any other currach did. They used to pay ten shillings a dozen for most of the year, but when they became scarce they were willing to pay up to a shilling per lobster.

It went on like that for two or three years, and soon another English company sent two more tank-boats to the Blasket, and they paid an additional shilling a dozen. It was always the new arrival, of course, who paid more. To make sure that the boats kept coming, the currachs shared their catch between them. *Page 199*

Lobsters were abundant at that time. It wasn't long before boats from France were paying a shilling a lobster all year long. That's how things went until a fifth company started blowing its horn on the coast of the Blaskets, looking for lobsters. We spent a few years like that, and the fishermen were never short of a shilling or two, what with the boats coming to our doorstep and plenty of money on board to pay for the catch, however plentiful it might have been.

Around this time a couple of boats came from Cahersiveen to Inishvickillane. They took Maurice Daly Senior and his two sons to help with the lobster fishing, as they too had a currach. So

Maurice Daly Senior, until he eventually left Inishvickillane, had a good life from that year on.

At the time the companies were sending their tank-boats, the initiative that was then called 'Rialtas Baile' came to Ireland — otherwise known as *Home Rule*. I often told the fishermen that, unbeknown to the people of Ireland, *Home Rule* had already begun on the Great Blasket. And ever since then the Islanders have continually told me how right I was. Everyone remained satisfied so long as English and French gold was paying for our shellfish right on our doorstep.

Nobody knows how much gold and silver the ships left on the coast of Kerry at that time. During the rest of the year other merchants were sending steamships to look for mackerel. One night in March I got five to six hundred spring mackerel and we brought them to Dingle. We were offered four pounds a hundred for them.

Page 200 While these ships were operating on the coast, no poor person went short of good money. I often used to bump into the fancy lighthouse boat, which had senior officers on board. Every year for six years they took everything we caught, at about a shilling a lobster, large or small.

When the regular fishing failed, there were phosphorescent fish[29] that could be caught at night. We could do this because we had large boats and the right tackle. One year we did a great deal of night-fishing. We cured heaps of fish, but there was no demand for it in Dingle. A report went out that there was a great market for fish in Cahersiveen, because fish was scarce there. The crew of the boat started egging one another on, saying that we'd be a poor lot if we couldn't manage to fill up our boat with fish. We should rig up her sails and set off to the south through Dingle Bay, because that's where we would have the best chance of selling our fish.

On the following Monday morning we filled *The Black Boar* with yellow mackerel — that is, salted mackerel. These fish weren't

---

[29] The lanterneye fish is the only known family of fish that have the ability to turn their lights off and on at will. From the Beryciformes order, these amazing fish carry luminescent organs just below the eyes.

too big or coarse. Thanks to a favourable northerly wind filling our sails we soon reached the lighthouse at the entrance to Valentia Harbour and from there we sailed on up to Cahersiveen, a town with a great bunch of men of the right sort.

We were delighted when we caught sight of Valentia Harbour and Beginish at the entrance of the harbour. There were two farmers living there who also acted as boat-pilots. Valentia Island is seven miles long. The Knight's mansion is at the western end of the harbour, at the edge of the sea, in a flat area they call Glanleam. Formerly it was called Knight Leam Valley. The lighthouse is further down, on a headland looking out over the open sea, showing the way to a safe haven to anyone who might have gone astray.

When we reached the town quay a lot of people came out to greet us. They thought we'd come from a large ship that had sunk, and so they were amazed.

We wanted to find out if there were any fish-merchants in the area. There were indeed, and some of them were nearby. One of them offered to buy the fish, but his bid was much lower than what we were hoping for. *Page 201*

Another man came down the slip, and gave us a great welcome. He had the manners and the bearing of a gentleman; although I was one of the youngest in the boat, we already knew one another well. He went with us from the boat and gave us plenty to drink. He bought all the fish we had for a crown[30] a hundred, and then he arranged lodgings for us at his father's guesthouse in the centre of the town.

His father had a fine house, with only himself and his wife living in it. We had something to eat there and handed over the fish to the man who had bought it. When we had settled up with one another, he gave us a few drinks, but wouldn't let us pay for them.

When we came back to the guesthouse we asked the man of the house if there'd be time for us to go for a stroll along the street. He

---

[30] Five shillings; a quarter of a pound sterling — worth about €25 today

said that there was an hour to spare, which should be enough for us. While three of us went off together, the other members of the crew remained in the lodgings as they were getting on in years, and didn't fancy going out sightseeing. We left them to it and off we went to a fine drinking house where we had a good look around.

Pretty soon the publican came out of the kitchen and welcomed us.

"How's life, boys?" says he.

We were a bit surprised to receive such a warm welcome, but we needn't have been, because he knew us all well. We'd got to know him from his regular visits to buy things in Dingle.

The jovial patron gave us our fill of drink, and after a while we left and wandered up and down the street. We went into another pub where there was a man from Dingle, who also offered us drinks.

Page 202 When closing time came, we set off to return to the guesthouse. About half way there, on the corner of a street, three women accosted us. They were some of the best-endowed, strongest and shapeliest women that any of us had ever seen.

One of us had grey hair, though, mind you, it wasn't from age. The women approached him first and starting speaking to him in English that was hard to understand. The grey-haired man had a bit of broken English, but he couldn't understand proper English. I was the last one to come up to them, and I stopped on my heels. The other man with us couldn't understand English in any shape or form. One of the women, with bright red hair, who was the one doing most of the talking, was a clean six foot in height and with the finest head of hair you ever did see — the same colour as this very fancy lamp I have on my table, which the gentleman from the Kelly family sent me.

Pretty soon I heard the red-haired woman telling the grey-haired man, in English: "*You must come along with me.*"

"*I won't not, ma'am,*" was his reply. He gave a jump and turned, and while he was turning, she put her claw into the back of his waistcoat, and ripped it off him, from top to bottom; (we had only our waistcoats on, having left our jackets in the guesthouse when we went out). The three women followed us to the doorway of the guesthouse, with the three of us panting for breath. When we were safely inside we all had a great laugh over the grey-haired man and his backless waistcoat.

We slept well at MacMurrough's, a generous, hospitable man. He hinted that there was a house in the town that didn't mind lodging male visitors, but he didn't say any more than that. The next morning we ate our breakfast and then headed off.

The grey-haired man had no waistcoat, and so he bought a new one, but he still had the front part of the other waistcoat, which was new, and he would have to buy a new back for it. Everyone was buying curious items around the town, with the result that not one of the crew of the boat brought a halfcrown back to the Blasket from the sale of the small mackerel. *Page 203*

While we were gathering together at the boat, the grey-haired man came with an armful of goods, but he still needed something that no one else needed — a new back for his torn waistcoat. After having taken two or three drinks, he passed by, proclaiming loudly:

"Damn it! The woman we saw yesterday, who ripped the waistcoat from off my back, was actually standing in the doorway of the finest house in the town today. What's more," said he to another man who was approaching, "Maurice saw her too, when we were walking together through the town."

"I'm surprised she didn't put another claw into you today," I replied.

"God knows, if she had, I would have done the same to her too!" says he.

Well, the boat sailed back home, with a favourable head-wind across from the south through Dingle Bay. And I'm telling you, dear reader, that when we reached the jetty we had nothing of value except a pile of worthless trinkets.

There was a tailor on the Island at that time, and two young apprentices with him learning the trade. No tailor ever play-acted and joked like him. When the grey-haired man's wife was looking through the bag that he had brought from Cahersiveen, she found the front part of his good waistcoat, with no back on it at all.

"Mary, Mother of God!" says she to herself, "what on earth happened to this fine new piece of clothing? I suppose it got caught in the mast of the boat when he was trying to put the sail up." She showed it to the old tailor, who was a bit of a rogue. He paused for thought and then said, smiling from ear to ear:

"There's a block of houses in that town this long while, occupied only by women, and these women are constantly on the lookout for men visiting the town. I guess the lad with the backless waistcoat must have met up with them!" She was a fine gentle woman, and she probably believed every word he spoke. It was almost as if she had been stung by a bee, as she came out the door to find me. She looked all around, saw me up at my house and came over to find out what happened to her husband's brand new waistcoat. I told her that it got caught up in the sail, and that he himself tore the back off it, because it was hanging off him, and he didn't want to make a show of himself in a unfamiliar place.

There was another man on the Island at that time who had nothing to do except make mischief, may God forgive him — and indeed all of us! He'd been with us on the trip at the time, as he owned the boat. When he was in the town and saw how the back had been ripped out of the grey-haired man's waistcoat, this gave him something to gossip about — something he was an expert at. This event was indeed something for him to talk about — three men in an unfamiliar place, their wives left at home, and nothing in the world to stop them from going to such a house. The rumour he was spreading was that while we were in the town the three of us had cheated on our own wives. He went on to say that, just as we were leaving the establishment, a red-haired woman had put her claws into the grey-haired man; and if the back of the waistcoat hadn't been ripped off, his wife back on the Island would have lost him forever.

After this tittle-tattle had spread throughout the village, the wife of another man who was with him was even more furious than the grey-haired man's wife. The row got so bad, the people in the village were amazed that they didn't leave their husbands. The situation didn't get any better, because there were

Page 204

troublemakers there egging the women on. What's more, the scandal-monger who was spreading false rumours probably didn't see the look on our faces when we were returning to the guesthouse. However, as with all rumours, facts never interfered with a good story, and that's how it was with him.

There was an occasional dig at me, too, and about my wife; but being a woman of character, my wife ignored the chatter, unlike all the rest of them, who wouldn't stop bickering, and nearly started hating one another. Anyway, the story wasn't as outrageous as had been painted, but even so, the older women failed to get the younger women to see sense, because the picture in their minds was too powerful. Just imagine it — a husband with the back torn out of his new waistcoat, and he in need of a drop of wine when he reached the guesthouse; the man who had reported what had happened just ahead of him, and me and another man just as upset as he was, although we hadn't lost even a stitch of clothing.

The mischief-maker and the wife of the grey-haired man were close relatives, but the mischief-maker didn't care about his relatives getting upset so long as he had his bit of fun. Things didn't improve for a long time. Once, when the Stations of the Cross were being held on the Island, it was said that these two men did them dutifully. Whether that's true or not, it wasn't long before they came to their senses. However, no matter how good the prices were in Cahersiveen, it was many years before the Island women allowed their men to go and do business there again.

A long time after that, there was the night of the mighty wind. The following morning the first people who went out saw that one of the big boats had vanished from the jetty. It was our boat. Off we went helter-skelter around the local area. What had caused it to disappear? Was it the wind that moved it, or did water get into it? The only clue as to what had happened was the tree it was tethered to. The wind had bent the tree so that the tether had slipped free, releasing the boat and allowing it to get swept away out to sea. It was a great loss to us because it was still a fine new boat, and while we had it we did good fishing with it every year.

Page 205

Page 206

There were many big foreign boats out looking for spring mackerel at that time. On one of those days, I was off to Dingle. It was a Saturday, and all these boats were moored from Saturday morning till Monday morning, many of them in Dingle itself. As I was going into a shop, I heard a boy say to the shopkeeper that one of the big boats had found a fine boat around the Skelligs. There wasn't a mark or a scratch on it, so he took it into the quay at Valentia Harbour. "They've handed it over to the priest on the island so that he could give it back to its rightful owners," says the man who was speaking.

"Perhaps it's your boat," says the shopkeeper.

"Perhaps it is," I replied, and from what we told him, he said that it was, because it didn't look like any other vessel.

"The coastguard's keeping a close eye on it," says he.

"I suppose the priest must have handed it over to coastguards to look after it until somebody came to fetch it," says the young man.

When I heard about it, I was more than willing to give him the best drink in the shop, especially as there was only one other man there. Even if there had been the crew of an entire ship, I wouldn't have cared. Wouldn't a drink be a small thing in exchange for news of my fine new boat — and by now I was certain that the boat that had been found was indeed mine.

I asked the shopkeeper to give them both whatever drink they fancied. He told them that I was going to stand them their favourite drink, whereupon the man who was talking burst out laughing.

"So, it's the person whose little boat has gone missing who's giving us the drink," says he. "We've got our own boat, and *Page 207* enough money for a week's drinking, and so, pour out the drink and one for each of the rest of our crew."

I had a drink with them and, when I went out, I met a man from Dunquin with his horse harnessed, all ready to go home.

"Are you ready to go home?" says he.

"I will be," was my reply, "as soon as I've collected my bits and pieces in that house over there."

"Bring them with you, and you can ride back with me," says he.

I thanked him, and ran off. I brought back the bibs and bobs I'd picked up, which I had brought with me to the big town. He was there waiting for me where I had left him.

"You're still there," says I to him.

"I am; didn't I say I would be?" says he.

"Well, I suppose we'll have one for the road before we leave the big town," says I to him.

"If you like," says he.

"I do, without a doubt," and in went the two of us. He had a bottle of black porter, and I had a glass of whiskey. There were a couple of tough characters from the street in there too, hanging around, looking out for country folk. They got a wee drop from us at any rate.

Both of us jumped into the cart and turned our backs on Dingle. There was no load in the cart and for that reason no grass grew under the feet of the horse until we reached Dunquin.

I stayed with him until morning. The next day was Sunday; it was fine, with boats from the islands out, but I sensed that when they heard that another boat had been saved in Little Creek, over in Valentia, they were happy and surprised. Part of the crew of the lost boat was out at sea and they decided to go south on the Monday morning in search of her.

Monday morning was very fine. We all gathered together and *Page 208* brought the other big boat with us from the south. There were eight of us in it, and four were to be in each boat coming back: at least, that was the plan we made — that is, if it turned out to be our boat.

When we arrived in the south, we made it to the quay at Valentia Island, and there right in front of us was our boat, without a mark or a scratch on it. We weren't there long when a coastguard approached us. He asked us if it was our boat, and we told him that it was, and he asked nothing else. We asked him if it would be alright for us to take it with us. If so, we would take it north that day, since the weather was fine. We had little help to bring the two large boats if the sea was at all rough. The man looking after it said that he didn't have any authority to hand over the boat, but that he had to safeguard it. He said that it was the island's parish priest who was responsible for returning it to its owner.

That being so, we had to look for lodgings in the town of Cahersiveen. We went to the same house where we lodged before. The old couple of the house had a great laugh at us on account of the fine red-haired women. The mischief-maker was with us this time, too, and this was another occasion for him to cause trouble. You may take it from me that after the lights came on that night we were out walking in the streets of that fine town again. We weren't a bit afraid of the police — but we were certainly scared of bumping into any of those red-haired women — believe you me!

Well, after we'd had a word with the mischief-maker about the red-haired women, the man of the house started telling us stories about the number of pleasure boats that had sunk in and around Valentia Island during his lifetime. Altogether he counted a dozen. Three boats had gone aground in the harbour itself; one person survived and two died, and one was never found, dead or alive, then or since.

Page 209 When it was time to go to bed, we went off and slept happily until morning, when the woman of the house had breakfast ready. The man of the house brought in a drink for the road — a gallon of black porter.

When the men were ready to go, we first had a drink to warm our hearts, and after that the food. We were taking everything as easily as if we were already home at the Blasket jetty.

"For Heaven's sake!" says the captain, "get on with it. When will you get these two dried-up boats to the Island jetty? And by the way, you still have to go and look for the priest, and that may take some time," says he.

The mischief-maker answered him, of course, and said:

"This is our special day, and maybe it's our last day in this town."

He was right, because no one who was there that day ever went back to the town since then.

Well, there were small, out-of-the-ordinary items we had bought in the town. We gathered them up, got the big boat sailing, and reached the quay. When we thought that we would be further delayed by having to look for the priest, we didn't have to worry because he was actually right there to meet us at the quay. The coastguard we had been speaking with was with him: there they were, waiting for us, and we'd been thinking that we'd be the ones waiting for them.

We greeted the priest, and he greeted us. He asked us if the boat was ours, and we said that it was. He said that the people who brought it in had given it up to him, until the owners came to claim it.

"But did they want to be paid for salvaging it?" asks the captain.

"Oh, indeed they didn't," says he, "even though they are poor people like yourselves."

"I don't know what we are to do then," says the captain. "We will do this much; there are eight of you there, so make up ten twenties[31] between you, and I'll offer it to them to buy drink. If they won't accept it, I'll give it to any man you want in a Dingle pub." *Page 210*

That's how it was. We went into the pub nearby, and we were the only ones in it. We made up the bill between us.

"Sure, it'll do us no harm to have a drink," says the mischief-maker, for he was a grand man when all is said and done, as I think I've mentioned before. And anyway, where's the man without his failings? He got his pint quickly and drank it down. Round after round of drinks followed, until we had spent the whole day until nightfall there.

We still had Dingle Bay to get across, but we were too weak to get the two big boats ready, and so we couldn't sail. For every man who was able to do his job, two were not. So finally we decided to take it easy and to start off early in the morning. The man of the house gave us somewhere to sleep, which we were glad of. The

[31] Probably ten pounds (there were twenty shillings in a pound)

next day was Sunday, which we thought would delay us even further, but the man of the house said that Mass would be around ten and so we'd have plenty of time to set off after that.

After breakfast we went back to Valentia, where the chapel was in the middle of the island. We were there early and were looking at everything going on around us. Some of the people there were great landowners, in the best part of the island, of course; but these were mainly blow-ins. Others had only small plots on the poorest land where it was impossible to make much of a living.

We reached the chapel by asking a boy from the quay who was accompanying us. It was an old chapel, built in the style of former times, with four wings on it. It wasn't high or large. There were two pubs in front of it, owned by the Sullivan family.

When the congregation was assembled, I could see that they were neatly dressed, and even though it was an island, you might have thought that they had been brought up in the middle of the country. Their clothes were clean and tidy, and all of them, both young and old, looked honest and refined.

Page 211

The centre of the chapel was open up to the roof, and there were galleries on each side of the wings. The edges of the galleries were full of people standing; I don't know whether they had permission to go to the edge of the galleries, or not. There was no bad behaviour or noise, inside or out, until Mass was over. Well, perhaps this church taught me something that probably no visitor learnt from such an establishment. At any rate, saying my prayers didn't stop me from observing the congregation, and noting that there wasn't a sallow skin or a dark-haired person to be seen in the community, inside or out.

When Mass had been celebrated we didn't bother going to the pubs. Instead, we set out east across the island, hoping to get home more quickly, even though the day was pretty well shot. We went into a farmer's house and got some milk to drink. There is no buttermilk in this part of Kerry; instead, they simply mix the whole week's milk together.

We told each other that it'd be better for us to go to the north to see how the sea looked. To do this, we had to go to the top of a small hill. When we reached it, there was a wondrous sight to be seen, namely, everything that had been excavated from the side of the hill. It was a slate-mine, and great work had been undertaken there, with big diggers working down to the bottom, and here and there right into the hill itself.

After being astonished by that sight, we turned to the other side of the hill, where there was another splendid view, the marvellous estate belonging to the Knight of Kerry. It was often called Glanleam because his fine mansion was situated in Glen Laom. People who have been abroad may have seen wonders greater than this place, but for us, of course, it was a marvel since this was the furthest we'd ever been from our homes.

Page 212

Below us was a magnificent sight. There were six copses in a line, like six racehorses getting ready to run. The mansion was in the centre of these copses, with three on either side of it, and the same space between each of these perfectly proportioned copses. Between every two copses, on a green, grassy lawn, there were objects carved from decorative Kerry stone. One of these was called *The Eight Points of the Rogue*;[32] another of them was *Castle Short*.[33] I've forgotten what the rest were called, although none of them was made for any practical use, I imagine.

There was a fine grassy park with twenty-two black Kerry cows on it, none of them spotted or yellow, but all of them jet-black. There were twenty-one calves of the same colour in another pasture alongside, and a big park, partly fallow and partly cultivated, with so many sheep that we couldn't count them all.

In Valentia Harbour at this time there was the greatest number of masts we had ever seen up till then — or since. The masts were on large boats and small ships that had come to Valentia Harbour from far and wide, fishing for mackerel. They made money galore at it, so that even a poor person wasn't without a pound or two.

On the other side of the hill we saw a huge mast, with as many ropes tied to it as found in any vessel that ever sailed the seas.

[32] Ocht bPointe an Rógaire — perhaps a sundial?
[33] Caisleán Gearra

Page 213 There were many gadgets tied to that mast; you'd have been blinded if you looked at them in the sunlight. It was the mast that carries the large cable bringing messages from Newfoundland to Ireland. A dozen experts are in charge of that mast.

The upshot was that we'd more or less squandered the day by the time we reached the quay — Cush Quay[34] — where our two boats were still waiting for us, with only four of us in each one of them to sail them to the Blasket. However, the delay was no harm as the weather was improving all the time. Although in the morning it had been lashing rain, by the time we were ready to leave there wasn't as much as a puff of wind blowing.

We dashed down to the boats and launched them, having put a lot of tackle into them. That was when the mischief-maker, who was always hanging around, pointed out that any poor soul who was about to sail across the bay would surely be in need of a drink. Another man replied that perhaps the men still had a little something in their pockets, and if so, it wouldn't kill them to take a drop before setting out across such a wide bay. It'd take a lot of rowing to get across the Bay of Dingle that day, since there wasn't a puff of wind to help us on our way.

"It's a poor pocket that has nothing in it to buy a drink for a few people," repeated the joker. "I'll buy a drink for every one of you, and then you can do whatever you want," and off he darted to the pub.

When we reached this wretched establishment, the joker ordered a gallon of porter, which worked out at a pint per man. And a miserable establishment it was indeed, as were all the others like it, for it's many's the person who has been brought to poverty on account of places such as these. When the man pouring out the drink was about to serve it, he noticed that one of the eight *Page 214* men wasn't there, and so he sent someone outside to see where he was. He found him in one of the boats beside the quay. He'd had a few drinks already and, because he hadn't a shilling in his pocket, he was probably shy about drinking with his pals. All the

---

[34] Cé na Coise

same, he was made to come in, and when he'd drunk his fill we all set off, and not one of us was thirsty.

Having reached our boats on this beautiful Sunday afternoon, we bade farewell to Cush Quay and to everyone standing there on the pier. There were quite a lot of people there, none of them looking either poor or miserable. However, I doubt whether I'd be able to say the same about them now.

We set the boat's stern to the land and the bow to the sea, as the hearty heroes of yore used to do, and reached the inlet from the north side. As we passed below Glanleam, we saw a well-kept road there lined with every kind of tree you'd ever fancy. There were four men with a wheelbarrow, going up and down the road carrying something in the barrow. We didn't yet know what they had in the barrow, although it amazed us that they were to-ing and fro-ing like that.

At the mouth of the harbour we met a boat. The mischief-maker asked them what the men had in the barrow. They told him that it was the old Knight, who was a good hundred years old. They had to carry him like that, so that he could get a breath of fresh air — and they did it twice a day.

"They wouldn't have to do it", says the mischief-maker, "if they'd thrown him down on the beach the first day!"

Our two boats set off across the bay to the north. By the time we were leaving the harbour, the light was shining from the lighthouse. Off went our two boats together and eventually we reached the jetty in the West Island. Because the night was short and fine, and since we weren't in a hurry, it was daybreak by the time we reached home. That was the second trip to Valentia for us, and I don't believe we've ever been back there since. *Page 215*

We had the two big boats, and by the end of the year we did some good fishing with them. During November we caught a good deal of luminescent fish. It went on like that for two or three years: lobster-fishing during their season, and some great foraging at other times. There was always something going on at that time to provide enough for those of us who were poor.

SEVENTEEN

Us stuck in Dingle because the police wouldn't let us
have our boats; The rents being arranged: a pound
a cow; Doing whatever we wanted; Death of my
father: he senses the end of his own life; My mother
on the other side; The end of the two who first put
the sound of this language of ours in my ears

Page 217

One day, about three years after we brought the boats back
from Valentia Bay, we took both of them over to Dingle,
full of all sorts of things — wool, pigs, sheep, fish, and
so on — that would make us a few quid. The boats were chock-
a-block, and there were sixteen men crewing them. We had a good
head-wind through the bay to the east until we reached the
harbour and finally the town quay. After we'd moored the boats,
we sold everything in them and then we had the night to spend
in the town.

That was a merry night altogether, but the next morning was
a sad one, because when we went back to the boats there were
some men there who wouldn't let us get to them. They were the
police, and they had a warrant to stop us taking the boats with
us. It was an order from the rent-collectors, since we were in
arrears paying our rent. Of course there was no way we could pay
on the spot, since we were prevented from going home and having
any access to our livelihood.

Well, the men from the Blaskets who had been stuck there
provided the only entertainment in town. Loads of people came

in from the country to see the wondrous goings-on, including the odd friend with a little money in his pocket to give a helping hand to pay off our debt. The entire rent of the Island had to be paid before anyone would be allowed to repossess their boats. Those who had a great deal to pay hadn't any connection with the boats. Two people came to me from the country offering money so that my share in the boats could be redeemed. I thanked them but didn't accept it, because I had a feeling that the boats wouldn't be released, no matter what. We trudged up and down the streets, with the odd decent shopkeeper offering us money to help pay for the boats, but not one of us accepted. We told them that if and when the boats were released we'd come for them again. And so we had another night in Dingle.

Page 218

The next morning we were gloomy and sad, and we went on grumbling just as we had the day before. We stayed there until mid-day. Then our patience gave out, and all sixteen of us moved out of the town in a rage, saying that all the stewards and landlords in the country could go to the Devil.

We reached Dunquin, with some of us riding on horses but most of us walking. We had to go back to Dingle to look for the goods we'd collected there, and which we needed. We hadn't spent much on the return journey, but even so we had to bring a good deal along with us and to carry on until we reached the land we had left behind us. As the old proverb goes: it's a good vessel that reaches its destination.

Since then the Islanders haven't ever had a large boat, and even now, in our golden years, we have only a couple of small ones. Since that time, the only boats you'd find at the Blasket jetty have been currachs.

The rent collectors went mad, because when they tried to sell the boats, no one would buy them, even for a pound for the pair of them, and they had to put them into a field until the worms ate them, and they never even got a sixpence or a penny for them. That broke the spirit of the bailiffs and the collectors as regards the Islanders, although a shopkeeper took a currach from a very poor man by stealing it from the jetty during the night. But the same thing happened with that currach as did the boats — he didn't get a sixpence or a penny for it. It ended, upside down, in the corner of a field belonging to the man who took it, looking just like a porpoise in from the open sea.

Page 219   Well, since they got nothing out of the boats on that occasion, everything carried on normally for a long time before we were asked again for any rent. That was the beginning and the end of it, and you could say that that was all the rent we ever paid since then.

After that we had to rely on the currachs and get what we could out of them by fishing day and night from May to August, lobsters by day and mackerel every fine night. We spent a few years like that, and plenty of outsiders came every year, looking for fish, until eventually there were five companies in search of mackerel. Although this kind of fishing involved very hard work, there was never want or famine, because of the quantities we got from this kind of skilled work. I believe that if we'd been as penny-wise then as we have been more recently, we would have avoided becoming so poor so quickly.

It wasn't long before this sort of life changed, and not just in one way. Some time after this, the steward had to give up the land, and a man was sent by the Earl himself to the Great Blasket.

At that time the rent was two pounds per cow, and so the total rent for the whole Island came to eighty pounds. This fellow gathered the Islanders together and asked them how much they thought they would be able to pay; and that was the extent of his business with them. After having had a good while to think about it, some chancer eventually said:

"The Devil take my soul! I wouldn't lift a hand to do a tap of work unless I got at least a pound for every cow." You never heard such laughing over what this chancer said; even the gentleman himself laughed when he was told what the fellow had said. It seemed to the poor sod that he'd have been in God's own paradise if he had only to pay a pound for rent, when his father had to pay

Page 220 five. They often had to sell most of their cows for five pounds, because those scoundrels were for ever making off with people's cattle. Those rogues had no sense of decency; they all ended up in either the poorhouse or the loony bin, which served them damn well right.

After that, things were easier, because from then on there was an end to the bailiffs and lawlessness. When you'd paid your rent there'd be no further demands until the rent was due again. We spent a good while like that, and the Islanders were entirely satisfied with the law as it stood, although there was the odd dig at the chancer who'd talked about a pound a cow, because it could have just as easily been ten shillings per cow.

At any rate, nobody minded this at that time so long as they could get ten shillings for a dozen lobsters and a pound for a hundred mackerel, which at that time were very plentiful, and there was a good demand for them. One day a tank-boat arrived from England in search of shellfish; it had three hundred pounds in gold sovereigns on board. That day the tank-boat offered a shilling for every fish, and the three hundred pounds soon ran out. There was no shortage of money in Great Britain at that time!

I suppose it's true, as people say, that the wheel of life is constantly turning. My life has certainly taken many a turn. And if the Blaskets got a bit of a shake-up at that time, and even with God giving us this sort of wealth, we probably didn't look after it properly, for everything we easily acquired we spent just as easily.

1888

While I think about it, that particular year, 1888, was when I had a small field of rugged land on a piece of high ground.

I decided to break it up, because it was too old and unprofitable as it was. With this rush of activity that came over me, I decided to work half of it one year, and the other half the next. *Page 221*

A person often gets an idea that isn't always the best, although at other times, under different circumstances, the same idea might be a good one. But when all is said and done, this decision of mine was not a good one. I had great trouble afterwards, and I got little benefit from it. I had to set out to the beach, to get fertiliser. I had an old black donkey, and the poor fellow had to take every load about a mile and a half, every step of the way uphill. Well, a person often brings work upon himself and soon gets fed up with it, and that's how it was with me. It wasn't too long before I became fed up with the whole business, especially as the old black donkey was starting to fail on me.

In the end, I sowed half of the small field with potatoes. At the time they were being planted my seventy-year-old father was still in good shape, although a bit stooped. At any rate, he used to make a trip to this field every day, even though he was gradually becoming weaker and slower, as age took its toll.

It wasn't long before he gave up going to the field, although he wanted to continue doing so at first. One day, I thought he was in the field but I was mistaken. When I put my head out that morning, there was no sign of him, and I found that odd. I asked a boy passing by who told me that he was in his daughter Kate's house, and that was where I found him.

"Father," says I to him, "I thought you'd been in the small field since breakfast?"

Page 222
"I don't want to go there," says he.

"But you said you wanted to," says I to him.

"I did," says he, "but not now."

It's strange the way we all go about things; later that day he told us that he'd never again see potatoes grow in that field. There are many things that don't worry a person until it's too late. After I had buried my father, we were sorry that we hadn't asked him whether he had seen or heard something near the field. No doubt something of that kind happened there, something that revealed to him the coming of his own demise.

My father was in his grave before the potatoes were up that year. That left more of life's hardship on the shoulders of poor Tomás, and it was only the beginning of it, may God have mercy on us.

Around May of that year there were plenty of mackerel, and we got a fair penny for them. I had saved five pounds after only one week, even after having paid for everything to do with the upkeep of the house. Well, as my father had recently died, I had to take the five pounds I'd saved to buy a coffin for him. Coffins weren't as expensive then as they are now, but it still cost around ten pounds for the entire funeral at that time. Nowadays, of course, funerals can often be as much as thirty pounds.

After I'd finished the work, I had to stir up my bones to do some extra work, and even after my hard time on the small field I didn't get the fill of two sacks of potatoes out of it. However, I managed to reap three crops of oats from it, and it was the final crop that happened to be the best of the lot.

At any rate, the next year I took on the other side of the small field. The yield from it was very good, because by then I knew more about the nature of the soil, and I spread fertilisers accordingly. This half of the field produced ten sacks of potatoes and enough wheat to last for three years, all because I'd looked after it better. And what's more, some of my neighbours gave me a helping hand, because I had often looked after them whenever they were short of seed.

Page 223

A short while after that, my mother, then about eighty years old, started preparing to leave this life. She hadn't a cramp in her foot or in her hand, and was as upright as she was in her youth. She wasn't sick for long, which was perhaps all for the best as I didn't have the means to look after her in addition to all my other responsibilities at that time.

One night when she was very poorly, and I was going to stay up with her, who should drop in to see me but my uncle Dermot. He immediately told everyone to go to bed, and said that he'd take care of the sick woman until the morning. Before daybreak he called to say that she was over on the other side. He told us to jump to it and to do what the law required for her since the weather was fine. And so I had to dress myself up and set off to Dingle, a splendid big town at that time, where most of the people were decent and friendly.

Well, the weather stayed fine until my mother reached her native church in the Parish of Ventry, a long journey from the Great Blasket, in terms of its duration both by sea and by land.

And, although it was a decent funeral with horses and carts being used for the most part, it was on the mourners' shoulders that she was carried to the churchyard itself.

That was the end of the two who first put the sound of this language of ours in my ears. May the blessing of God be on their souls!

EIGHTEEN

My brother back from America for the second time;
The two of us out fishing; The steamship and the
sailing-ship; The bottle of booze that knocked me off
my feet; At the back of the creek until morning;
'There's many a shilling to be found in the sea!';
The droning of the seals; Gathering wreckage
around Beginish

My Brother Paddy Back from America for the Second Time   Page 225

I was very surprised when I heard that he had come over again
for the second time, now that his two sons were grown-up, sturdy
young men. They'd all been in the States for seven years, and in
my opinion they did pretty well over there.

Well, after he arrived back, there was no get-up-and-go in him.
You'd have thought that he'd lived in the woods during those
seven years. His clothes were in rags and he himself was in poor
shape without as much as a red cent in his pocket. His two sisters
over there had to pay his fare back home for him.

Although he was never idle for a single day during those seven
years, he spent every penny he'd earned on his two sons, and he
wouldn't let them work. Then, he had the habit of taking every
other sixpence he'd saved — after paying for their board — and
of going to the pub, where he would drink whatever was left —
and I don't suppose that ever amounted to very much.

I'm not criticising Paddy and his two sons one little bit, but
I'm going to say what I have to say and that'll be the end of it. I'll

tell you what happened to them and how those young fellows treated their father, and behaved towards him — the same man who had spent seven years in America, and who by the sweat of his brow had managed to make men of them. The long and the short of it is that neither of the two lads ever sent as much as a penny or even a letter asking about him since then. Nobody

Page 226

knows where the youngest man went. The older son got married and is living there, to this day. The father is still alive and has a pension. This is the best law that ever came into force for the elderly, as it benefits both sons and daughters.

Well, after he left Dingle and came back to the Blasket, Paddy was moseying about from place to place. He didn't want to stop anywhere until he reached his old homestead. I well knew his character and his ways beforehand but, even so, what was I to do? I couldn't very well turn my back on my only brother just after he'd come home from the New World. It was difficult enough for him to remain sane, and even taking that into account, he'd never be in anybody's way because he was one of the best workers you'd ever meet — and sure, haven't we all got our faults?

Now, during that time there was fine fishing around the Blaskets for mackerel and lobsters, both of which were in great demand. Since Paddy was going to be staying with me, I thought I'd better try and get some use out of him. I got him to come along with me and to take a section out of my old currach so that it would be easy for the two of us to bring it up and down. At that time most of the currachs being used for catching lobsters during the season were designed for two people. We had twenty pots in our small currach, and it would have done your heart good to see the two of us battling with the sea in it. And I'm telling you, we were getting some real fishing done, although we weren't going far from the house. We usually did our fishing around Beginish, and so we were able to have a morning meal, a meal in the middle of the day and an afternoon or evening meal wherever we happened to be — whether we were on dry land or out at sea. (At that time those were the names we used to call those meals.)

There were other currachs making long journeys — out as far as Tearaght, Inishtooshkert, Inishnabro and Inishvickillane; those islands are called the Lesser Blaskets. People setting off on such a long trip would have to take food with them, and stay out from dawn to dusk. Needless to say, they used to be pretty well shattered at the end of each day. There was a great quantity of lobster near these islands that wasn't to be found closer to home. But of course, a man who fished closer to home could catch up with them, because he could check the pots more regularly.

Page 227

We sold many a pound's worth to the ships that used to go up and down through the Blasket Sound. They'd have white-sheeted billowing sails raised up, even when there wasn't a puff of wind in the air. We often ate our dinner with them. We used to give them crabs and other fish. They, in return, used to give us tobacco, and other things too, like a glass of whiskey. I often used to get two glasses because Paddy never touched a drop after he left America. He'd acquired some common sense.

One fine day, a medium-sized, fine-looking steamship came towards us through the Sound from the south. Another ship was being towed behind her, with a single set of sails in every colour of the rainbow. There was a throng of people on the sailboat, and as far as clothes and ribbons went, every one of them was looking more refined than the next. These ornate small ships were going quite slowly, so that people who'd never gone through the Sound before could get a view of the Blaskets they would never forget.

It happened that I was pulling up a lobster-pot close to them, and what was in it but a blue lobster and a craw fish. As they were heading north and passing by us, I held up the craw fish in one hand and the lobster in the other. No sooner had I done so than every hand on the ships was raised, with men and women beckoning to us. They stopped near the shore and waited until we reached them.

There couldn't have been a greater welcome than there was for the two old fishermen, but our little currach wasn't empty: there were a dozen lobsters in it, two dozen crabs, and three dozen other kinds of fish. The gentry didn't care about our appearance or that of our currach, but were only interested in what we had on board.

Page 228   Until we encountered those splendid boats, I'd thought that my travels in this life would have been complete if I had gone as far as Limerick. As for the *Yank*, I don't think he was a bit interested because of the worldly sights he himself had seen. However, he often said afterwards that they were amongst the most magnificent sights he'd ever witnessed on sea or land; be that in Ireland or over yonder in the States. (Well, enough of this blather, because I'd have to do a lot of writing before I'd finish telling you all he had to say on this matter.)

One of the men let down a bucket to pull up the lobster. When I saw the fine bucket they lowered, it looked so grand that I thought they wouldn't put any lobster in it for less than a fiver. He let down the same bucket again to carry the crabs up with it, and then again for the left-over fish that were lying about on the bottom of the currach.

Well, as soon as he'd taken up everything in the little currach, it wasn't long before he let down the same bucket again, and I swear I thought that it was a chunk of bread that had landed in the stern of my currach. I didn't see what else it could have been. But I was mistaken, because when I took it in my hand and looked at it, I found that it was money. The man who let it down spoke in beautiful English.

"*You have a shilling there for every throut you send up,*" says he.

My fine gent pulled the bucket up again, and it wasn't long before I saw it being lowered once more, full to the brim. This time it was a fine lady on board who was lowering the bucket. I'd say that she had the most refined nature and beauty of anyone on the ships. The bucket was as full of good things as it was when it arrived with the money. It was crammed to the brim with every kind of food, as well as some tasty nibbles I'd never seen before. After I'd emptied it into the stern of the currach, I took off my beret and went down on one knee in order to express my gratitude to her.

We were about a mile from land at this time, because the tide was dragging the ship out to sea, but all the same the day was perfect, with our little currach going back full of every kind of luxury. The things we'd given weren't worth a pin in comparison with what we had received in return. It wasn't long until another man spoke up. He had a bucket in his hand; it wasn't a fancy bucket (although, no need to say, its entire contents were magnificent) but it was full of bacon. To be quite honest, the thought did occur to me that these good people were trying to give us enough so that we would never need to go out fishing again.

Page 229

After a while a man came to the centre of the ship and asked us to send up the empty bottle that was in the currach. I did so and in a little while it returned filled with pure water. Then he asked us again if we had any more bottles in the currach, but we didn't. He left us again, and it was some time before he returned with a remarkable-looking bottle, full of drink — rum or brandy. The bottle was full, with about six glassfuls in it. He sent it down, warning us that what was in it was mighty powerful stuff, and suggesting that we should add water from the other bottle.

The long and the short of it was that we bade one another farewell, and by this time we were about a mile and a half from land, which wasn't far. It was a fine day and there wasn't a puff of wind blowing.

Shortly after we left I wanted to taste what was in the bottle, to see whether it was whiskey. But Paddy suggested that we should get to shore first before tasting it, and then I'd have plenty of time to appreciate its contents. For once he was quite right, but I said that I'd only have a small taste of it, to check out what it was. I thought that if it wasn't poison I'd be safe enough, but like everything else, the sinner cannot do as he wants.

We had a small wooden cup for bailing the currach; it was actually my baptismal cup. I poured a spoonful out of the bottle, and about a glass of water out of the other bottle. I mixed them together; far from being poison, you'd have thought that it couldn't harm a one-year-old. Although the *Yank* had tried to stop me from touching it until we reached land, now he said:

Page 230

"Since you've started, why hold back?"

"Better to check a river or you may end up in the rapids," says I to him, and that was the last word he got from me for the next two hours. By this time we had cut the distance by about a mile, and there was still another half mile or so to go. To make matters worse, a sudden gust of wind blew up out of nowhere, bright and brilliant. I'd spotted it before I started drinking this potion, but oh, my goodness, wasn't I the keen one to slug the drink back so that it might put a bit of jizz back into me and help me to get through this disastrous gust that was really beginning to blow hard.

Anyway, down went the draught and immediately, if Paddy is to be believed, I stood up and collapsed into the back of the currach. The poor man thought I was dead, because he figured that it was poison in the bottle, and that the good people of the boat had given it to us by mistake. Such a thing could often happen too, of course. My poor brother had to give it all he had in order to reach land.

Just as he reached the shore, he was at his last gasp, having had to shelter in a cove. He had only just made it when I came out of my stupor, without a bother in the world, and in top form.

Page 231 "Well," said the *Yank*, "you've had a good sleep if anyone ever has. But I don't care, since you're still alive, because I was afraid you were a gonner. Perhaps you'd better take another wee drop!" I knew right well that he was just having a dig at me.

Well, the gale was still blowing and there was no sign of it abating. All the same we had the shelter of land now and, of course, we had plenty of food and drink on board — enough for a month. Although we were near Beginish, and not far from the house, and although there was only a mile of sea between us and the Great Blasket, we had no thought of leaving the cove.

Then the gale started to abate so Paddy said:

"Why don't we pull up the pots; these rocks should shelter us from the wind."

I didn't fancy doing this, but he's a man who likes to get what he wants, and if you cross him you get no good out of him for the next three days. We started to do it his way, but Paddy ended

up with the hardest job, because he had to do the rowing and all
I had to do was to lift up the pots.

We'd only finished part of the work when the gale started up
again. We'd got a dozen lobsters out of the pots, about twelve
shillings' worth. At that time they were more or less a shilling a
head.

By now it was late afternoon, and our little currach was still
quite a way from home. Other boats tethered to ships could see
us, as well as people on the hills, but it wasn't too long before some
people were saying that we must have been lost near the ship, and
that we had gone missing.

Fearing the worst, a large currach had been launched with four
men in it, and off they went to Beginish. They had to search for
quite a time before they found us, and it would have taken much
longer if they hadn't called out, because we were hidden away in
a cove, having decided that it might be better to wait there until
morning. We answered as soon as we heard the shout, and they
soon found us. They asked us about the ship. There were many
things for them to see: meat, bread and much more.

It wasn't long before one of the crew reached out for the black *Page 232*
bottle. While he was looking at it my heart sank, because I knew
he wouldn't be able to resist tasting it, and who knew what might
happen then. I told him at once that it was a purgative, and that
really provoked his curiosity. He took hold of it, removed the
cork, and sniffed it. Then he said with a smile on his face: "Oh
King of glory, it's brandy!"

That floored me, because I knew full well what he was like, and
that it wouldn't be possible to get the bottle off him. I realised
then that although my brother and I had first acquired the bottle,
it was the gang that now had their hands on it. When this wretch
lifted the bottle, I warned him only to wet his tongue on it and
told him how it had affected me.

"If it were Satan's brew itself," says he, "I'm sure that a
mouthful won't do me any harm!"

To tell the truth, I don't know how much he drank, because I
turned my back on him in disgust. He then handed it to the man

next to him, who also took a slug out of it. I couldn't say whether they drank much or little of it, but however much it was, it wasn't too long before the two of them were in the back of the boat, apparently stone dead. The two of us knew that they weren't dead, because we had both experienced the same affliction already. Their two companions thought that they had kicked the bucket, and so started mourning their lost companions, but they stopped when we explained to them that they were merely unconscious.

It seems that the big currach was to bring us a man and two oars to get us home, so there'd be three in each vessel. The storm was still rather strong, but appearances can often be deceptive.

Wasn't it dreadful the way matters turned out for us in the end? We'd had all that fun getting the goods from the gentry's ships, and when we left, not one of us was poorly. And now, here we were at the back of a cove, with two at the stern of the currach as good as dead, because nobody knew what they had drunk from that bottle.

Page 233

> *Oh King of Glory,*
> *For what the ship brought in our way,*
> *To thee alone our thanks we pay,*
> *Although this gift was sent by thee,*
> *The drink that cleared our misery,*
> *Has made a show of us today,*
> *And sent our fishing boat astray.*
>
> *A boat arrived to save our skin,*
> *They came to rescue kith and kin,*
> *Who can tell what they've imbibed,*
> *No man can really know,*
> *If sleep or death now grips them so.*
> *No joy for us in this dank cove tonight,*
> *Cold in the dark we must sit tight,*
> *Until first light — unhappily we wait,*
> *Praying for this wild storm to abate.*

Around about two o'clock the first of the unconscious men awoke, and the second one immediately after him.

Shortly after they woke up they both said that they were going to head home, and so we left the cove. One man said there was a sort of lull in the gale, and there was, too, at that time.

The large currach sent a man over to us with two oars; that made three in each currach. Off we went together to reach the Great Blasket, and it wasn't long before we arrived. When we reached the jetty we saw that there was a great hullabaloo going on. Everyone was there who was able to make their way to the jetty. There was much crying and confusion, with the whole Island worried that we'd all been drowned.

Although everyone looked gloomy, the gloom soon gave way *Page 234* to laughter over the magic potion carried by ships from another world, lowered by men for other men to drink — a mixture reeking of spirits brewed in the pits of hell.

"Wasn't it lucky they didn't drink the whole bottle," said one man. "Then their women would have had it in for us!"

This topic of conversation went on for a good many years. Wasn't the stuff in the bottle amazing! A pen-full of it in a cup of water would be strong enough for anyone. It's a long time since I ever had a drop of anything like it in my hand. Nobody rightly knows what kind of ships they were, but it's been said that they left the great city of London in order to make a map of the whole of Ireland. Others said that they were returning from Brazil because they were coming from that direction when we met them. Yet others suggested that they weren't from this world, and didn't look like human beings at all.

It was a great year for fishing. Every time you lifted the pots you'd get a dozen lobsters, which were worth a dozen shillings. For that you'd get a half bag of flour. A half bag of meal cost eight shillings. So it wasn't difficult for a poor person to make a living at that time.

After the ships had left, there was an extremely fine month when there wasn't even a ripple on any pool. That was the sort of weather that was best for the kind of fish we were looking for.

Even better than that, there was great demand for any fish you might catch. The *Yank* and I were doing well with the little currach because we had a wide area to fish in and no one to compete with. The lobsters used to enter the pots in the late afternoon. One evening we were very late, and the lobsters were storming into the pots.

Page 235
"Wouldn't it be a great shame for anyone to go home on a nice quiet evening like this, that's neither too cold nor too long," says Paddy to me, "and gold to be had in the pots? But if people had been in the position that I was for the last while, they'd surely know better," says Paddy. "It'll be daylight by the time we get home now," says he, "so let's wait here with the pots a while, and we'll be sure to get the same amount again as we have managed up to now, or close to it at any rate. For wouldn't it be a crying shame to be leaving them there?"

He was the kind of man who, if you didn't give him his way, you wouldn't see him the following day, even if you had good need of him. Although the situation didn't appeal to me very much, I had to agree, or else be prepared to go fishing on my own in the little currach the following day. Well, I had to pay the bills, so I did the sensible thing. I used to pay for the upkeep of everything, while all he had to worry about were his board, clothes and tobacco.

"Let's go," says Paddy after a while; "they've had plenty of time, and if they're ever going to be in the pots, they'll be in them by now. Let's go and have a look." When I pulled up the first pot, there was a tremendous clattering in it.

"I think there's an eel in it," says he.

"I don't think so," says I to him.

I put my hand down into the pot and I took up a whopper of a lobster, and another one after that.

"Are there two lobsters there?" enquires Paddy.

"Yes, and two fine ones indeed," says I to him.

"That's two shillings," says he. "Oh good Lord! you'd have to sweat blood and tears in America to earn yourself two shillings, and all you need to do here is to lift a pot through twelve feet of water and toss it into a boat!"

By the time we had lifted the last of the pots, there was a dozen fine lobsters in them.

"I bet you'll get your dozen out of them!" says Paddy.

"Yes, and a good dozen at that," says I to him.

"They'll be a better dozen than we had in the middle of the day and they're easier to catch," says he. "Mary, Mother of God! isn't it many's the shilling to be easily found in the sea, unlike other places where you have to sweat blood and tears to earn anything like as much. Upon my soul, if people in America could make money as easily as this they'd neither slumber nor sleep, but would be continually hauling up lobsters. What's more, you need so little bait for them." *Page 236*

Although he used to talk a lot of nonsense, so that I was often disinclined to believe him, I well and truly believed what he said this time, because I wasn't so green that I didn't know what happened in rich countries abroad — gruelling work and a couple of foremen constantly peering over your shoulder.

We'd had about an hour's rest when I noticed him putting the oars out again.

"We mustn't be nodding off," says he. "Since we're spending the night out here, let's get something out of it," whereupon he threw out the pot-rope, which was tied to the bow that anchored the currach while we were out at sea.

As I've already said, I had to be his servant and not his master, or we'd never have got anything done. We set about our work again, and when we got to the end of the pots, we had another dozen. We anchored once more, and I started counting the lobsters; I had exactly a dozen.

"How many have you got now?" asks Paddy.

"Exactly a dozen," says I to him.

"Oh, it's no wonder that a lot of folk living on the coast of Ireland are poor," says he, "and it serves them right! Anyone snoring away on a calm night like this deserves no sympathy when there's gold and silver to be got for such little effort."

I suppose he was partly right, but a poor sinner can't keep at it day and night, even if it were raining gold. We stopped for a

while. I don't know if I nodded off myself; he said I did, and that
I'd had a good nap.

Page 237 "I think daybreak is coming, so we ought to haul up the pots
again and then we'll head off home; no one will know how we
spent the night," says he, throwing the rope off and putting out
the oars.

I promise you, I wasn't feeling too great by this time, what with
the cold morning creeping in. I felt hungry, had tired bones, heavy
eyes, and a numb chill stealing over me. And I don't know how
the chancer at the bow was feeling. But I pulled myself together,
since I had to, and by the time I'd finished there were another
fourteen lobsters in the pots.

When we turned back towards the house, what should we see
but a vessel moored where it should be, and it was evident to us
that it was a foreign vessel. It met us in the Sound, and it was close
enough for us to go and talk with the crew. When we came
alongside, it had an unusual name — none other than *The
Shamrock*. It had a tank in it which meant that it was looking for
lobsters. A fifth company had dispatched it in search of lobsters;
and they were after lobsters if anyone ever was. They asked us how
many lobsters we had, and how much we wanted for them. We
told them that we didn't have any on board, but that we had some
in a storage pot nearby. What's more, we told them that we'd only
ask them for the same amount that we would ask from any other
vessel.

"Off you go, and bring back everything you have in the pot,"
says he.

Off we went, and the pot wasn't too far away. Then we
returned to the ship, with the six dozen we had. They were
counted one by one, and three gold sovereigns were handed to us.
A day and a night's fishing had produced that. I told the captain
so, and that we had spent the night up, so that we were good and
weary but, even so, we had the earnings for the night. When he
heard this, he gave the order to come on board immediately. We
excused ourselves, saying that we were near home now. He would
have none of it, so we had to go on board. First of all he filled a

glass for me, but Paddy refused to take a second glass. Then the captain said:

"The food is ready, so please eat your fill."

Again we tried to make the excuse that we weren't far from *Page 238* home and that it wouldn't be difficult for us to reach our own houses now. But it's many a hungry man has expired while the food was being cooked for him, so we had to accept the invitation. This splendid vessel was the captain's current home. I had never before seen, on sea or on land, anything so ornate as this. As for us two, we were like a couple of well-fed rabbits at the table. One of the men advised us that we should go out to sea as far as we could when fishing, because it was out at sea that the best fishing was to be had.

We ate our fill. I was mildly ashamed for being dirty and shabby in such a place, but my brother was only concerned with filling his belly. While he was abroad he had lost any shyness or sense of shame that he had when he was young. He told me that if I had spent any length of time away from home, I too wouldn't be too choosy about where I got my food.

When we went up onto the ship's deck the captain was pacing up and down. He started asking us about the lobsters: whether there were more of them in the area. We answered every question, and after a while we left and bade him farewell. When we reached the jetty some people were leaving the harbour, and others were still asleep.

When we had bailed the currach dry, the *Yank* said:

"We'd better get a bottle of milk and a dozen eggs to take out to the vessel. We won't be long; it'll be something to offer the gentry — some of the finest people I ever met."

I liked the decent way he spoke, although he often used language that I didn't like. So, while he waited, I went up to the village and brought back two dozen eggs and a bottle of milk.

Out we went again to the small ship. The look-out recognised us, and I handed up the bottle and the box with the eggs in it. One of the men took them quickly, and hauled them up. They were *Page 239* unusual items for them, because neither eggs nor milk could be procured out at sea. The captain spoke to the fellow who hauled them up, and after a while he came with a box filled to the brim. There was a bit of everything he had on board: biscuits, tobacco, a nice chunk of meat, and all sorts of other stuff. And apart from all these things, I came upon a half-pint of spirits. We headed back and reached the house. We slept until dinner-time, which was a new rule that we had made for ourselves.

After dinner we set out and started lifting the pots to get them ready for our early morning fishing; that's the time the lobsters tend to go into the pots. They don't like the middle of the day, because it is too bright. When the sun was setting, we'd pull the pots up, and there'd be a good number of lobsters in them. We spent all night out there, and by morning we had a good catch. Then we realised that they were best caught at night-time, so any night that was fine we were out, getting a good catch without anyone noticing.

One fine autumn night, while we were dealing with the pot-ropes, we heard a song being sung long, softly and sweetly. It came from away to the north of us, seemingly from some rocks about half a mile from us. It made my heart jump and greatly upset me.

"Do you hear that?" says I to Paddy.

"I hear it well," says he.

"Let's go home," says I to him.

"Yerra, I pity you, aren't they just seals!" says he.

"Seals don't have human voices."

Page 240 "That's exactly what they do have," says he, "and it's easy to see that you've never heard them before this. They sound like human voices when there are many of them gathered together on dry land. Look, there's a crowd of them beached on those rocks back there. And more to the point, it doesn't matter what species they are, they all do it."

I gave him the benefit of the doubt, because I knew that people who go abroad aren't afraid of anything, living or dead. Keeping this thought in mind, I put my fears to one side. We spent the rest of the night like any other night, although I wasn't really happy in myself.

Before long I heard the long, soft, sweet singing again. It reminded me of someone singing *Éamann Mhágáine*, but I just had to keep that idea out of my mind. As for Paddy, he just whistled up a tune — the seals in the west and Paddy in the east. I suppose he was only trying to raise my spirits.

Well, we got a good yield out of the pots with about a dozen fine lobsters in them.

"Do you have a dozen?" says he.

"I do, exactly one dozen," says I to him.

"The devil! 'tis well you didn't go home on account of the murmuring seals! You wouldn't do much good if you had to go and earn your living in foreign parts," says he.

Doubtless he was right in what he said, although at other times he used to be wholly mistaken. He didn't stop until we had anchored again on the same rope. And to top it all, he chose the best place to hear the singing seals! While we were getting ready, there wasn't a peep out of them. But it wasn't long before they all started off screaming together, so that they would have been heard no matter which way you went.

"I wonder what makes them go mad like this every now and again," says I to Paddy, "when at other times they're so peaceful?"

"They're like this whenever one of them comes back from sea. There's another one, just now beached on the rocks, and they were all asleep until he arrived," says he.

By this time no one had ever heard, whether at a market or at a fair, the sound of so many songs intermingling with one another. Well, I accepted what he was saying about them, because he knew more about the world than I did. He had travelled to many places, unlike myself who had never been further than my fireside. He'd spent a long time in the New World, where he used to do seasonal manual work quite a distance from where he lived. Moreover, he was twelve years older than me. *Page 241*

"Wait until daylight — I don't suppose it's far off now, and then you shall see the seals beached on the rocks yonder," says he.

"But I often saw one beached on a rock," says I to him.

"But you wouldn't be so scared if you were more accustomed to being out at night. You'll not think twice about them the next time you hear them," says Paddy.

I understood what he was getting at by the time he'd finished dropping hints about me coming with him the following night. Before long he said that the day was dawning in the east, and that there was no need to be shifting any more pots.

"Wait till it gets brighter; then we won't have to go searching all over the place," says I to him.

Well, the upshot of it all was that it had become good and bright by the time we got going, which was just when the singing seals went completely crazy, every last one of them piping up in unison.

"It won't be long until those lads back there will be leaving," says Paddy.

Soon after that it was bright daylight and the ridge of the rock was thick with seals: some of them had their heads in the air; others were snapping left and right at each other but one big hearty chap up above them wasn't budging as yet. Paddy told me that he was still fast asleep but that when he woke up, there'd be all hell to pay on the rocks.

Page 242 From what he said, you'd think that he'd spent his whole life studying these seals, because he knew so much about them, unlike myself.

We remained anchored to the pots until, one by one, all the seals had gone down into the hollow. This business took up most of the morning. Finally, the big seal woke up. When he lifted his head, he let out a terrible scream that could be heard over the entire area. It wasn't surprising that this scream was heard by all the seals on the rock because he was the leader of both the big and the small seals. Soon he started heading down, as big as any bull that was ever found in a field. He put his snout under the seal nearest to him, and lifted him as high as the mast of a boat, and he didn't stop until he had driven him out into the sea.

That was when all hell broke loose. When the others saw this going on, every one of them made for the water with all their might. Any of them that were slow had the bull's nozzle thrust under him to lift him high into the air and then chucked out into the sea. This happened to a lot of them.

The big fellow stayed for a while on the rock, drawing his breath and checking whether he'd got them all together. Then he himself went down into the sea, and the wave he created would have sunk a small ship. Believe you me, while this hullabaloo was going on, there wasn't a peep out of any of the other seals.

We could have had our pots well and truly ready while this show was going on, but I never thought that Paddy would wait as long as he did. I suppose the tricks that were going on at the time amazed him as much as they did me.

Well, after this we weren't too long pulling up the pots, which were now clearly to be seen, without any water whatsoever covering them. We had a good catch that morning: a clean three dozen in all. I'm telling you, even though our currach was small, the catch we had was large.

For the rest of that season we spent every fine night like this. *Page 243* For one thing, if the sea is rough, not much goes into the pots, day or night. The lobster likes the sea to be calm before he'll try peeping out.

One particular morning, when we were ready to come home, there was a little puff of wind from the south, and then when we moved out we saw some pieces of timber from a wreck. We picked them up, only to find more in another place. Our currach was soon full of them, with more floating in on the tide.

We had to return to Beginish to empty the currach and then to push out again. The wreckage was coming thick and fast on the tide that was swirling round the point. There were new, clean, white planks floating, for which there'd be a good demand. We had to take a rope from a pot and put it around a dozen planks to tow them after us. Then we had to turn back to get the rest we'd collected. We got sixteen of them in one go, and we were hoping to get the rest while the tide was still on the move.

The only thing hampering us now was hunger. After the night, it was heavy work gathering these planks. But we decided to carry on doing this job as long as the driftwood was afloat. As for my brother Paddy, he never seemed to get hungry, thirsty or sleepy.

I told him I was getting famished, and that it was time for us to have something to eat. I was just trying to see what he would say.

"Yerra, man, don't you remember that proverb — how does it go: 'Catch the fish while it's there to be caught,'" says he. "Do you imagine there'll be wreckage to be found any time you want it?"

I guessed that this would be the answer I'd get, and I knew, too, that he was right. Indeed, things like that aren't always to be found, and people who delay often find out later that they've missed their chance.

Page 244

Well, we didn't stop as long as the tide held and we were able to collect more of them. By now, when the time had passed for us to get food, our hunger had abated. When this happens, a person gets weaker, and that's how it was for us too.

Later in the day we saw several boats here and there collecting wreckage in the same way, some of them at Gob Point on the Great Blasket Island and others over near Dunquin. By this time we had around sixty white planks on Beginish, all saved with the help of our little currach.

My brother Paddy, the poor plodding *Yank*, did great work that day — never mind all he did in America while he was over there. We often had a good distance to go, to tow the planks to dry land, and when we got there, it was often Paddy himself who carried them ashore without any help from me.

We'd done well for ourselves, but what about our people at home? We'd left the house after dinner the day before; it was now dinner-time the following day and we still hadn't returned. What would our people be thinking but that we were dead? There were very few currachs near the houses at that time, because they were out at the little islands, laying pots. The rest were out looking for wreckage. So there wasn't an oar or a currach at the jetty to go out searching for us.

By now we ourselves were completely exhausted, the tide had turned, and the wood had become scarce, so we set off for the house, and believe you me, if there'd been as much as a puff of wind against us we'd never have reached home.

Afterwards, all that anyone spoke about was the wreckage that had been picked up around Beginish by the two lads' little currach; and indeed it was many the day after this that we continued to collect planks, flotsam and jetsam. We sold over half of it on Beginish, but we had to bring the other half home, because any bit left on Beginish would have been stolen.

When the season was over, no boat had caught more lobsters, or gathered more wood, than our little currach. It wasn't difficult for a poor person to get a bit of tobacco at that time, unlike today *Page 245* as I scribble on this paper. There has been no wreckage afloat since the Great War and the year of the *Quabra*.

NINETEEN

Page 247 The year after we salvaged the planks — and I suppose we'd made a dozen or so pounds out of it, not to mention the lobsters — we got down to business as usual. We were doing well at the beginning of the year, but a horse doesn't always have a good run.

At the time of year when young fledgling birds were almost mature, boys used to go out looking for them. My eldest boy and the King's son decided to go somewhere or other to find a young seagull, because a young fledgling bird would often live in a house amongst the chickens for a year or two.

The two of them went off to the nests in order to bring home a couple of seagulls. They went to a dangerous place, and while my boy was trying to catch hold of a young seagull, the bird suddenly jumped and knocked him off balance. He fell off and down into the sea, may God save us from all such things! It was a long time before he went under and resurfaced. The body floated on top of the water until some currachs spotted it. His grandfather was in the boat that picked his body out of the water. The only consolation we had was that there wasn't a mark or a scratch on him, even though he had fallen from a great height. His death was a cross I just had to bear. It meant a great deal to me that I was able to bury him on land and not to lose him to the sea.

That was the first thing that happened, and it wasn't a good start, God help us.

Page 248

The accident occurred around 1890 when the boy was just starting to get a sense of responsibility, and to run messages for me. Well, the one who departs doesn't feed the one who remains, as the man said long ago, and we had to get back to our work again and to continue plodding along.

That year wasn't nearly as good as the previous one. We didn't catch as many lobsters during the night, because the weather never settled and there used to be a constant current under the rocks, which wasn't good for that kind of fishing. It so happened that this year green fish came in close to the shore. The sea was full of them. This kind of fish was called pollock, a big, coarse fish that would keep you busy trying to get it over the gunwale of the currach. To catch them we used fishing lines baited with slices of mackerel on a large hook. One day, using gear like this, we went fishing for them. We got a huge catch, so much so that we had to leave the fishing-ground early, because our little currach was full and the sea was so unsettled and choppy. When we got to the jetty, there were many people who were amazed at the amount of fish our little currach held.

We spent part of the year fishing for pollock until every container in the house was full of them. Altogether we'd saved three hundred of them. Around Christmas there was always a great demand from country people for these rough fish — when they were going cheap, of course. I brought home fifteen pounds from Dingle for my share of the pollock. In addition, many of my relatives got a couple of them, since we had loads of them in our house.

A while after this, the daughter of Mr Daly Senior, the caretaker of Inishvickillane, came home from America. This was the girl

the rake Dermot, my uncle, had in mind for me in my early youth.
She spent a few years over there, but her health failed, as happened
Page 249 to many others like her. She didn't get better when she came back
but fell sick again, even though she came to the healthiest island
in Ireland.

Eventually, after only being there for a season, she died on the
island. There were fishermen from Cahersiveen on Inisvickillane
at the time; and when people heard that she had died, everyone
tried to get over there to attend the wake. You wouldn't meet
better people anywhere; the most generous folk around, and
because of this, everyone would turn to them when in difficulty.
Many people were gathered there for a good part of that night,
and currachs were still arriving at the island up to ten o'clock in
the evening.

Well, there was a great crowd gathered in the evening, and
another large crowd were going westwards along the bay in the
morning, as it was a splendid day and the sea was fine and quiet.
There was a fiddler from the parish of Moregoch there, who had
arrived at the Blasket at the same time. The fiddler went along
with us westwards on the first night. He never stopped telling us
stories until the morning came. He didn't even stop in the
morning either. He lay on the flat of his back in the grass telling
stories until the girl's body was removed. Since then I have often
thought about that man Daly. If he were alive today it would be
easy for a Gaelic writer to have enough material to write a book
about him.

The day of the funeral was one of the finest days I have ever
seen, and one of the warmest. It was an amazing sight to see
everyone gathered at the top of the jetty. The coffin was placed
into a Cahersiveen currach, with three good men in it, because it
wouldn't have fitted four. When they were ready, they turned away
from the island and set out across the bay.

There was a large, red-faced man in the bow of the
Cahersiveen boat on whom the heat was taking its toll and he was
sweating profusely. However, even with all that effort, his strength
Page 250 did not fail him all the way from the Great Blasket and on to

Dunquin. From time to time everyone imagined that he would have to give up, but he didn't. This was one of the most remarkable feats I have ever seen a man perform, especially across that exceedingly wide bay.

When we reached the Blasket Island jetty for the funeral, there were already currachs moored there. We still had to row for another three or more miles. I'd never seen so many boats moored in the one place, and so I decided to count them; there were eighteen boats in all. Since that time the most I've ever seen at a funeral has been fourteen or maybe sixteen.

May God preserve all the souls I have written about on these pages! May He not give any one of them an evil place to dwell in! Although the Inishvickillane man had a full household at that time, only three of them are around here today. Some of them are in America, others in their graves, or scattered to all corners of the earth like many another.

Life went on from year to year, and I was still living in the old ramshackle house. Suddenly, I got the idea of leaving it and building a new place, so that the hens would no longer be making a racket in the thatch over my head. All the same, in times of need, I often got a small pile of eggs up there; but on the other hand, it was those same hens that caused the roof to leak.

The kind of houses that were being built at that time had a wooden roof on them, with felt and tar outside under the sheets. They were as slippery as a bottle, so when a hen wanted to go up to lay eggs there, she wouldn't be able to stay up but would fall down into the dung-yard; this discouraged any hen from trying it again.

Once something comes into a person's mind, I suppose it can get stuck there, and that's how it was with me regarding the new house. I knew that I wouldn't get much help with it, but that was *Page 251* no great problem for me, because I already had an old house, and therefore I could take as much time as I needed to build the new one.

Well, I only had to go across the street to find stones lying around. As the little Yellow Dwarf said long ago, it's easier to knead where the flour is. It was a great thing for me to have the raw materials all around me. After I drew a plan of the house, it became clear to me that I would have a mansion fit for a king if I could get it built and roofed. I was always at it, adding a bit any time I got a chance. Bit by bit it started to look like a house, and before long it was the height of a person. I only had to put up the two gable ends; these were narrowing rows of stones, one on top of the other.

Well, I kept working for a solid three months, and finally I was able to put the keystone in place on the top of the gable-end. This work was done without a stone or any mortar being handed to me. The rake, Dermot, often came round to see me, but I used not to detain him.

I took this work upon myself in the depths of winter, because I'd have no business doing it when there was fishing to be done. When I'd put up the keystone, around the middle of March, there was all kinds of work needing my attention: turning the soil, bringing manure by boat or up from the shore, and it was also the time that people would go to visit the seal caves.

On one of these mornings, when it was fine, soft and pleasant, there was a knock on the door before daybreak. Since I wasn't in a deep sleep, I jumped up with a start, opened the door only to find it was Dermot outside.

"Throw on some clothes," says he; "the day is splendid. Let's go off to the islands. Who knows what we might find hanging around in some seal cave or in a creek. Would you have a small chunk of some baked bread?"

"I have plenty of bread," says I to him. "But I don't want to go out to the islands, because it would be a wasted trip, so early in the year."

Page 252 "Stop your babbling!" says he. "We'll find something — a string of rabbits or perhaps something even better. How do you know that we won't come across a nice young seal? I haven't any bread; bring along a good chunk that we can share."

"Yerra, isn't that a sturdy little laid-back wife you have!" says I to him. "I suppose she must be using the flour sparingly!"

"Divil a bit of it," says he, "when she is wasting food or looking after her own needs! But whenever her own belly is full, she thinks that every belly in the district is full too. She's a damn fool of a woman who has always been clueless."

I grabbed a good triangle of bread, and out the door we went. The rest of the boat crew had arrived and were waiting for us. We launched the boat, and off we went. We didn't stop until we got to Inishnabro, where there was a cave famed for its seals, and where it would be a rare thing indeed not to find one. A fine spring-tide was flowing, so we decided to investigate.

The four of us were soon inside the cave and all of us were keen to get out of the boat. We were closing in on the cave, and one man began peering down into a large pool.

"Yerra, I wonder what sort of things those are down there?" says he.

One man after another looked down and we could see that the pool was full of whatever it was that was there. However, none of us could actually make out what it was we were looking at.

One of the men was a great swimmer and was used to swimming under water. We called him over; he came quickly and looked down.

"Yerra, the devils!" says he, "they're copper and brass bolts. Don't you know that a ship was wrecked here a good while ago and that it was carrying a lot of bolts like that? Didn't the boat from Dunquin salvage a good load of them a while ago, and got good money for them too!"

No sooner had he said this than he took off all his clothes and *Page 253* dived headlong into the pool. It was no more than about six feet deep, and he wasn't long down before he came to the surface holding a copper bolt that was at least four feet in length.

"'Pon my soul!" says he, "I hope you're not relying on me to bring it all up. Tie a rope around someone else; better still, send two people down at a time. We'll need to put a good spurt on before the tide comes in; it'll be difficult to see them if the water is disturbed."

There was nothing for it, but where would we find two willing
men to go down? That was the question. Some of them had never
been in sea water, and others, who could swim well, weren't
accustomed to going under water. There were six of us in the cave
at this time — the crew of the boat and the two who were in
charge of it. When they heard that there was something of value
in the cave, they wanted to go and look at it. They weren't too
keen, however, to go down themselves to retrieve it.

Dermot made a dash across the shore to find me, and said:

"You're usually a good swimmer — even though you don't
often gain much by it. Come over here; I'll put a rope around you,
and we'll bring up some of those gold bars. Let's not leave it all to
one person, or even to two."

Well, even though the situation didn't greatly appeal to me, I
had no desire to get this maniac's back up and so I did what he
asked. I undressed and quickly went down to the bottom of the
pool. The rake wasn't too happy when I didn't put the rope
around me as he had told me to do. He thought that I was
annoyed, but I wasn't; I simply had no need of a rope. I was a good
swimmer so I could dart up to the surface whenever I wanted.

While I was going down, my foot struck a bolt. I looked around
for another one so that I could surprise the rake by coming up
with two. The other men were only bringing the bolts up one at a

Page 254 time, which was a good feat in itself. These men earned what they
found — unlike the onlookers who weren't going down to get their
share of the bolts.

Well, I was searching eagerly, and pretty soon I noticed another
bolt, and I shifted it easily. I had one under my arm, another in
one hand, and with my free hand I was helping myself up. I bent
my two legs and pushed up easily towards the surface. However,
when I got there the weight of the bolts brought me back down
again. When I resurfaced in the middle of the pool, the rake was
ready, waiting for me. He threw out the rope, and I caught it with
my free hand.

As soon as he saw me coming with the two bolts, he started
humming a tune. I was alive and had something to show for

it. He showed me no pity because he was a very hardened forager.

"Well done yourself; even though you're slow, you've come heavy-laden! Down you go again," says he. "Today's the day to do it, because as soon as the word gets round about the bolts, people will be here day and night and there'll be little left for us."

There was another man standing on the edge of the pool; Maurice Bawn was his name. He was a broad, strong man, but he had never swum a stroke. He felt that it wasn't right for us to be going into the pool while he just looked on. So he said to Dermot:

"Put the end of that rope around my body and I'll go down, and I'll bring an armful of them up with me, since they are so plentiful."

"Yerra, your soul to the devil!" says Dermot, "you must be losing your mind. You might as well send down a bag of salt. Can't you see that even the swimmers are barely alive when they come up?"

Maurice turned to another man and asked him to put the rope around him. This man, Liam, was the rake's brother, and was the one who had dropped his load of seaweed into the sea when he was looking at the two cocks fighting. I've mentioned him already in this book; he was the kind of man who couldn't have cared less whether Maurice was brought up dead or alive.

Liam put the rope around Maurice, and lowered him into the *Page 255* pool. As soon as he hit the bottom, he immediately started pulling himself up the rope to the surface, not even waiting for Liam to pull him back up. And it was just as well that he did, because Liam would have given him as much time as he had given the two cocks!

While the tide was out of the channel we got twenty-one bolts between the two of us — a fine pile of both copper and brass. Hell would freeze over before the rake would tire of bringing them up to the boat. When we'd finished, we started eating our bread, without anything to go with it. No one spoke a word until we'd finished, but now and again a man dipped his hand into the water and swigged back a handful of the brine in order to clear his throat.

While we were pottering about like this, and getting ready to head off home after we had finished, Liam spotted a trawler making towards Inishvickillane. He spoke up and drew our attention to it.

"They're bringing something with them today," says the rake.

When the ship reached the island's beach she dropped anchor.

"Well," says Dermot, "put out your oars and let's see what brought her this way, and then we can head off home, God willing."

We set out to cross the short distance between the two islands. It wasn't long before we were alongside them. The trawler was full of people, important dignitaries, although none of us recognised any of them. They were all out enjoying themselves around the islands.

The bolts were hidden in our boat, so that no one could see them, but in the end we said to one another that it'd be a good thing to show one to them to see what they'd say about it. When one of the gentry saw the brass bar he was very surprised and wondered where we had come across it. He immediately asked us if we wanted much for it. But it was a hell of a long time before Page 256 he got any answer, because none of us knew how much they were worth. In the end the captain of the vessel said:

"Here's a man who buys this sort of thing; he'd like you to sell it to him."

We soon found out that he was willing to buy all we had of them. In the end, to make a long story short, we sold the whole lot to him for sixteen pounds. I suppose that if they'd been in any other place we would have got a pound for each one of them, but we were far from the market and it would have been difficult for us to get them there.

We had to go on board the trawler to have something to eat and drink, and there was plenty there for everyone. Where else, of course, except where the gentry were, would there be so much to be had? And now, instead of the bolts, we had money in our pockets.

The day was getting on by the time we finally said goodbye to the gentry. Then we made for the other island, which is called

Inishnabro, where there were rabbits to be seen dancing on every blade of grass, enjoying the balmy, sunny weather. Suddenly, while we were still at the bottom of the island, the rake spoke up. Although I often describe him as a rake, instead of calling him by his proper name, Dermot, he wasn't actually a rake at all, but quite the opposite. He was the captain of our great boat, and a right good captain he was too, especially at foraging. Suddenly he stood up and said:

"It's a fine afternoon, and there's nothing left for us to do now but to go home. So, since we've got two good dogs and a couple of decent spades, why don't we make a quick trip over to the island, and each of us will be able to bring half a dozen rabbits back home with us."

One man thought it was a good idea but two didn't. All the same, the suggestion of a hunt appealed to everyone. The boat stopped at the jetty, and out we got, two men on one side and two on the other. By the time we got back to the jetty it was late in the afternoon. The rake had quite a sizeable catch — about the same *Page 257* amount as the other two together; but he also had a good dog, and both he and the dog were as fit as fiddles.

After everyone returned to the boat, they piled up all their catch together. We had eight dozen rabbits, a dozen per man. When we returned home, the oldest man in the boat said that it was the largest catch in such a short time that he ever remembered catching. And luckily enough we also had a fair wind to carry us home quickly.

Most people can't keep a secret, and indeed one of us let the story out, about where we had spent the day, what had happened to us, and about the gentry who had bought the brass and the copper we'd found. As a result, we retrieved no more of it, because, before we got together the next day, all the village boats had already gone out. Well, to finish off the story, not much was salvaged from the cave after that. It seems that we got most of the loot on the very first day. Anyway, since then only the odd bolt was found.

The two pounds I got from the salvaged bolts paid for the roof of the house. Things were cheap at that time, and it didn't cost too much. There was much about the new house that appealed to me. It was small, although when I designed it I thought that it would be like a mansion compared with my old cottage beside it. There was one good thing about having the cottage to live in, and that was that it allowed me to take my time in building the new house. Moreover, I didn't need to take any parts from the cottage to build the new house.

I worked on the house every free moment I had until I had finished it. When the work was completed, who should come round but the rake? He stood looking at it for a while, and finally said:

"Mary, Mother of God! how did you put that together so quickly, without getting any help from a living soul? May God *Page 258* preserve us! sure no hen will lay its eggs on that ridge. For if it tries, it will surely slip over the edge."

Although it was finished, the house remained empty for a while before we moved in. There weren't many felt-roofed houses on the island at that time, but now there isn't a house that doesn't have a felt roof on it, except for those that have slates.

We moved into the house around the year 1893, at the beginning of spring. The main reason for going so soon was that manure was very scarce that year, and there was enough soot and manure on the roof of the old house to cover half the potatoes on the Island. Another thing; the rake Dermot had been at me every day, because nothing he had sown had ripened. This was because he was a poor man, living on his own, who used to do a lot of travelling here and there. This prevented him getting things done, as often happens with people like him. Mind you, I did feel sorry for him as he had lost his first wife, and she was good to him. His second wife was the local birdbrain, useless and clueless. Another reason I was well disposed to him was because he'd be the first to help me out whenever I'd be in trouble of any kind.

As soon as the rake saw a fire lit in the new house, he'd drop in to see us without delay, so that he could claim the soot for himself.

"For God's sake, don't let anyone have it except me!" says he.

He was very sharp about making sure he got his share of whatever was going round, but then again he'd be the first to share out whatever he had himself.

"I'll not give it to anyone else, don't worry," I reply. "Have you anything important to do today?"

"Mary, Mother of God! sure I've nothing on; why are you asking?" says he. "Have you anything you want me to do?"

"Yes; come up to the top of the old house and collect your manure."

Page 259

We'd been in the new house for a while and were doing well. We were happy there. It was a nice clean house, smoke-free, with no condensation. We hadn't been long settled in when whooping cough hit the village, and measles along with it. I spent three months during the worst of it looking after the children, but in spite of my best efforts two of the finest of them went the way of all flesh.

Our spirits were truly broken, God help us. It seemed to last a hell of a long time, to be sure. The deep sorrow of losing our children took its toll on my wife, and she was never the same afterwards until the day she died — so she didn't make old bones either.

Well, after this personal ordeal, I tried to pull myself together. It was brought home to me that the only cure for things such as these is to endure them patiently. I was trying my best to make it through another slice of life — one good year comes along, then it's followed by two that aren't so great.

A few years after this a young lady from Ireland's capital came to the island on her holidays, and it wasn't long before she became friendly with one of my daughters. A person often takes an interest in one special person apart from all the others that are around. The two of them spent time together each day. They used to have a day in the hills and then another day around the beach and by the sea, and when the weather was mild and sultry they used to go off swimming.

One day when they were doing this, there was a flood tide that was too strong for them. While they were trying to get close to land they were actually being carried away from it until they became exhausted. One of my sons happened to be digging potatoes in the kitchen-garden beside the house — it was the beginning of autumn. He was a spirited young fellow and was able to swim well. At that time he was eighteen years old. He saw the two women in the sea, and immediately recognised who they were and that they wouldn't be able to get back on their own.

He threw down his spade and went the quickest way down the cliff and shore, until he came to the beach. He didn't take a stitch *Page 260* off himself, shoes or anything, because the girls weren't too far out. When he went into the water he saw the young lady going down.

Out he went and spoke to his sister, telling her to keep floating on the surface, that the young lady had sunk and that he would go to rescue her first. But when he tried to, he and the young lady went down together. Another man brought in the sister who, by this time, was barely alive. The boats eventually brought in the bodies of my son and the young lady. When Paddy and I returned from our fishing, this was the sight that met us.[35]

Well, I had to handle this ordeal too, and get through it somehow. On the day of the funeral — it was the largest funeral that had ever been seen in Dunquin — both of them went in the same funeral cortege for a good while, until they split up as they drew towards their own family churches.

The family of the young lady were very kind to me for years after that. I don't know if they are long since dead and buried. As her father and her mother only met me for the first time in Dunquin, I had to introduce myself to them. I suppose they thought I was furious with them, as it was their daughter who had caused the death of my son. But I was never so insensitive as to think anything like that. If she herself was in any way responsible, they certainly were not, as they were far away in Blackrock, near Ireland's capital, when this tragedy occurred.

[35] (*Trans.*) "Donal was drowned at the age of 18 in the incident that occurred at Trá Bhán in August 1909 … Eileen Nicholls was also drowned." *Cérbh É Tomás Ó Criomhthain?* by Micheál Ó Conaill (*p. 16*), *Ceiliúradh an Bhlascaoid 2*, in eagar ag Máire Ní Chéilleachair, An Sagart, An Daingean, 1998.

I suppose that if it were not for my uncle Dermot, and the help of God, I would never have got back to being my old self again. At times it was touch and go whether my daughter would ever recover, as she was still only barely hanging on. It always seemed to me that if she were to recover, then I wouldn't be doing too badly at all.

The rake used to come to see me every day and night, pooh-poohing the gloom and doom he'd hear in our house. To give us courage he talked about other things that were much worse than what had happened to us — for example, the ship that went down with hundreds in it, a bank collapsing and killing a lot of people, and miners dying in their droves. *Page 261*

Things didn't go too well for the rake himself, the poor chap. He had sturdy sons at this time and he believed that he would soon be able to do as he liked, provided his sons managed to make a life for themselves. Then he'd have nothing to do except to have them at his beck and call.

A short while after this, he dropped in to see me and I didn't know what was up.

"Something has brought you here," says I to him.

"Misfortune," says he.

"What misfortune?" says I to him, as I waited for his reply.

"Well," says he, "late yesterday evening, the best fellow I had, my son Paddy, was running after sheep when he tripped and hit his head on a sharp stone. He bled profusely. The wound wasn't big, but the stone made a large hole in the bone, and I think that there's a piece of the bone lodged inside."

"And what are you going to do now?" says I to him.

"I want to fetch the doctor and the priest," says he. "Since the day is fine, get yourself ready."

"I'll be with you straight away. You get the rest of the crew," says I to him, and I collected what I needed.

When we got to Dunquin, two of us had to go for the priest, and the other two took the road to Dingle. The priest was from the north, and that was where I headed with another man, Pats Sheamus. The rake himself and his brother Liam went for the doctor; they had a long road ahead of them, believe you me, going there and back by foot, without a horse or a foal.

Page 262 The priests weren't at home when we got there, so we had to wait until they returned. The parish priest asked what had delayed us. We told him what had happened to the boy, and that we had been here a long time. He asked us if it was a matter of life and death. We said that it was, and that two others were getting the doctor. The two priests conferred with one another, and the young one agreed to come along quickly. He told us to go on ahead of him.

We thanked him, and set off along the road and went as fast as our legs would carry us, because we knew that, however hard we tried, the priest would be ahead of us, even though we were taking a short cut. But we weren't so slow walking as we thought, for when we reached the jetty of Dunquin neither the doctor nor the priest had yet arrived. It was late in the day by this time, but we had to get back, and there wasn't much of the day left by the time we reached the Great Blasket. It wasn't long before the priest reached us, and then we had to launch the boat, of course.

There were only the six of us, but enough of us as the afternoon was fine, because the other two had gone for the doctor. We didn't know when they'd reach us, whether they had found a doctor or were still on the lookout for one. By this time we'd given up on them. Then, as we faced the cliff, we saw the two of them at the top with the doctor. We had to turn back and take them on board. The night was pitch black by the time we reached the Island as, of course, we had to go back — and set off again.

Both the priest and the doctor thought that the boy was dangerously ill, but the doctor said that if there was even a fragment of broken bone inside the fractured skull, it would always be a source of trouble for him. "But", says he, "there won't be a bother on him if that isn't the case."

Well, the day wasn't a complete waste for the eight of us, and that's how it always is on an island like this one: constant hardship in times of distress. Alas, the poor lad never did do a decent day's work from that time on, until the day he went into his grave.

TWENTY

A year of famine; Meal and flour donated; The old captain and his old crock of a vessel; The King's Man and the King of the Blasket; The way in which the old tub finally sets off; Buying piglets in Dingle; No more charitable donations

T hat was a year of famine on the Island — and in a lot of other places as well. A gentleman from Ireland's capital city came to find out where the need was, and he came as far as the Blasket. He sent an order for meal and flour to Dingle. Page 263

There was an old trawler in the harbour, which hadn't been in service for ages. There were two metres of seaweed growing on it — periwinkles and limpets, mussels, and so on. The old captain in charge of it seemed to be in as poor shape as the ship. You wouldn't think that a single drop of water, either brine or fresh water, had touched him since the year of the Great Famine. The bristle that had been growing on his face from his youth was still there and hadn't been touched. It had grown down his chest in a thick stubble like a goat's beard, to be kept for gloomy, wet days, and only to be shorn when drier weather arrived. He wasn't a day younger than eighty. Someone in Dingle told him that he should earn himself a few bob from that old wreck of a vessel that had never moved from the harbour mud for the past fifteen years.

By the time the meal and the flour were ready at the quay, the old crock of a vessel was up alongside the quay, too, with nobody on board her except the old captain who had left the cargo-bay. You'd think he'd been told to tell every cart driver to put his load Page 264 on to the ship. It wasn't long before the loading was finished and a coastguard arrived at the quay. The coastguard went straight over to talk to the old captain. He brusquely asked him where the rest of the ship crew were. The old lad explained that he only needed a small crew, though he could manage pretty well on his own too. If there was someone to help him put the sails up, he could easily manage to get to the Island by himself.

The official was a tough, no-nonsense type, and became impatient with the old captain.

"It's not what suits you, but the poor people whose food it is; it's being provided for them as a charitable donation. They'll be going short if they have to rely on you and your damned wreck of a vessel. And I wouldn't give half-a-crown for that old tub's chances," says he.

The reason he was so annoyed with the old grey-haired captain was because he himself had planned to go with him in order to keep an eye on everything in the boat. When he saw that the old captain didn't want to take him along, he lost his temper.

"Have a crew put together by the time I come back. If you don't, I shall take the cargo out of it and I'll put it all into another ship," says he, heading off down the quay.

While this was going on, the grey-haired captain was fuming, his grey appearance turning blue with rage. He was in an awful state; he rushed down the quay after the official, and would have followed him further but was stopped by the Island people. Then he yelled aloud, like a mad bull, screaming:

"You can go to hell, because you have no jurisdiction over my boat — who the hell do you think you are, anyway? Is there Page 265 anyone from the Island that would go with me and put the sails to the top of the mast for me?" the old captain enquired, with a wild look in his eyes. He didn't care who was in the boat, as long as it wouldn't be anyone likely to boss him around. He must have realised that there was some justification for the coastguard to be talking to him so boldly.

Even though the meal and the flour were badly needed by the Islanders, they weren't too ready to answer him, and one of them even said that he didn't know how to do this kind of work and so he'd be of no use to him.

"But don't I have the know-how myself?" the captain insisted. "All I need is some help to put up the sail-cloth, and then I'll do the rest myself."

Hardly had he said this when the coastguard came back down the quay again, going at a fair pace, with a neatly-tied package in his hand as though he had made himself food provisions for the day. He appeared to be trying to reach the old barnacled wreck as soon as possible. The grey-haired captain didn't notice him until he had hopped on board the boat.

"Have you managed to get any help?" says he to the captain.

"What the devil is it to you whether I have or not?" replied the captain. "I'll get them when I want them. What business is this of yours, anyway? You don't have any damned authority over my ship."

At this time, there were two policemen standing on the quay near the old wreck of a boat. The coastguard called them over to arrest the old grey-haired captain, on the grounds that the food intended for the poor was being ruined because water was already seeping into the meal, and there was no one on board to pump the water out of the ship.

The two policemen came on board, grabbed hold of the old- *Page 266* timer and took him away from the quay.

"Keep him in custody for the time being," says the man left on board. "Perhaps I can find another two good men to help me."

This coastguard would have liked to have had a colleague to help him, or perhaps the King of the Blasket himself. The coastguard knew the King well, and as the King was near at hand on this occasion, he asked whether he would be willing to come along on the old jalopy of a ship if he, the coastguard, were able to find another good man to help.

No wonder the King took this as a great compliment. After all, he was the crowned King of our Island, and could turn his hand to any task, from sowing and fertilising potatoes to being a sailor, if needed. What's more, the King would be the first up and out in the morning, on his old short-tailed, light-grey donkey, while everyone else would be still sound asleep in their beds.

"I'd be delighted to go with you, and I'll get another man to help as well," says the King to the coastguard.

"Thank you very much," says he.

The King came to me before he set out to sea and, of course, I knew there was no way he'd leave without saying goodbye to me first. He called me over, gave me a glass of spirits, and had something else for himself. He showed me a box full of beer, and asked me to look after it. He said he'd be grateful to me if I'd get it home safely for him, "because", says he, "if I took it with me on board I'd smell of drink and feel awkward not handing it around to the others. I don't think it'd be a very good thing to do, anyway." The King had another bottle of spirits to give later to those who were going along with him.

"I'll look after the box for you — and not touch a drop of it. All the same, I'm a bit concerned about you, with that old grey-haired man who, I think, intends to go along with you."

"We'll be well able for him," says the King.

Page 267 Well, we went out and joined the rest of them. The King called another man with whom he got on well, and shouted that there were two others ready to go along with him if that was alright.

"It is of course," says the coastguard. "In you go."

My two companions went in quickly. The coastguard who was already on board gave them both jobs to do — pulling and slackening ropes, dragging ropes through pulleys — so it wasn't long before the old crate was ready to move out from the quay.

While all this was going on, the old captain was still on the quay without a peep out of him. Anyone who knew anything about people would understand how the grey-haired man must have felt. However, there can be no success without discipline. Nevertheless, it was just as well that the policeman had intervened, because otherwise the old captain would have had the ancient tub, the meal, himself, and the Island people sunk.

When the tub was ready to sail, the coastguard sent word to the police asking whether the old captain was willing to come along with them. They insisted that he should not be allowed to be in command of the old boat until he himself was capable of bringing it back to Dingle. Although the grey-haired man wasn't too pleased with this, he knew well that if he himself weren't on board, he wouldn't get paid, and it had been a long time since either he or his ship had had an opportunity such as this. And so, when the police asked him, he told them immediately that he'd like to go along too. The coastguard asked a young lad from Dingle to come home with him as there were two Blasket lads remaining in the town when the trawler was setting off. The young lad went with them. Then the vessel turned its stern to the land, its bow to the sea, and sailed away.

Off went all the rest of us then, plodding down the road, carrying small items, but we weren't able to carry them on our backs. Therefore, we had to have a horse, and we all understood that there was a box belonging to the King that had been left in someone's care. It wasn't too long until they realised what needed to be done, and so they asked me to go and fetch a horse. Since I had promised the King that I'd look after the box, this was foremost in my mind. I brought back with me a man who had a horse for us.

Page 268

Six of us altogether had small loads to bring back, but the others, including myself, had nothing much to carry. As for me, I had only the King's box to think about. The people who had nothing to carry didn't need a horse, but they were happy enough to chip in to pay for a horse for those who had baggage. The fellow who owned the horse wanted a shilling per man, which he thought was a fair price for the trip to Dunquin. It was certainly a good long way, and so he also demanded an extra shilling, making seven shillings altogether. No one was willing to give him another penny, and so it looked as if the deal was off. The man who owned the horse was just about to leave when I told him that

I'd be willing to provide the seventh shilling, as I didn't want to leave the King's box behind. My only condition was that I should be allowed to ride.

"That's alright," says he; "I don't have much to carry."

"For God's sake, jump to it then and bring the horse, so that we can get cracking," says I to him.

Off went the fellow, and he didn't let the grass grow under his feet because he was back in a jiffy with a pack-horse that was so powerful it could have carted away half of Dingle. We tossed in everything we had, and it wasn't too heavy a load.

"You hop in, too," says he, "since you are so high-spirited."

I climbed in and it wasn't long before Dunquin came into view. The King's box was soon at Slea Head but the King himself was only at the mouth of Dingle harbour. We could see this from the road after we cleared Slea Head. There wasn't a breath of wind to move a sailship, no matter how good she might have been, but Page 269 by the time we had got as far as the top of the Dunquin pier, a good breeze had started up. Then we realised that the old captain would make it to the Island before us as he had a good wind. We brought down our boats and currachs, and got into them quickly as we were anxious to beat the old rust-bucket of a ship.

We needn't have hurried at all, because there was neither sight nor sign of it when we arrived at the Island. It wasn't long after we had eaten a meal before the families of the two who were in the ship came to enquire as to what might be delaying them. They were told that probably the bottom had fallen out of the *Wise Old Nora*, that their two family members had gone missing, and all of this on account of charity donations that weren't even needed in the first place.

People went to the hill to see if the ship was to be seen in the bay. There was a large shape like her to-ing and fro-ing beside the Ventry harbour mouth. Well, it was good that it was there at all. People were very glad to think that their folks might be in it. From hour to hour we thought that the old rust-bucket would soon be approaching; however, there was no sign of it while it was still daylight, and we couldn't understand why.

Someone from each home stayed up until morning, because there was something for every household on the ship: as it was charity no one was going to be done out of their fair share. Morning came and still there was no sign of the ship. Finally, in the mid-morning, the old wreck of a ship was to be seen off Slea Head, with only a stitch of canvas about the width of a woman's shawl on each of her masts.

Well, it didn't matter what condition the ship was in as they were all still alive and she was on her way, ploughing along through the waves. The Islanders had ceased being anxious by now, so a man here and there went off to have something to eat, killing time until the ship reached the jetty, where it could be unloaded. We didn't think twice about doing work like that, since we were getting something for nothing, and whatever shortcomings we ever overcame, we never overcame that shortcoming. That is to say, if there was ever anything going free, it'd always be us who'd be the first on the scene before anyone else got there.

Page 270

It was late in the day and there was still no sign of the bearded old captain or his wreck of a boat reaching the jetty. It wasn't too long before a few men came down from the upper village to the jetty, from where they went out with a couple of boats — a currach and a small boat — to meet her. The larger boats had been laid up for a long time.

When we reached the vessel, everyone on board looked the worse for wear after having spent a night on the old wreck — even the King didn't look too great. I suppose he'd had the toughest time and didn't get much sleep. The King greeted us, and we greeted him, like the old heroes of long ago. There was a man continuously pumping the ship right through the night; a man who was in good physical shape, because it's tough work pumping a ship.

Then the King asked me if I had brought the box along. I said that I had, and that it was up in his home, safe and sound. He was over the moon when he heard this, and even though he'd been down in the dumps, this certainly cheered him up.

Two ropes were tied to the rim of the trawler and, because the tide was with us, it wasn't long before we had her anchored and every man praying that it would sink as soon as it had been unloaded. There were eight tons of meal and flour on board — a good load of provisions for the Blasket at that time. When we started to carry it home, you would have thought that the jetty was an anthill, with everyone carrying a bag on their back.

When the two men from the Island had left the old tub of a ship, there was only a crew of three left on board — the official, the old captain and the boy who had helped them. The anchor was raised and taken on board.

Page 271 People said that the old captain had been left in port when he was a strong young man, because he was so bad-tempered that nobody could work with him. It had been a while since he had been out at sea, which was why he was available at this time with his old tub of a ship.

Well, I haven't yet finished the story about the King's box. There were eight pint bottles and a flagon in the box and, although the King was on friendly terms with everyone in Dingle on this day, you might note that it was me whom he asked to look after his beer. You see — his sister was my wife! By then, some of them might very well have got a delicious whiff from the box and would have liked to sample the contents. And, another thing, on previous occasions, after he had solicited their help in suchlike matters, when the goods were returned to him it was clear that the 'rats' had been at them.

Woe to him who wanders from the straight and narrow, and does so in many ways. It's many the person, for many's the long year, who has visited me on this Island. There's many a so-called gentleman who wasn't a gentleman at all until he spent time here. But every person who has visited me still keeps in touch, and quite regularly sends me a little something, although it's sixteen years since the first of them came to visit. Don't have anything to do with someone who doesn't show respect to his betters or isn't obedient to his superior, whatever sort of man he may be. If anything is to be got from the poor it will be achieved by means of civility.

The King had many a relation who, I believe, got little in the way of beer from him, although he never had a bottle that he didn't share with me. Whenever I'd be off to fetch a load of turf or on my way back, he would be in the doorway, saying:

"Oh, come inside for a while; what's your hurry?"

I never liked to refuse the King whenever he asked me to do something, especially since he became the King of the Island — and even before that, too. I used to be reluctant to accept things he offered me, but that doesn't mean that I was a pushover either, of course.

The people of the Island weren't the slightest bit interested in *Page 272* king or knight — through ignorance, I suppose. It was all the same to them whether it was the King passing by them on the road or a tramp with a begging bowl, but I never let him pass me by without raising my hat to him. And why wouldn't I? — isn't his title just as good as the king of Spain's, and what's more, isn't he a Catholic king into the bargain?

Well, if the Blasket homes had been short of food up to then, that certainly wasn't the case after the old wreck of a vessel managed to make port. There is an old proverb that goes: 'God's help is closer than the door.' This is perfectly true, all praise be to God! And may He bestow upon those who have been generous of heart, and have given gladly to the poor, a peaceful and joyous end to their life. It is my hope that the One who placed us on this earth will not inflict hardship on the human race: Amen.

Now that so much had arrived, and so unexpectedly, our first concern was that the food might go off before we had even eaten the half of it. We decided to get the most we could out of the food while it was still fit to eat. The plan we came up with was to buy piglets, and when they had eaten the last of the meal, we would then apply again to the authorities for more.

It took an hour to come up with this plan of action. Every man on the Island had to have a shave and put fresh clothes on him before we set off. Then all the currachs on the Island headed off towards Dunquin. The first locals who saw all the Island currachs arriving on the mainland in the early morning soon spread the news. They thought it must be a funeral procession, although they hadn't any idea who had died.

When we reached the cliff where the pier was, everyone from the parish was there, and they nearly sank the currachs, trying to see who the corpse was.

Page 273

One of my relatives came over to me from across the shore.

"Yerra, my dear fellow," says he, "it must have been something serious to bring you over here, as well as all the currachs."

"Didn't it occur to you to ask one of the other men you met?" says I to him.

"Ah, go on with you; some of them only tell fibs and cod around, so I'd have a problem believing much of what they'd say," says my friend.

"I don't know what they're thinking, any more than you do, but I do know what brought me over," says I to him. "I'm going to buy piglets, and I guess that's what the others want to do too."

"Mary, Mother of God! I had the impression that most of the people over there hadn't a bite to put in their mouths," says he. "So isn't it a very queer thing that they're now buying young pigs, not to mention having the money to do so!"

This kind of talk annoyed me, even though he was a close relative. But he was a miserly, lanky lump of a man, whose manner didn't appeal to me. So I decided that before he walked away I'd get my own back on him.

"If that's what you heard, why on earth didn't you ask your relatives on the Island whether they needed anything? You yourself had plenty but you never thought of finding out whether the Islanders were short."

"You seem to be angry, and that's not like you," says he.

"It's just as well for you that your ignorant blather didn't get you a taste of blood on your teeth," says I to him.

When the currachs were well and truly secured, in the way Fionn moored his own boat, we set out for Dingle. The market had been running for a good bit before we arrived, but the piglets we wanted were usually sold at the end of the day.

On reaching the town we went to the people who had piglets *Page 274*
to sell. They weren't expensive in those days, costing from ten to
fifteen shillings. The largest sum ever paid for a piglet was nine
pounds; a man from Dunquin gave that amount for one, the year
the Great War started. Well, my story doesn't follow that one, as
the storytellers of old used to say. The country-folk were utterly
amazed when they saw that each of us wanted to buy two or even
three piglets.

"Yerra, luv," said the old woman, a relative of mine, from
whom I bought piglets, "of course it is a long time before the
potato harvest for you to be buying piglets. Isn't it amazing how
many piglets they've bought today — most of them have bought
three! And another thing; I heard that some of the people of the
Island hadn't a bite to eat, not to mention buying young pigs. So
tell me, where did you all get the help from?"

"Och, are you really so dumb that you don't realise that the
One who creates scarcity for a while is the same One who provides
us with abundance another time? And didn't you hear what
happened to us? This is what happened. An official from the
government arrived the other day advising us not to stint on the
food, for we would soon have plenty of it. So as soon as they had
received notice of this, the Island breeders decided to make up a
herd of pigs."

"Oh Mary, Mother of God! it'd be a long time before other
people would get such a notice," says she.

"But didn't you get it before we did?" says I.

"How's that?" says she.

"Didn't God give you enough when we were in need? Then,
when the wheel turned, He provided us with plenty in our time
of need. But it seems more than likely that you'd take our share
too if you were able to get your hands on it," says I.

On this occasion, forty-two piglets came to the Blaskets
altogether, but I only bought two, which was enough for me. In
the long run, anyone who had three might as well have had the
third one drowned because, from the day we bought the piglets, *Page 275*
we ceased to get any more charity. It was said that a malicious

rumour went out about us; two or three people told me that that was so one day when I was going to Dunquin. Anyhow, my two piglets got on beautifully, and they weren't too long on my hands before I got nine pounds for them; no other two pigs that came in our time sold for more than eight pounds.

Whenever we used to bring pigs to the market we usually had to spend two or three days in Dingle with them, and often a week during the bad weather. On this occasion my two pigs and I had to spend three days and three nights in Dingle, which cost me half the price of one of the pigs. And that's why, for more than twenty years now, we've given up keeping pigs altogether.

TWENTY-ONE

The wake in Dunquin: drink, tobacco and pipes;
The man who fell off the chair on top of two
women; 'It's better to have them like that than for
them to start singing'; Dermot's second son half out
of his mind: bringing him to Dingle hospital and
back home again; He running off one night and not
being found in the morning; The sea brings in his
body, which is buried at Castle Point

I n those days there used to be a market every Saturday in the *Page 277*
big town on the mainland. I had just paid for the pigs, and
was thinking about dragging myself back to the house
without further ado when I saw a man from Dunquin coming
towards me along the street. He had a horse and cart, the horse
foaming at the mouth and sweating profusely.

I approached him where he had stopped to unbridle the horse,
because I got the impression that he was in a bit of a hurry. As
soon as he had unharnessed the horse, I went up and asked him
what he was doing. He said he was trying to organise a wake for
his mother, who had died at noon the previous day. There was a
woman from home along with him — which had been traditional
for generations there.

I gave him a fourpenny[36] glass of the hard stuff, and half a glass
of the same stuff for the woman along with him. The dead wife
had been a close relative of mine and so, of course, I gave up any
idea of going to the Western Island, or heading home.

---

[36] 'gloine thoistiúin', *a teston glass*

Page 278

The man organising the wake told me that he'd brought another horse with him, which I could ride if I wanted to tag along, as it was carrying only a barrel of black porter. He asked the shopkeeper to pour out a drink for us since I wasn't heading home. Well, having run into them on the way, I didn't have the neck not to go along to the wake and so I remained with them.

We hadn't gone far when a man came along with another horse. The two men chatted, and while they were talking, the man I was with asked the other if he could give me a ride, and then he suggested that I should go along with him. The other fellow boldly replied that if I were going his way there was no need even to ask. We decided to go for another drink in the same establishment. Inside it was the other man who offered the first round. Everyone had a drop before we left.

"I ought to go and check whether the coffin is ready," says the man who was organising the wake. "Hopefully, they have everything ready by now, and there'll be no need for any further delay."

Off he went, and his woman companion along with him. It was then that I asked the other man about the black porter he had to bring with him. I enquired whether they were having both a wedding and a wake at the same time.

"Certainly not. Sure, won't the barrel be at the wake!"

"I must say, I've never heard or seen the like of that at a wake before," says I.

"Oh, that's been happening for quite a while now," says he, "so you can be sure there'll be a barrel at this wake too."

Pretty soon the two came back, and the coffin was ready. Each man went off to harness his horse.

"Why don't we walk," says the man carrying the barrel, "so that we can put this into the cart."

Page 279

Off I went with him along Green Street until we reached Middle Street, where we put the barrel into the cart. Then we turned on our heels without delay, and soon found the rest of the family waiting for us.

The horses were all facing westwards towards Dunquin on the Dingle peninsula. We didn't drive quickly because there were fragile items in the carts. We passed the time lilting our way along the road until we reached Vicarstown where the corpse was laid out.

There were lots of people gathered there, lilting the night away. Everything was taken inside, and the horses were unharnessed. By this time a lamp had been lit, with a couple of candles burning beside it. Two women jumped up, took hold of the candles and positioned them in the correct place at the top of the table.

I sat beside the door when I went in, and before long the man of the house came over and showed me to an empty chair in the corner. He asked me to hold on to it before someone else took it from me. I must say that I was grateful to the man of the house for taking such good care of me, because I was fairly worn out after the days I'd been away from my own home. And that chair wasn't located in a gloomy corner of the house, either. I had a good view of everything and could clearly see all that was going on. The feet of the corpse were towards the fire and her head towards the door, and to the front of her all the food and drink had been laid out.

I hadn't been too long in the corner when the proceedings started to resemble a wedding-reception, just as I had suspected when I had first seen the barrel in Dingle. There was a good roaring fire, with a kettle hanging over it, and two kettles beside it. And then the fun started, with men and women leaping wildly up and down.

At this time four people were putting strange clothing on the corpse, "clothes for the road into the beyond", as one of the women said when they had finished doing it. Soon after they sat *Page 280* down, four young women jumped up and placed an old door between two stools to make a table, and it wasn't long before I saw all the delph being gathered together and arranged on the table. Then three pots of tea were brought to the hearth, one woman carrying two of them and another woman with one. Tea was put into them, and then boiling water, until the three pots

were full to the brim. The other two women were bringing white
bread until the table was full.

I watched all these goings-on with great interest and then a
man came over to me from the back of the house carrying a big,
white bucket. It was full to the brim with black porter, and in his
other hand he had an empty mug that held about a pint. When
he met the first man as he came through the door, he thrust the
mug down into the bucket, filled it, gave to him and said: "Take it
from me," — and I thought it was an odd thing for him to say. I
knew well that it wouldn't take this fellow long to swig it back,
because not only was he known for being a hopeless drunkard
but even his appearance told the whole story.

From what I could see, nobody refused to take a drink from
the bucket until it reached me. I declined. The man who was
giving it out was amazed. It isn't that I wanted to break a tradition,
because I would never do that, but I had never been interested in
the drink that was being distributed from the bucket, since I never
liked the taste of it. With that, the man of the house, who knew
what I liked, came with a bottle of whiskey and a glass and said
to the other man: "Don't you know that this fellow doesn't drink
porter?" He filled up the glass from the bottle, and I drank it.
Actually I sort of needed it, because I wasn't really feeling myself
yet as I'd been so long away from home. Mind you, I didn't have
such a bad time of it since I'd left home. But how right the man
was who said there's no place like home.

Page 281

I glanced at where the candles were burning at the top of the
table, near the feet of the corpse. There were two men sitting
there, panting and puffing away at their pipes, and the whole
business was rather unpleasant. One man was cutting tobacco and
squeezing it, the other man was grinding it small and putting it
into the pipes. I was pitying them more than envying them
because I had often seen a good man faint from doing the same
sort of thing.

No sooner had this thought crossed my mind than one of the
men fell off his chair and crashed down on two well-built women
who were, themselves, busily trying to light a couple of long-

stemmed pipes that had been freshly stuffed with tobacco. They were trying to get the pipes lit using matches, but it would have taken a machine a whole day to make all the matches they managed to waste, and even at that they didn't get their pipes lit.

Well, I haven't yet finished telling you about the man who fell. The women didn't thank him for falling on top of them and breaking their two pipes at the stem, after all the trouble they had gone to, trying to light them.

While the man was being helped to his feet he was still in a faint. Actually he doesn't deserve to be called a man but rather a rascal, because any man worth his salt would have stopped a lot sooner. The fellow was trying to show off, but was so badly affected by the tobacco that he simply looked ridiculous. One person suggested giving him a drop of water; another man said to give him a drop of the hard stuff; I myself told them to give him his fill of tobacco, as perhaps that was what he wanted! Page 282

I wasn't too pleased with him after I saw him fiddling with the tobacco, because I knew he had only himself to blame. I advised our host to chuck him over to the back of the house, which wouldn't have killed him. The wretch was then taken from the place where he had fallen. He'd only just been carried out when I heard one of the women say: "Let's hope that the next time pipes are smoked it'll be at your own funeral!" Then she glanced at the woman beside her and pinched her, but she didn't wake or move. "The devil take you! It didn't take you long to fall in a heap!" says she, shaking her more firmly, but to no effect. A couple of women came over, and a cup of pure water arrived; she was given a spoonful of it to drink, and then she started to come round slowly.

I had a good view of everything from the corner where I was sitting, and what's more, I was pleased to be just an observer, because this was the first wake I'd ever attended outside the Island.

There was a man sitting beside me, a decent, well-spoken fellow, taking a puff out of his fine white-stemmed pipe.

"I wonder whatever happened to the man who was putting tobacco into the pipes," says he, "the man who fell over — I haven't seen him since. It was his own miserable nature that was his undoing, because he wasn't up to the job. And another thing, he'd already drunk a whole pint bottle of the hard stuff, as had the two women he fell on."

"But that woman over there must have a good head for drink if she was able to consume a man's share of the bottle," says I.

"She got the bottle from our host to share amongst the three of them, but I suppose she must have consumed half of it herself," says he.

"And weren't they very rude to you, not offering you a drink," says I to him.

Page 283 "It's fifteen years since I've taken a drop, dammit!" says he. "And whatever you might say about the tinker-man, those two women could easily knock back all the hard stuff and tobacco in Cork. And the pipes they were smoking had already been filled three times since the beginning of the wake."

I saw the makeshift table all this time in the middle of the kitchen, the 'wounded' had been attended to and wherever they'd been put to keep them quiet; by now the tea was being poured. There was masses to eat and we just helped ourselves. There was white bread, jam, and tea; but there was no butter, which was not unusual in a house like this. I wasn't the last one to get to the table, because our host had come to me earlier on, and had taken me and my chair along to where I could more easily help myself. Then, turning to me, he said:

"It's different for you; their homes are nearby but you've a long way to go to get to yours."

I consumed a fair amount, but I didn't overdo it, because I didn't want to make a show of myself in such a place, where there were people from all over. Even if I'd been born on an island in the middle of the ocean, no one could ever accuse me of making a fool of myself or being ill-mannered, wherever I went. And it's not that I'm looking for praise, even if I have earned it. I like to be fair with everyone, so why shouldn't I be fair to myself too? I take no credit for this; credit is only due to One who is far greater than I.

A fresh group came to the table when the others were finished, until everyone in the house was satisfied. Then the whole house was chatting as buckets of porter were being brought around now and again. That's how it went on for the whole night. Some were smoking like chimneys, some filling their pipes two or three times until the morning dawned.

Around two o'clock the man beside me pointed to the other side of the house where there was straw and hay, on which most of the women were snoring, their jobs finished by now, and their bellies full too. The man whispered in my ear: *Page 284*

"This is at least better than their singing," says he.

"Yerra, pal," says I to him, "you know that it would be highly unlikely anyone would be asked to sing at an occasion like this."

"And more's the pity!" says he. "Not long ago I was in a house like this in the parish of Ventry. Some people sang a short song, about three verses. Nobody bothered about it until they started another song, and then they were put out of the house — not by the host, mind you, but by others."

"Weren't they old enough to know any better?" says I to him.

"They were married women, so they were," says he.

"Had they taken a drop of beer?" says I.

"Yes, and some kind gentleman had given them their fill of it," says he.

As dawn appeared there was another meal, and a drop of the black porter along with it, but the people who lived nearby didn't touch it. Around midday or one o'clock the people were all gathered together for the funeral, and when the priest came they set out for the graveyard. It wasn't far, because the family's local church was in Dunquin.

It was the wake that most interested me, mainly because there was drink there. Wakes from then on had to have a barrel or two at them. I don't agree with this practice because where there is drink, horseplay tends to follow, and that isn't appropriate when a house is in mourning.

The funeral was held on a Sunday. A number of people from the Island who happened to be in the town were also present, and *Page 285* it was late afternoon by the time we got home. I often used to hear the old people saying that a trip to the town takes more out of you than a week's work at home — how true that is. We'd been a week away from home this time because of the pigs. All the same, one of our men always said that he wouldn't mind living there for ever.

Well, there was an end to all the pigs acquired by means of the charity meal. All the pigs were bought on the same day at market in Dingle, and if one puny pig had been left unsold it wouldn't have been much use anyway.

"It'd be obvious to anyone that nothing good would ever come of them," said the poet to me one day.

"I suppose you have a good reason for saying that," I replied.

"Oh, I'm quite sure about that," he affirmed. "The charity meal was shipped for us, and then everyone was off buying piglets at Dingle Fair to eat the meal — what a great story."

"But you haven't explained what you meant in the first place," I repeated.

"That's only half the tale," says he. "Have you never heard that there's two sides to every story, and there is with this one as well. While this meal and the piglets were being brought to the Island, no one in Kerry was talking about anything else but that. They were all nattering about the Island piglets. And gossip is never the harbinger of good fortune or joy."

"I fear that there will never be a pig or a piglet again here," says I to him.

Page 286

"That's what I think, too," says he.

He was right in his opinion, too, because there hasn't been a pig or a piglet in the Blaskets since then. If young people were to see a pig or a piglet in this place, they'd freak out altogether. The Island people have had to make do without a pig or a piglet since then. And those who know what they're talking about say that, after you take all the costs into account, there isn't much profit to be made from pigs anyway.

Soon after we came home my uncle Dermot bumped into me, with rather a sad story to tell. It was that his second son was failing, and that he hadn't slept a wink the night before.

"What brought this on?" says I to him.

"Oh, my dear fellow, the lad is half out of his mind," says he.

"Perhaps it is the start of an illness," says I to him.

"I don't know," says he "I'm afraid that his time is up."

"Yerra, man, take it easy; don't people often shake off such things?"

Well, I didn't see him for a couple of days.

Then I thought to myself that it wouldn't be too great an inconvenience to go to their place to find out how they were getting on and to see whether they were managing, because he was always decent when times were tough for me.

That thought spurred me on, and I didn't stop until I reached the house. When I arrived, the poor fellow wasn't looking too happy at all. I didn't like the look of him. How I wished I could have done something for him, but unfortunately I couldn't.

The son was being well looked after by them, and he needed to be, too. The uncle told me how he'd spent the time since I had last seen him — without sleep or slumber, without joy. I enquired whether he was getting better or worse.

"He's going downhill," says he.

I felt very sorry for my poor old uncle, because he often used *Page 287* to stand by me when I was in a bad way, giving me words of comfort and wisdom. In my opinion, the son would have been better off dead, which is preferable to a lot of other things that beset poor sinners.

I headed off from the rake's — a nickname I've often used for him throughout this book. Actually, as I've said before, it is an unwarranted name for him, because he was in fact quite the opposite. However, this particular morning he seemed to be in a wretched state altogether with the way things were going.

The next day my uncle came over to me early. When I saw him coming, I knew well that he wasn't bringing good news.

"'Tis yourself," says I to him, as he came through the door. "I suppose it wasn't any light-hearted matter that brought you to me today."

"No, my dear fellow, it's a miserable matter that has brought me," says he. "People tell me that he should be in hospital because that'd be the best place for him. But I don't imagine it would be an easy task to take him in the currach."

To tell the truth, I didn't like the sound of this at all. I would have much preferred to be doing almost anything else, but what could I do? When the going gets tough you've got to stand up and be counted.

We went together, four of us, to see how we might manage it, with none of us feeling too confident, as we set out to sea. We were well aware just how dangerous it would be.

Well, when you've got to do something, you had best just get on and do it with the right attitude. So, with that, we hopped into our best currach, rigged it up, and then went back to collect the sick man from the house.

Page 288 Things are not always as you imagine, and that's how it was this time. You wouldn't have imagined that there was anything in the world wrong with him while we were putting his clothes on him and getting him ready, and he went with us down to the jetty as well as ever he did before.

Off we went, his father with him at the back of the currach, and four of us rowing hard until we reached Dunquin. Then we set off along the road to Dingle. The boy didn't pull any stunts on his father during the trip. The man who brought us along on his horse and cart remarked that we wouldn't have had such an easy time of it if the boy's hands had been untied. The father came home the following day after we had settled his son down into the place that had been arranged for him. As soon as I heard that my uncle was going home I set off with him to keep an eye on him, but there wasn't a peep out of my uncle the whole way home.

It wasn't too long before I had even more misery to deal with, because after getting over this matter my wife died, and I had to make all the arrangements for her burial. That left me dazed and very confused. Although I had two small girls who grew up with me after she died, they were not of much help at that time. And even if they had been, when one spouse dies the remaining one is very often left to blunder on foolishly and that's how it was with me. I had to deal with everything and, in spite of my very best efforts, often everything I did ended up in a shambles. The grief didn't lift so quickly this time, even though of course I was trying to shake it off every day. I couldn't manage it, of course; something would always happen to blow upon the embers of my sorrow again.

The season for night fishing for mackerel was approaching, and here we were, trying to work during the day.

One night we were out, and it was a night to remember. It *Page 289* started looking ominous, and we had to get to land in order to find some shelter. It wasn't long before another currach joined us, carrying a large catch of fish in her nets, which showed that it would have been possible to catch fish if it hadn't been for the bad weather that had prevented our efforts that night. After a while there was a break in the weather, and we put out four of our currachs.

When we reached the place where the other crew had spotted the fish, we cast out the nets, and hardly had the last mesh left the currach when it started pelting rain, with lightning and thunder, so that you couldn't see which way to go.

I said that we should pull the nets in again, and no one disagreed. I happened to be in the stern of the currach, and I jumped up, grabbed the rope and pulled away until I had the net. Two of us were drawing it in, one of us at the corks and the other at the base. It was rare that any two had so much trouble dragging a net on board, with such a gale and the sea blowing over us. When we got the last bit of it in, we couldn't see anything with the pelting rain and the wind.

We got our oars rigged up and went at it together. There was nothing for us to do while we had our heads down and were pulling on the net, because that's what we were meant to be doing as instructed by the man at the bow. He was holding his head up in order to keep his eye on the land, although he, like us, couldn't see very much either.

Finally we reached the place we had left, and one of the currachs was there ahead of us; this was the currach that had taken us out of there when it had spotted the fish. They had cut the nets, and there was only half their catch on board, but that didn't worry them. There was still no sign of our two other currachs, but it wasn't too long before they managed to reach us.

Page 290 This was the first time I was ever really frightened at sea, and it wasn't the last time either. It doesn't matter if one or two are frightened if that's their nature, provided the other members of the crew keep calm. But every one of us in the four currachs thought that night was one of the worst they had ever endured.

Well, after we arrived at the jetty, the stormy weather had mostly died down, so we decided that we might as well do some fishing, as fish usually come to the surface after a storm. We might even get a good catch, which would compensate us for all the hassle we had endured.

And that's how it was. We pulled the currachs just above the waterline; everyone went home and had a good meal in the middle of the night. The night was calming down beautifully, and when I was finished eating I made my way out to the jetty. One by one the men were coming from the houses and going to the currachs. The other fishermen of the Island had been fast asleep all night.

Off we went in our four currachs, and didn't stop until we reached the area where we'd been during the storm. We cast out our nets, and it wasn't too long before we could hear the clatter of fish filling them up.

If a currach didn't have a full catch, it could get fish from another currach that couldn't manage to take any more. Indeed, after all our efforts, we had to throw some of the fish back into the sea, as well as some of the nets. Morning was drawing in on us, and four of the currachs came into the jetty full to the brim, with as much mackerel as they were able to carry.

The morning was beautifully quiet and our four currachs made their way across the sea towards Dingle, where there was an extra shilling to be had per hundred-weight. We decided to do this because we had so much fish, and we thought that it would be more profitable for us to go straight to Dingle than to take it to Dunquin and then pay for a horse to carry it. *Page 291*

We hoisted the sails, and there was a good following wind, which we needed badly as the currachs were down to the gunwale. It didn't take too long to reach the quay, where one buyer bought the entire catch for fifteen shillings a hundred.

There is an old proverb that says: 'The lazy loafer doesn't catch a fish.' We had fish because we weren't lazy loafers, and the folks who were asleep had none.

We had a purse full of money by this time; every one of our currachs had over three thousand [shillings]. First we went to get something to eat and then we went to the pub, where we sang half a dozen songs. That was no wonder, because if there were poor people in our community at that time, we weren't amongst them. We drank and ate our fill and were still in good voice with money galore in our pockets.

Before we left the big town, we were told that the Island boy, Uncle Dermot's son, was doing well, and that we were to tell his father to come and fetch him. Although it was well on in the night when we reached home, I naturally didn't go to bed until I took the good news to my old uncle.

The next day was Sunday, and I thought I'd have to be on my travels again, since it wasn't a night for fishing. My uncle realised how exhausted I was and so he didn't bother me.

Well, the boy returned home late on Sunday and of course everyone in the village was asking about him. There didn't seem to be anything wrong with him and he looked much as he would have on any other day. People concluded that he was over his illness now. *Page 292*

Unfortunately, this was only wishful thinking and wishful thinking is usually way off the mark. About three months after that, people noticed that he was becoming somewhat distracted, and that his family were keeping a close watch on him. One night, when everyone in the house was asleep, he ventured out, and he wasn't to be found anywhere the following morning.

The poor rake came to me early the following day, not looking too happy. Everyone in the town went looking for him, but he wasn't to be found dead or alive, and we had to give up the search.

This Island is three miles long by the old measure, with Black Head being right at the end, and furthest west from the houses. For some reason — hunting, I suppose — two men and their dogs went west towards Black Head. The dogs went under a large stone, and although the men whistled several times, the dogs wouldn't come out.

The two rushed down, looked under the slab, and what did they find but the clothes and the shoes of the missing boy. They got the heebie-jeebies, and set off home straightaway, all thoughts of hunting having been quickly forgotten.

When they reached the houses, they didn't want to tell their news to his father. One of these men was a friend of mine, and so they decided to tell me first, so that I could inform his people. It wasn't much easier for me than it was for them. However, when I bumped into his father unexpectedly, I had a word in his ear:

"I'm afraid your son has gone, but you've already wept a lot for him, so hopefully this news will bring you peace of mind," says I.

"It will, of course," says he.

The upshot of all this was that three weeks later, the ocean brought his body ashore.

Page 293 A currach from the Island came across him, and they brought him in. He was buried at Castle Point on the Great Blasket. The place where his clothes had been found was the very place where he had gone swimming — so it is said. Blessings and grace on his soul.

A few days after getting over this tragedy, I put my head out early one morning. It was a pleasant, quiet morning. I stood for a while facing my wall, thinking how I should best spend the day, since it was so beautiful. I decided to gather some crabs and then go fishing for wrasse. Wrasse is as good as meat if properly preserved. Off I went and got all the crabs I needed as they are the best bait to catch wrasse.

I got my bag ready for the road. There were crabs, drink, a few slices of bread for the day, and some hooks, and so on, in it. I reached the hill, and dashed across two-thirds of the Island before I stopped. Then I set off down the slope until I reached the sea. I caught a good fistful of wrasse there and I had the time to do it.

When I glanced over towards a point to the west, I saw the stern of a currach coming towards me, at a fair speed. One man was in it, rowing stern about, which I found very odd indeed. As he approached I realised who it was. It was none other but Maurice Daly, the shepherd from the Western Rock. Apparently, part of the cliff had fallen on his currach, and he was coming to get it mended. It was the bow that was broken, which was why he was coming stern about.

TWENTY-TWO

*I learn to read Irish in Dunquin; I read the old
stories to the Island people; Carl Marstrander
staying with me: a fine gentleman; Tadhg O'Kelly
has a Gaelic school on the Island: preparing word-
lists to send to Scandinavia; A gale at sea; A man on
his own being blown through Dingle Bay; The
arrival of the man from the Government: the
channel repaired; A giant creature in the net: its
huge liver kept the Island lit for a year; The man
who escaped from the shark*

Some years before this, we often used to be held up on the
mainland because of bad weather. The children in the house
where I usually stayed always used to be at school. The
Gaelic language was being taught at Dunquin school at this time,
one of the first schools where it was taught in Ireland, as far as I
know.

Whenever I was with them, the children of the house were
forever reading me stories, until I myself got a liking for it. They
gave me a book of my own, and one of them did his best to
explain the difficulties in it, such as an aspirated letter, a
lengthened letter and an auxiliary letter like the 't' in 'an tsráid'.

When I understood all this, it didn't take me too long before I
was able to manage without them to read stories on my own. By
then my head was full of information so that if I came across an
awkward sentence, all I had to do was to think hard and I'd be
able to understand it without bothering anyone else.

It wasn't too long before I had lots of books, and the people on the Island used to come to listen to me reading the old stories. Of course they knew many of them themselves, but when they saw how deftly they were presented in the book they lost all interest in telling them themselves. It would be a long time before I ever got bored reading to them, because I really enjoyed doing it. From this time on, the odd person was coming out to see the Island. *Page 296*

Carl Marstrander

At the beginning of July, on a Sunday, a currach from Dunquin brought a gentleman to the Blasket. He was a tall, slim, fair-skinned man with grey eyes. However, he had only a smattering of spoken Gaelic.

He met all the people and took notes about them. One afternoon he asked some of them to recommend a place for him to stay. They told him about the King's house, and arranged for him to stay there.

It wasn't too long on the Monday before he had his bits and pieces gathered together and had settled into the King's house. He was asked why he had not remained in the parish of Ballyferriter, where he had spent a fortnight. He replied that there was too much English in their Gaelic, which didn't suit him because he needed to experience the purest form of the language, and it was here that he had observed the best Gaelic.

He asked the King who would be the best person to teach the language to him. The King decided that I would be the best one, because I was able to read it, and because I had fine stylish Gaelic even before I had learnt how to read it.

He came to me straightaway and questioned me. He handed me a book, *Séadna*[37] — no, not that one, I tell a lie — it was *Niamh*.

"You are good, but do you speak English?"

"I haven't great English, Sir," I replied.

---

[37] Séadna and Niamh are personal names.

"That's fine," says he. "But you wouldn't be able to do the job without a little English."

The first day that we got together, he gave me the title of 'Master'.

He was a fine man, with a gentle, humble style that, of course, is common amongst many like him who are well-educated. He spent five months in the Blaskets. We had a two- or three-hour session together every day for half the time, and then he got news that he couldn't stay as long as he had intended because he had too much to do back where he was employed. And so the two of us had to work out a change of plan. The gentleman asked me if I could spend two sessions every day with him. "And", says he, "you'll get as much from me for the second session as you get for the first."

Page 297

I used to go to him after I had finished my day's work. At that time of year the nights were long, although there used to be some fishing going on. As I had my own currach, and had another man along with me, I wasn't able to take time off to be with Marstrander.

Well, I wouldn't be able to have a second session with him except when I was fishing during the day. All the same, how could I refuse the gentleman? I said that I'd do my best for him, but that if I missed once or twice he would have to excuse me. So this is what we did: after I'd return for my dinner I would go to see Marstrander, and this didn't detract too much from my fishing.

After leaving us on Christmas Eve he sent me some money when he reached home. I don't know if he's alive or pushing up the daisies now. I don't like to think of him being dead.

It was around 1909 when this gentleman, Marstrander, visited us.

Soon after that another man arrived by the name of Tadhg O'Kelly, who was on his holidays. He was a good Gaelic speaker. Every night he had a Gaelic class in the schoolhouse for a couple of hours. I never let any afternoon pass without spending some time with him.

At that same time a letter came to me from Carl Marstrander, the Scandinavian, full of paper, asking me to send him the name of every land animal, every bird, every fish and every plant that was growing on the Island.

He specifically asked me not to get help from any book, and that I was to spell the names according to my own pronunciation.

Page 298

Well, my boy, I wasn't too skilled at writing Gaelic at this time, and wouldn't I have to be really good indeed to spell all their names correctly! I referred the matter to Tadhg. "Oh," says Tadhg, "we'll easily do this together!"

Tadhg wasn't a bit reluctant to undertake this task, because he already knew a good deal about such matters, but there were many names I knew that he had never heard of before. We spent some time every day working on this project, and when we had finished we sent them over to Marstrander.

Soon after this, word came to Tadhg that he had to leave. He was with us only a month, although he thought he'd be staying for three.

A year after Tadhg had left us, there was an abundance of fish to be caught every night. There used to be half a dozen currachs from Dunquin coming too, but they weren't as skilful on the seas at that time as they have been since then.

Well, this particular night was mild, quiet and wet, so all our boats set out to sea. We spent half the night fishing, and then returned to the jetty, having caught nothing. I said to the two with me that perhaps the end of the night might be better, as that was when the fish usually came to the surface. I also said that it might be a good idea for all of us to get a bite to eat first in order to get ourselves good and ready for the job ahead.

And that's what we did. After we all helped to bring the currach ashore, each of us went to his own house.

A short while later we moved out again, although some of the crews didn't come back because they had fallen asleep.

There were Dunquin currachs that didn't go home, but remained floating around the Island jetty for the whole night.

Page 299

When I was ready I made my way back to the jetty. The rest of them were already assembled, preparing themselves to head out to sea again. It was still a good time for fishing, except that there was no let-up in the rain. Off went all our currachs; some went a good way out and others stayed close to the jetty. We ourselves weren't too far from land.

We let out all the nets we had. They had hardly been let out when we heard a noise coming towards us. What was it but a gust of wind. It was so powerful that it knocked everyone down into the back of the currach, and the currach itself got tossed around.

I dashed to the rope that was holding the nets from the stern, and started pulling them towards me. The other two were telling me to check if there were any fish in the nets, but there were only very few. "Let the nets out again," they said. So that's what I did, as there hadn't been a squall for a good while.

Hardly had we let out the rope than there came a noise that was seven times greater than the first one. It didn't leave a drop of brine in the sea, but lifted it up high into the air, shaking the currach, and dashing it to and fro.

"Jump to it," say the other two to me, "and pull in the rope. The net will be blown away any moment."

"We'd be alright now if we had stuck to what we were doing originally," says I to them, dashing quickly to the rope. However, I wasn't able to budge the seine-net an inch. I had to face the stern of the boat, but the net was rigid and I was finding it difficult to pull in.

Well, we eventually did manage to get the net in safely, but never was there such dreadful weather as there was on that *Page 300* occasion. The sea was being whipped up into the sky by the wind and rain. We were just about making our way towards the jetty, one of our men rowing and two others steering. I was at the stern and although I had two iron thole-pins, even they got bent, such was the strain while steering.

The tide swept us into the mooring, but we were nearly thrown over the jetty, no matter how hard we tried. When we reached the jetty, it was full tide — a high, surging tide. The shore was full of currachs, some from Dunquin, some from the Island, and as the landing place was quite narrow there wasn't much room for us to secure our boat.

When we got the rope onto the shore, we heard that a currach from Dunquin had gone east through the channel with only one man in it. Two other members of the crew had come ashore, leaving the one man to go off on his own out through the channel. It was unfortunate but unavoidable, because there were just too many gathered at the jetty.

The gale continued to blow furiously throughout the night, and the little one-man currach was being blown across Dingle Bay until late into the morning of the following day. The man was blown into Cahersiveen Harbour and there wasn't a scratch on him or on his little currach. He was given a great welcome there, having overcome the storm all by himself. All were greatly amazed that the fear alone hadn't killed him during that long, stormy night.

Immediately after I came home, I had to go out again to see if my relatives were safe and sound. I had to check that the children were alright because their own uncles were out at sea, and they would be anxious to know whether the storm had caught them. The rain was still pelting down heavily without any let-up, and I had to go from house to house practically on my hands and knees. By the time I got back home, dawn was breaking and the weather was beginning to improve.

I threw off my clothes and went to bed, and it didn't take long *Page 301* before I was fast asleep.

Two days after this, the people of the Blasket went out lamenting the man they assumed had drowned, but he was waiting for them at home. It was a great surprise. A steamship brought him across to Dingle, along with his currach and nets.

The story spread across the land that this had happened to a man from the Western Island, and it wasn't too long before a representative of the Government appeared, to find out about the channel he went through and how he made it to the harbour. The Government representative said that it was a tragedy that anyone who was already in such a sheltered harbour would have to leave it again. "And", says he, "it was sheer bad luck that he just happened to be the last person who came through the channel into the harbour that day."

When this man came back, it wasn't long before they started to do whatever was needed to repair the harbour wall. There was ceaseless work going on until the wall was higher than any other place around it, and since then there hasn't been any trouble, because if you are inside, there is no way out of it, dead or alive. There was good work to be found there for a long time. I myself earned fifteen pounds out of it and was only working there on the occasional day, as my expertise was seldom needed. Two other men from nearby were more frequently employed than I was as their skills were needed more.

Soon after the work had been finished, two others and myself went fishing one fine evening. We didn't have to go far from home. At any rate, we weren't having much luck with the fishing, so when we reached the White Strand we cast out our nets again. It wasn't too long after the nets were out that we noticed a commotion in the back of the net. I said to the other two that there was a seal in the net, and that any mackerel in it would quickly be eaten. But the other two didn't pay any heed to what I said — my words just went in one ear and out the other.

Pretty soon after this, one of the men at the bow said that there was some sort of devil in the net dragging both the line and the *Page 302* currach along with it. "And", says he to me at the stern, "pull the rope in, and be quick about it!" "But I would have had it pulled in long ago if it wasn't for you lot!" I replied.

Hardly had I spoken before the thing in the net went wild. It pulled the currach and the nets for about a mile, and it nearly drowned us in doing so. Fortunately, however, there were twenty fathoms of rope at the end of the net, although I had to let out all I had in my hand of it. There seemed nothing we could do but to cut the nets, which would have been a great loss to any poor fisherman. The man at the bow told me to pull the rope again, which I did, and we dragged a piece of the net on board. That was when we had a few choice words to say to one another!

It was a moonlit night, and when we saw the huge, shapeless mass, somewhere behind the currach, the three of us went pale with terror, not knowing what to do. The man at the bow told me not to let go of the nets, saying that he'd prefer to be drowned rather than have no nets. I did as he asked, but I had to let the net out before I could bring it back in again. This beast was huge. There were six of the seven nets twisted around it; and when it went down we had to let the rope out each time until it reached the bottom.

Well, we were struggling with it until we drew near the jetty. I had a good knife opened all the time to cut the rope, but that would have been of little use to me if the beast had gone berserk. Finally, we reached the jetty, where we got help from two other currachs. The beast completely filled the pool of water at the landing place. Soon the man at the bow said he'd get out on the beast so that he could pull the nets off it while it was still in the water. None of us were too keen for him to do that, as we weren't certain that this was a sensible thing for him to do. Soon we could see it thrashing around in the pool, so much so that it drenched everyone nearby. Its fin smacked against a rock and knocked a half ton out of it.

It nearly frightened everyone on the jetty to death when it was *Page 303* finally beached. It had a liver that kept the whole Island alight for a year. It was no easy job getting the nets off it. After this we were left without nets and only a few ropes that were torn and ripped apart. The three of us have never been the same since. The strain was too much for us, and we would all have been drowned if we hadn't been as close as we were to the shore.

Another day, with the currach tied to a stone on the road, we were fishing with lines. It wasn't long before a shark went under the currach, persistently going back and forth, so that it was impossible for us to get rid of him.

One of our men was stretched out across the thwart, and of course his two feet were out over the gunwale. I myself was at the stern of the currach and, when I looked up, what did I see but the shark with its maw wide open, heading straight for his feet. I yelled at the man to pull his legs in. He did so in double quick time, and the shark rose right out of the water. We were nearly drowned by the wash.

We had to head for land and it followed us as long as there were two fathoms of water beneath us. We were of no use for the rest of the day, I can tell you, and we didn't recover for a week after that.

Since then I have never seen a creature on the surface of the water that would terrify me as much as that one did. After that, currachs and boats often capsized, sometimes at night and sometimes during the day, without people knowing what had happened to them. I'm strongly of the belief that it was a giant beast that attacked them, trying to overturn them. It's many's the thing lurking out there in the deep for the unwary seafarer.

TWENTY-THREE

The building at the edge of the harbour at Dunquin;
The man from the Island and the man with the gun;
The Island under the Deprived Districts Board; Five
new houses built; The foreman who didn't know Irish;
Three uncles and a pot; Flower staying with me: we
compile a book of folklore; My daughter married in
Dunmore: she lived there twelve years and left six
children; The Great War in France; The Quabra;
Brian O'Kelly: after he leaves I send him my daily
diary and the story of my life; C.W. von Sydow;
George MacThomas, Father MacClune; A young lady
from France; I finish the book, 3 March 1926

Early one morning some people from around here spotted Page 305 a big, white building on the edge of the harbour out at Dunquin. We found it rather odd, although we knew that the landlord had been threatening us for some time. Some of us said that it was bailiffs who were there; others thought not. Whatever the reason for the white house being on the mainland, none of us had any desire to go over to see what it was, even though most of us were mumbling about things we needed.

A very fine day came, and a middle-aged man with a medium-sized currach said he would go over if he had two lads to accompany him. Being related to him I said that he would be better staying at home because there was nothing good happening on the mainland.

Well, there was no good talking to him, once he got this idea into his head. He rounded up the lads and off he went across the

Sound over to the mainland. He was a small, arrogant man, with a tuft under his chin, like that on a billy-goat. He didn't delay leaving or cool down until he reached Dunquin harbour. You would have thought that he had spent his life on board a destroyer. Nothing would stop him until he got in sight of the shack, in which, so he was told, was a force that had been brought in to deal with the Blaskets. Even this didn't satisfy him until he could see the sort of men who were in the white building. He managed to get near to the doorway, where he noticed a couple of guns.

Page 306 There was a grey-haired man a bit like himself in the building, with a goatee on him. He suddenly noticed our friend peering insolently in from the door at everything that was going on. The next thing, the man inside took a gun and aimed at the Islandman at the door.

When the Islandman saw this he took off as fast as his legs would carry him and headed straight for the harbour where he had left his small currach. The grey-haired man with the gun followed him down just for the fun of it, and fired a shot to scare off the intruder.

The man from the Island called the two young lads to the currach. They dragged it after them from the high tide to the low tide. When they launched it, the young lads soon noticed that the water was coming up to their knees, so they yelled that they'd be drowned. Although they weren't far from land, the older man wouldn't let them turn back for fear of the grey-haired fellow with the gun. He stuffed his waistcoat into the crack the water was coming through, and one of the boys bailed her until they reached their own jetty.

It happened that I was there to meet them. I asked the older man to tell me what had been going on over on the mainland and what they had been looking for. In a gruff manner he replied that they were indeed over on the mainland and that if I wanted to know anything I could go and find out for myself.

"But didn't I say before you left", says I, "not to go there, because you're totally clueless!"

I took the flat of my hand and gave him a smack in his earhole.

I had given good advice to that cheeky old lad when he was leaving in the morning, and see how rude he was to me on his return. This isn't the first time either that this sort of thing happened; look how he made me so angry that I raised my fist to him, something I've never done to anyone in my life — except to him. But the grey-haired man with the gun on the mainland scared him so much that he's never been the same man since.

When the Islanders heard about this, they were all greatly upset. Most of us were very poor at this time and we had nothing that anyone would want to buy except perhaps a jacket, half a packet of flour and other things not worth more than a ha'penny. *Page 307*

The parish priest didn't like the sound of it, and he wasn't satisfied until he knew whether there was some way to pay off the Islanders' debts. The Deprived Districts Board had already been operating for a while; it was asked if the Blasket could be put under the authority of the Board. News came back quickly that they would be willing to undertake this responsibility.

The priest sent for us to come immediately to see him on the mainland, where there would be an official from the Board with him on the appointed day. However, that day turned out to be too stormy, so we had to go to Coosaraha instead. The man from the Board and the priest were there to meet us, sheltering under a projecting rock called the Priest's Rock. The Islanders often have to take refuge in this creek, because whenever there is a strong northerly wind it isn't possible to find haven anywhere outside Dunquin, and this creek has the advantage of being a lagoon.

When we reached the end of the creek, the two gentlemen were there before us. You would have liked them because each one of them had an honest look about him. While I'm on the subject of Father O'Griffin, it's now only a week since he left us, after having been our parish priest for the past twenty years. Anyway, he was a great support to us that day. Wherever he resides now, may he be content.

We spent some time discussing the problem with the officials, and finally they convinced us that we wouldn't see the white house any more. They bade us farewell. It wasn't too great a day out at sea, but equally it was not up to much for those on dry land either, because snow showers from the northwest were blowing the eyes out of their heads as well as out of their horses.

When we reached our own landing place, everyone on the Island was down there to see if we had any news for them.

Page 308 However, the news we had for them was good, for God's help is closer than the door, and so we were delighted to relate the good tidings, unlike the man with the goatee who had gone to the mainland and had nothing but bad news for us all.

The next day the white house was gone, and soon one man after another from the Board was coming to enquire about us. As I've said before, there's an old saying that God's help is closer than the door, and who can say, sure isn't it often the worst thing in the world that happens to us that is the making of us, and that's how it was for us with the white house. And however great the intentions of our political masters may be, the power of the Great Headmaster in the Sky puts a stop to them now and again.

Not many days passed before the head of the Board arrived. He put up his cabin, and spent time amongst us measuring and dividing up the land. I myself was at the other end of his measuring chain. He used to give me a fine glass of the hard stuff every morning and afternoon, and I assure you that he was a fine man in every respect, with whom it was easy to get on.

He took down our names because, as we were tenants of the Board, he wanted to know if we were satisfied with this or with that. He had a foreman along with him and all kinds of equipment that they brought over from Dingle in a trawler. That trawler made a lot of money out of the works on the Blasket.

After the official told the foreman what to do, he left him to get on with the work; even so, he used to pay a visit every now and then. The paymaster used to come once a fortnight, bringing the wages. To make a long story short, whatever difficulties may have confronted us, and although we may have thought that we were in dire straits with the white house spying on us from the mainland, we, in the end, had a guardian angel backing us, glory be to God.

The Board spent a year and a half working on the Island at that time, and most of the villagers had plenty of work. We used to get two shillings a day — a good thing, considering we were working for ourselves. I paid the Board seventeen shillings a year for my holding — and it's still the same. Compare that with the ten pounds that my grandfather had to pay in the old days. How things have changed.

Page 309

The foreman lodged with me for the seven months he spent on the Island. He was always very friendly with me, because I knew how to do things that no one else could do. What's more, I was always there for him whenever he needed me.

There were gulleys on the Island that used to become water-logged whenever it rained. The other man and I had to put up bridges over all of them, which was hard work in many cases. Bridges couldn't always be built in the same way as a house wall was.

Five new houses were built there, entirely by the foreman and myself, and it was often enough work to keep the two of us fully occupied. We had to build a wooden form for each of them, to hold the gravel and cement in place, and then we had to make sure that they were as straight as the barrel of a gun.

Before the houses were built the foreman was recalled, and a new man came in his place who didn't know anything about how to build houses, especially gravel houses. The situation was bad both for the new foreman and for another man who also didn't know his business. As a result, the two of them were soon for the high jump.

This was a matter of concern to the first foreman and he thought up a strategy in order to get the work finished. This was his plan. He took me, who always used to be with him around the houses, to the other foreman. He asked me if I thought I would be able to finish the rest of the houses on my own, because the other fellow knew nothing about this kind of work.

This is how I answered him:

"If I were a young man and I were to take an interest in any trade, I would only have to spend a month with you to learn every aspect of the work as well as you do. However, since I'm now on in years my only interest is to live each day as it comes."

Page 310

"I believe you," says the foreman; "but what would you say about finishing the house with this fellow?"

"I shall do my best for your sake," I reply.

"Thank you very much," says he. "I've been in your debt ever since I arrived on the Island."

"But since there isn't anyone else on this Island able to do this kind of work, what shall I gain out of doing it?" says I to the old foreman.

"What more do you need," says he, "except to be paid for the work you do every day?"

"But perhaps when the two of us have finished building the houses, this good man won't give preference to me over other workers on account of my being accommodating in this matter."

The previous foreman then turned to the other foreman, and said to him:

"Whenever you need only one man, give Tomás the work and let him have it until it's finished."

He shook hands with me, because there was a boat already waiting for him. The Islanders said that he was the best fellow that had ever been put in charge of men.

Well, the following Monday the work was going on as it had been for more than a year. The new foreman and I worked together. I had enough work ahead of me, because I was both a labourer and a steward at the same time; both the responsibility of the foreman and the workload of the labourer were upon my shoulders.

There were five houses altogether, all still unfinished since we'd had to spend time on each individual house. One needed a chimney, another two chimneys; two gables were needed for the walls of one house and another house also required a gable. We couldn't just stand around gawking at them; we had a fair bit of work still to do on all of them.

Page 311   I set to work and did whatever had been left for me to do. I did it well so that people wouldn't laugh at the work of the Great Blasket Man, who was now foreman for the new houses, many of which still remained unfinished.

Well, the two of us were doing well and getting through it splendidly. I was chief foreman, and the other man was my assistant. He had to do what I told him to do, and he couldn't have been happier than he was when he saw the first house completed.

I didn't get any bonuses in addition to what everyone else got for their work. Later on I got some extra work to do, when there was only enough work for one person, so I was the one who got it, which was how the former steward had arranged it. The day finally arrived when we completed five houses, and although that was fine with me it was even better for the other man. He shook my hand warmly and said he'd never seen a better person in charge than me.

"Do you think so?" says I to him. "Does the work that we have done together look any different to the other work?"

"If it does, it can only be an improvement," says he.

By then the two of us were over the moon, having finally completed the hardest part of the work.

There were lots of other fittings that hadn't been fixed yet, but that job wasn't as difficult as putting up the houses themselves. There were floors still to be laid in the five houses, and carpenters and slaters to be sent up. Often there used to be only enough work for very few — some days, only two were required; on other days only one, and that person was always me.

When the day came to lay the floor there were four men at the board stirring the mortar. The foreman wanted to tell them to mix a certain amount of cement with such-and-such an amount of gravel. But those workers had no English, and the foreman had just as little Irish. This made it difficult for them to get along together, and the foreman was as ill-tempered as anyone could be.

I was up above under the slates, plastering. I soon saw him *Page 312* approaching me and he seemed to be in a foul mood.

"Would you come down here," says he; "those people stirring the mortar are as dumb as four donkeys!"

I hopped down the big long ladder, and didn't delay till I came to the board. He told me what he wanted done and I translated his order to the rest of them, telling them the right mixture.

"These are the dumbest individuals I've ever seen," says he. "I'll have to let them go."

"But they say that if the houses are to be finished, it's you that will have to go, and be replaced by someone they can understand. It's just too bad that they don't understand you, nor you them."

There wasn't as much bellyaching out of the foreman from then on as there had been up to then, because he knew that he himself was partly to blame, as well as the people who had sent him to the Island when he didn't know the language of the Islanders.

We continued to put up with one another until the work was done, although I had to continue giving out to them to get them to keep their minds on building the houses. I had to do most of the talking from then on, and I got work every day until the job was finished. However, in my opinion, it was no thanks to this foreman, but rather his predecessor who really deserved my gratitude.

We were promised a lot of things that weren't done and still haven't been done these many years since, because in those days the people who were on the Deprived Districts Board worked hard, not like today. In any case, the plan saved us. It stopped the force, which was looking for any opportunity to take the clothes off our backs, from spying on us.

The Board improved our living conditions so that we were able to sow our crops whenever we liked. That wasn't how things were previously, for, if a neighbour wasn't going to plant anything next to you, you couldn't plant anything yourself, as it was impracticable to erect fences since each person's holding would have been too small.

Page 313 We've had nobody pestering us since then, but I'm afraid it won't always be like that. It's a long time since we've been asked to pay rent or tax; I suppose that's because the whole world is in a state of chassis.

One day, while I was trying to bring a load of turf down from the hill, what did I see but a huge trawler from Dingle approaching from the west, at the south of the Island. Every sail was hoisted, and a strong northerly wind was blowing. A powerful gust came down the side of the hill; I heard it coming towards me but I didn't think much about it, because I'd often witnessed such a thing before.

When it reached the donkey, which was right in front of me, it ripped the harness off him. It blew the donkey and me off our feet and knocked me out. When I got to my feet and had a look around, there stood the donkey but there was no sign of my harness. While I was looking for the harness, my eye caught sight of the trawler. To my amazement there wasn't a shred or a tatter of a sail up but only the masts. She was sitting there like a fool of a woman, motionless, because no boat had a motor at that time.

When I looked more closely, what did I see but my harness out on the ocean, about twenty yards from the vessel devoid of its sails. What was I to do then? There wasn't a sod of turf at home or anything that could be used to carry it. I stopped for a while, wondering what I should do. And then I had the idea of taking out two bags that were in the pannier on the donkey and to put turf into them, one on each side of the donkey.

Uncles

I had three uncles, three brothers from my mother's side. All three were married and they'd all been living in the same house for a long time. A woman from the mainland was married to one of them, and she was a good woman. Well, however long they'd been together, they couldn't stay together forever, and so they decided to split up.

It was good and early when I got myself ready to go up the hill. *Page 314* I had a sickle and a rope and I'd had a bite to eat. My plan was to take a bundle of rushes to a cabin I had, which was leaking, and to leave a handful of potatoes there.

I hadn't gone far from my own house when I heard a noise behind me. When I reached the place where the noise came from, who was there but my three uncles, battering one another, and trying to grab a pot from each other. They were all out for blood;

each with one hand gripping the pot and with the other trying to take the contents out of it.

As usually happened to me when I had decided to do a big job, the day would go entirely against me, and, as usual, I'd get nothing done. So that's how it was this day too. Well, what do you know, didn't I get the sudden urge to become involved and sort matters out. I went over to tell them to stop, and not to lose all sense of dignity over a belly-pot.

They didn't heed me. All three of them were tall and strong at that time. Each of them had a hand on the pot, with the odd punch being thrown at one another from time to time, although not killer-punches. Their three wives were out on the dungyard, laughing their hearts out, mocking them, and rightly so, of course. One of the women would speak now and again, saying: "Good for you, Liam, don't let them have it!" just like people baiting dogs fighting.

The women's attitude made me angry, so I jumped up from where I was sitting on the flat wall and put my claw into the pot. I asked my uncles if they would leave it to me to sort things out, since they were worn out from having been at it ever since breakfast. By now it was nearly dinner time. As soon as I put my hand in the pot, each of them took their hand out and leaned back to catch their breath. I had the pot then and no one was taking it from me.

Page 315 I asked them whether they'd be satisfied to draw straws; whoever pulled the longest straw would be the one to have it.

"That'll do fine," they agreed.

"But shouldn't ye have done this in the first place?" says I to them.

"But the devil wouldn't let us do it," says Dermot.

So that was the upshot of what I'd hoped would be a worthwhile day! But look what happens when the wind is against you. The day had been wasted, so when I'd finished dealing with the old pot I set off home.

I had dire need of a roof for my cabin and so, as the weather was fine and dry, I decided that I'd still be alive the following morning and there'd be nothing then to stop me getting on with the job.

And so, after an early bite to eat, off I went on my travels. When I was clearly out of sight of the houses, I was free to do what I wanted. I told myself that there would be nothing to stop me, the hill was ahead of me and I was fresh and ready to do a good day's work.

Just as I was in the area which is called *Buailteán*, I thought I heard a voice from the dead or the living, but it didn't stop me from continuing on my way. I carried on walking doggedly towards the place I intended to reach, but I didn't get far before I heard the voice again clearly calling me by my name and surname.

I looked carefully towards from where I believed the sound was coming, and saw two men a good way down the slope from me. One of them was beckoning to me with his hat. I set off down the slope of the mountain, and I didn't stop until I reached the two men. It appeared that they had a cow that had lost its balance, and they were unable to lift it. The cow was on the flat of its back, in a place where there was very little room to manoeuvre. Even twelve people couldn't have moved it one way or the other, as it was a heavy cow, and there was no flat place to get purchase on it.

I'd brought a rope with me to bring a bundle home. I tied it around the cow, but we ripped the rope to pieces, and didn't free up the cow at all. And so we had to give up, after trying every which-way, and by now we were exhausted. *Page 316*

We had to think of something else, and so we decided that one of us should go home to bring back help and a good rope. There was no way we'd leave the cow in the hole, dead or alive.

One man went off home, and the other said to me:

"I believe you've wasted both today and yesterday too."

"Yesterday, certainly," I replied, "whatever about today."

"Off you go to your business," says he. "I'll be able to keep her head free until help comes."

I did as he said and off I went towards the mountain again as I had planned. I started cutting as best I could. I bound up my bundle, and headed off to my house. The cow had only just been pulled out of the hole when I caught sight of them again.

Bláithín[38]

When Bláithín came to Ireland, a friend of his met him in the capital city, and told him about me, and where I was to be found. He had already heard from Carl Marstrander that he had spent some time with me.

On reaching Ireland this good man didn't tarry until he reached the Great Blasket. From then on the two of us used to spend a couple of sessions together every day, although they weren't long. He spent a month the first year, and five weeks every other year for the next five years. He stayed for a couple of months during his last visit. In the year 1925 he came again in order to compile every word we had written while speaking with one another, until we had it all finished and nicely put together.

Page 317   The book[39] will be a description about every misery, big or small, that occurred around the Blaskets, and the hardship that befell some island people. It will describe the way in which some of them lived on the small islands for a while, their appearance and their way of life. It will deal with a shipwreck, as well as the fairy voices, and other visions that often used to appear to them — that is, if they are to be believed.

When the land had been allocated by the Board, and everyone had his own field, all laid out and fenced off, there was nothing to stop us sowing as much as we wanted. We sowed enough and more than we needed. If we had friends on the mainland that hadn't enough seed, we often used to help them out.

Before the Board came, we used to sow a small patch, which often produced good potatoes. We had pigs and donkeys that weren't tied up at night, and because the little fields weren't fenced off properly, hard times befell us in spite of all our hard work.

I spent many a year working all day after spending many a November night out fishing for mackerel. Very often I went a week or more without a wink of sleep until I had the potatoes gathered into storage. Then, when we got the gardens fenced off

---

[38] *Little Flower* — Robin Flower, author of *The Islandman*, The Talbot Press Limited, Dublin & Cork, 1934

[39] *Seanachas ón Oileán Tiar*, which wasn't actually published until 1956

to prevent deer or eagles getting into them, nothing would have stopped us sowing and reaping.

At this time a know-all came amongst us. He decided that there would be food for him without his having to work for it. He just sat twiddling his thumbs and, as with all such villainy, it wasn't too long before some young lads decided to follow his example, and so a lot of people started taking it easy. This son of iniquity used to say that work was only for fools and horses.

Two or three fields became a wasteland since nothing was planted in them. The one who set the bad example went to *Page 318* America, and you can be sure he didn't find bread in a ditch over there. The supports that the Board had provided, along with the fittings that they had put up, were lost, and we had been slaving to keep them up. As a result, there's nothing growing there now but *flukes*.[40]

Many people came to see the Island after Bláithín left. Most of them would spend a month and I used to have to listen to them. I used to give them a session or two during the day, as well as having to do my own work.

The Board's Superintendent

The Board's superintendent spent seven months lodging with me. One of my daughters was living with me at that time; she's the one who survived the battle of the White Strand. One of her aunts lived in Dunmore with her husband McCarthy. They wanted my daughter to live near them, because he wanted to give half of his land to his brother. The people from Dunmore didn't give up this idea until they removed her from my house, which, as you might well imagine, left a huge void in my life. There I was, without anyone to look after me, just blundering along, with the whole world upon my shoulders.

The superintendent had to leave me but I found it odd when he asked me three times if I'd let him stay on. He even said that he'd be perfectly satisfied letting things go on the way I ran them.

---

[40] i.e. weeds

Unfortunately, I was not able to oblige. It's a sorry state of affairs for anyone who finds himself in a predicament he can do nothing about, and has no choice but just to put up with the situation he finds himself in.

I was absolutely desolate, bidding farewell to my daughter. Seán O'Corcoran from County Mayo, the Board's official, was affected every bit as badly as myself. Afterwards, he often said to me that the seven months he stayed with us passed quicker than any other period of his life.

My daughter lived a dozen years in Dunmore after this. When she died, she left six young children, and it was tough work for the poor father having to look after them. Of all the terrible things that have ever happened to me, dealing with death has always been the most difficult of all.

Page 319 ### The Great War in France
Soon afterwards, fleets started to founder out on the ocean — some of them were sunk deliberately. Strangers from virtually every part of the world came ashore in lifeboats. A brother of mine, who was twelve years older than me, was the only person living with me then. He was receiving the basic pension at this time.

Around this period a ship struck the Blasket. It went down near the rock a couple of miles out from the jetty. There was an incredible amount of cargo on that ship.

The Quabra
The name of this ship was *The Quabra*.[41] Its captain said that it contained a bit of everything necessary to sustain human life — with the exception of drink.

He was right about it, because the sea was filled with everything that folk from this Island had either seen or had never

---

[41] *The Quabra* sank in 1916, off the Blasket Islands. It was a steamer en route from America to Liverpool with a diverse cargo of watches, ammunitions and foodstuffs. She changed course off the Cork coast in order to avoid a U-boat and ran aground on the rocks off the Blaskets.

before laid eyes upon. Huge amounts of cargo were rescued from the wreck, and the Islanders made a lot of money out of it, although what they made off with wasn't rightly theirs.

All I could do was to watch them, because I had no wish to go out in a boat. The whole shore was covered with leather from the ship, which made a lot of money and clothes for the Islanders. The leather is still being washed up today, after any major storm.

Brian O'Kelly

It was the Great War that brought Brian O'Kelly from France to the Blasket Island. The Islanders were very grateful to him. He soon came to me every day for a couple of short lessons of Irish. Even though I personally got no benefit from *The Quabra*, look how God sent me a gentleman so that even I didn't lose out completely. Isn't God's help often closer than the door.

I was all the stronger because of the six years he spent amongst *Page 320* us. He spent Christmas on the Blasket the year he lodged with me.

For five years after Brian left I sent him recollections of every day he'd been with us. Then he wasn't satisfied until I had jotted down an account of my life and how I had spent it. Since I never liked to refuse anybody anything, I got down to getting the job done and have carried on for the last fifteen years until he stopped enquiring about my writing. This surprised and hurt me because of all the work I'd put in, but it so happened that another good man asked me to send him the last part of what I had written, which I shall do with great pleasure.

My life carried on in the same fashion for another while, with several visitors arriving, one after another. Each of them had a session with me, and even though some of them were less interesting than others, all contributed equally to my finances. I used to go fishing from the rocks and I'd have my fill of potatoes every year.

The Gaelic League had been established five years by the time I got involved. However much trouble I took upon myself, from year to year I was working harder and harder, and today I'm working even more intensely than ever for the sake of the language of our country and our forefathers. If I have written in this language as much as anyone else, I've done my bit, though lately I've had a lot of help from the splendid League, may God preserve them.

C.W. v[on] Sydow — O'Sorcha — (Sweden)

This gentleman came to us a couple of times. One Sunday he was with me, and he read the tale *Fionn agus Lorcán* with a better accent and pronunciation than many others going around in this country of Ireland. He invited me to go on holiday with him, some time in the future. On his last trip he told me that he'd be teaching Gaelic when he returned home.

Page 321

George MacThomas

George came from King's College Cambridge, in England. He spent three periods amongst us, in three successive years, and he still wants more of the same.

Tomás O'Reilly often came to be amongst us on his annual holidays. It is he who sent me most of my books. When he's away he sends me many books, which I enjoy reading very much.

Seán Ó'Coileáin from Duncormac spent three consecutive years with me. He didn't want to do an office job or its like, but to acquire a better knowledge of his ancestors' tongue. In my opinion, it wouldn't be easy to find a man who would be more proficient in the language than Seán Ó'Coileáin.

Tadhg O'Kelly, Patrick Brennan, Seán Kissane, etc — I can't remember the half of them.

I didn't have much to do with any of them really, and indeed I was never in any financial difficulty from the moment I saw Marstrander, up to this very day, thanks be to God. May none of them ever be struck down or be in want.

Father MacClune

This priest spent three weeks with me the first year he visited. We used to have Mass every day from him. He came back and we spent a month together, helping each other correct the whole of

Réilthíní Óir.[42] We'd have eight hours sitting down together every day, two periods in the day — four hours in the morning and four hours in the afternoon, for a whole month.

That month disrupted my fishing and my work on land more severely than any other had ever done. But what infuriated me particularly was when I found out that the person with whom I had worked so hard didn't even mention my help in the work. I suppose that it wouldn't have been so bad if it had been some academic, either in Ireland or abroad, who had done such a thing, and not a member of the church. But wouldn't we have it easy if our road to paradise was a straight one, and not a crooked one!

However, it will be a long time before paradise is full, and the world will not come to an end as soon as people imagine. May God not bring an end to the human race, however crooked or straight our roads may be!

Page 322

One of my sons had been in America for twelve years. He came home with his wife and two children. He was on board the same ship as Archbishop Mannogue when the latter was taken captive in Cork Bay. He stayed with me for only six months, and then he went off again and left me. There was no fishing or anything being done when they came over, and they were spending whatever small amount of money they brought over with them. He said that if things were to carry on like this much longer, the money he had brought with him would be spent, and then he'd be in a queer fix. I didn't contradict him, but said that perhaps he might be right.

My brother, the old pensioner, left me when they came home. He was taken in to a house in Dunquin, and at eighty years of age he is still there. Another of my sons is with me, and it's hard for him to stay here around the house, because I'm not much good for anything now except talking. We haven't a cow, a horse, a sheep or a lamb, a currach or a boat. All we have is a handful of potatoes and a fire.

[42] Little Golden Stars

I've been involved with this language for twenty-seven years, and I suppose about twenty years writing it. And, as I've already mentioned, it's seventeen years since the Scandinavian came to visit me. We've been receiving bits and pieces now and again from abroad, and so we have never been short of the necessities of life. I've heard many gasbags saying that you won't make money out of the native language, but I don't agree, because I'd be depending on handouts if it weren't for the language.

A young lady from France is my latest visitor. She and I went through the *Réilthíní Óir* together.

Page 323 As the storyteller used to say long ago after telling his story, "That's my story and if there's a lie in it, let it be." Here is my story and there is no lie in it, only the bare truth. Before I die I'd like every Irish and foreign student to have this book, as well as my other book *Seanchas ón Oileán Tiar*,[43] which is about to be published soon in the great city of London. The two books are in no way related to each other, although there are a lot of words in them that come from the same source. This book is about my life, with references in it to everything that happened, either significant or insignificant, around the Blaskets, but which were not mentioned by me in the other book.

To anyone who takes my books into their hand, however much they have paid for them, may God grant that they may receive their value sevenfold in wealth and in health!

And may He make room for all of us in His Blessed Kingdom!

The End, 3 March 1926, Tomás O'Crohan, The Great Blasket

---

[43] Traditional stories from the Western Isle

TWENTY-FOUR

From the Blasket, 27 September 1928; Well, I've reached the end of my story; Casting an eye on my life and my work; We are simple poor people; This is a rock in the middle of the great sea; Life is losing its big-heartedness and fun; I'm old now; I remember being at my mother's breast

From the Blasket
27 September 1928
In the Name of God
Well, I have slithered along to the end of my story. There is nothing in it but the truth. I didn't need to make up anything because over a long life I've gathered a lot of memories — and there are still more in my head, if anyone wants to ask about them. All the same, it was those things that interested me the most that I jotted down. For ages I'd been mulling over everything I was most interested in.

I brought other people into it besides myself. It wouldn't have been a proper job if it hadn't been done thoroughly. There wasn't any hatred between me and my neighbours. I spent nearly all my life amongst them, without ever falling out with any of them. Thankfully I've still never seen the inside of Dingle courthouse. Nor do I remember the law having to be brought against anyone at all except by my sister, who had to sue her own brother-in-law and another man.

Page 326

That sister was married in this village. However, her husband lived for only a couple of years. They lived in the family house, while her brother-in-law lived in his own house on the mainland. When her husband died he left everything he had to her and the child. My sister left her husband's family and brought the child over to us. My mother brought the boy up well.

Then my sister went to America, where she spent four years. Her brother-in-law was back in the old house, and bitter because she had left.

When she came back from America she went looking for justice for the boy, but little good did it do her. Her brother-in-law had selfishly appropriated everything for himself. She took an action against him, and got everything that she demanded. Whatever was owed was requisitioned from him immediately. That was the only time I remember the law being instigated on the Island, apart from the matter of the Dun Sheep in Tralee. Actually, I don't remember this event myself, although I do sort of vaguely recall it, because everyone is still talking about it, and will, I suppose, continue to do so, for the memory of an evil deed is long, and never dies.

We are a poor and simple people, barely getting by, day by day, one following the other. I think it's just as well that we weren't greedy people. We were skilled and we were satisfied with the way of life that the Blessed Master had ordained for us — to do everything without shirking; to plough the waves, often without hope of making headway, but our hope was always in God. We had differences of opinion with one another. We had our own virtues, and our own small faults. I never shied away from writing about the worthy traits or the small failings we had; neither did I hide the hardships that befell us, and which we faced, because we had no alternative but to endure them.

This Island is a rock in the middle of the sea, and very often the foaming sea rises up with the full strength of the wind, so that you couldn't stick your head out, any more than a rabbit could, crouching in its burrow while outside the sea raged and the rain swept down. We often used to head out to sea in the early morning whenever the day was suitable. We had to do this as fishing was our main means of livelihood. But by the end of the day the people back on the Island would often be worried if ever the weather might have turned nasty by the afternoon.

There is no way to describe the hardship involved in this sort of fishing. I consider it to be the worst of anything I've ever been involved in. Very often the waves rose right above us, so that we couldn't catch sight of land or shore. We'd spend long, cold, stormy nights struggling with the sea, very often without much to show for it, often yearning for God's help. It was seldom that we used to catch what we needed, and so we used to have to cut the nets and to let them go — both the fish and the net; the net being a very expensive item for us to purchase. Other nights after all the toil of the catch, and our currachs fairly full, we'd still be out on the open sea unable to get to harbour or land. The swell would rise up high, reaching as far as the green grass. Unexpected storms would break upon the banks, the sea engulfing the high grazing grounds. We would often have to put up the sails and flee away from the bad weather, some of us to Cooncrome Harbour, others to Ventry Harbour and yet others to Dingle. Then we'd have to come home against the storm, only to be back on the wave of fortune once more on the following morning.

Page 327

That is why there can be no comparison between us and people in big cities who have fine flat land. We had our small faults, of which we were accused at times, particularly whenever we'd get together for a drink. The drink used to affect us more than it did other people because we used to be constantly worn out by our way of life, like a horse that never has any respite or peace.

Life used to be good at that time. You'd never be short of a shilling, there was plenty of food and things were cheap — including the drink. It wasn't the desire of the drink itself that made us long for it, but to have a merry night instead of the hardship that often awaited us. The drop used to raise our spirits, and we used to have a day and a night now and again in one another's company, whenever we'd have a chance to do so. All that's gone now, and the great-heartedness and the craic are dying out. Then we made our way home, nice and decently, after all the carousing, like small children, not doing any harm to one another.

Page 328 I wrote in detail about a lot of all our goings-on so that there'd be some recollection somewhere about them, and I have tried to describe the character of the people who were around me so that there might be an account of them after we're gone, because our likes will never be here again.

I am old now. I am sure that many other things happened to me during my life up to now, if I only could remember them. People came into this world during my lifetime and have left before me. On this Island there are only five people left who are older than I am. They are on the basic pension, and I'll get it in a couple of months, too, having reached that age in my life, not an age of my choosing. Actually there are many people who would prefer to be old and getting the pension than to be young and without it. These are greedy and fearful people.

I remember being at my mother's breast. She used to bring me up the hill in a creel for carrying turf. When the creel was full of turf, I used to be under her arm on our way home. I also remember being a boy, and being a young man in my prime and strong. Famine and abundance, success and failure have come during my lifetime; a person who takes note of them can learn a lot.

One day the Blasket will be without any of the people I have mentioned in this book, or anyone who will remember us. I give thanks to God that He gave me the ability to observe what I experienced, so that after I've gone people will know what life was like in my time. May there never be a bitter word between me and the neighbours who were alive then, or between me and those of them who are still alive today!

Finally, there isn't a country, a region or a nation where people don't do something better than anyone else. Since the first fire was lit on this Island, no one has written about their life here. I'm proud to be the one who did it. This book will tell how the

Islanders got on in the old times. My mother was carrying the turf so that she could send me to school when I was eight years of age. I hope to God that she herself and my father will get their reward in the Blessed Kingdom and that I and everyone who reads this book will meet on the Island of Paradise.

THE END

Perhaps it hasn't got a short tail on it now! If there is a sentence there that you don't like, leave it out.

Tomás O'Crohan
The Great Blasket

Appendix 1

The houses we used to have: their construction and furbishment; Hens in the roof of the house: the chicks that fell on to the table; The most important leaders on the Island; Devices for providing light and the food we ate

[From the first edition, 34–40]

Perhaps this is a good place to give a short account of how we managed things on this island during my youth, especially since that way of life has gone, and is only remembered now by a few old people. As regards the houses that were around when I was young, and for a good while after that, they weren't like those to be found in any other place. Some of them were more elegant than others, but most of them were very wretched-looking. Some were only ten feet long and eight feet wide, and others were up to fifteen or twenty feet in length. In order to divide the house there used to be a dresser across the middle of the house, which came out from the wall on one side, with a corresponding partition joining it from the other side. There used to be two beds below them, with people in them. Two pigs would go under one bed and there were potatoes under the other. There'd be a large chest between the two beds up against the gable-end. On the other side of the partition, the kitchen side, was where the family — up to ten of them, perhaps — lived during the day or part of the day. There might be a coop, with hens in it, beside the partition and a broody hen nearby in an old pot. At night there'd be a cow or two, one or two calves, a donkey, as well as two dogs tied to the side of the wall or running all over the house.

A house with a large family would have two post-beds over in the corner, or perhaps a bed on the floor.

The bed near the fire was for the old people. They'd have a *Page 332* stump of a clay pipe going. If there were two of them they'd both be puffing away. There'd be a good fire of top sods glowing away until morning. Every time they woke up they used to shove in a twisted wisp of straw that they used as a spill, and then take a puff out of the pipe. If the man had an old woman with him, he'd stretch over towards her and stick the wisp into the pipe. Then smoke from the two stumps would curl up the chimney, and when they were at full blast the couple's bed looked like a steamship going at full blast.

There might be two or three dogs lying at the foot of the bed. Any cows would be below them, with their heads turned to the wall. Calves usually had the run of the kitchen, with their snouts to the fire. The donkey used to be tied to the other side of the house, opposite the cows; and the cat, and perhaps a couple of kittens, would be lying by the hob. At night, all the rest of the odds and ends in the house used to be put under the post-bed, which was made of wood or iron, and was several feet above the ground.

Some of the houses had no division to make a room. Instead, there'd be a post-bed in one corner and a floor bed in the other corner, with a dresser against the wall or up against the gable-end. The pigs, when we had them, went under the high bed. There'd be two or three barrels of fish in every house; and along with all the animals perhaps you'd find a pet lamb or two running around the house as well.

Those houses used to be made out of stones and clay-mortar. Most of them weren't in too great a shape because they used to be built in a hurry, with everyone lending a helping hand. The roof was made of rushes or reeds, with sturdy thick layers of turf underneath. The roof wouldn't have been so bad if only the hens would have let it alone. However, as soon as the rushes began decaying and worms got into it, even a man with a gun wouldn't be able to stop the hens from scratching and nesting there. Then it would start leaking dirty stuff with a lot of soot in it. The hens used to make such deep holes that they could disappear into them. A broody hen might well not respond to the woman of the house when she called to it at feeding time. Young girls often used to bring down a hatful of eggs from the roof. The young chicks also used to damage the roof because they were forever looking for nests. It'd be as good as a day at Puck Fair, listening to a couple of housewives from two adjoining houses squabbling over a few eggs.

Page 333

The better houses used to be from twelve feet in width and from twenty to twenty-five feet in length. There'd be a cupboard and a dresser across the floor in order to make a room out of part of the house, and two high post-beds. In these houses there might be pigs in the kitchen but there was never a sty for them outside. These houses used to have the same kind of roof as the small houses, and as these were low, it was easier for the hens to reach the roofs.

I remember a funny story about hens that happened in one of the large houses, the like of which didn't happen in any of the smaller ones.

The family were all together, eating the evening meal, their table loaded with potatoes, fish and milk. Everyone's jaw was keenly grinding and swallowing. The man of the house, sitting at the head of the table, had a wooden mug full of milk in front of him. Just as he reached out to take a chunk of fish, he noticed something falling into the mug. When he looked into the mug, something was submerged in the milk. The tongs had to be brought to take out whatever it was that had fallen into the mug. No one had any idea what it might be. "It's a chick," said the woman of the house. "What the devil made it fall in there?"

"It doesn't matter what the hell it is," said the man of the house. "Have you lost your mind or what? Where do you think it has come from?"

Everyone at the table was going crazy, and goodness knows how it would have turned out if another live chick hadn't fallen onto the potatoes.

"For goodness' sake! Where are they coming from?" said the woman of the house. *Page 334*

"They're certainly not arriving from hell," says the man of the house. "You should be glad at least that they're falling from above!"

A bright lad at the bottom of the table glanced up at the rafters and saw the sky and the sun shining through.

"You bunch of eejits, there's a hole in the roof!" says he to his father. "Come here and see for yourself."

When the man of the house saw the hole he exclaimed:

"Oh, wisha, may the Big Man up above take every hen, egg and chick and dump them all in the sea!"

"May God ignore you!" says the woman.

When they looked closer, they saw another ten chicks up there, with the mother hen.

My cradle was in one of the medium-sized houses. It was a rather small, narrow house, but it was tidy — what there was of it — because my father was very deft with his hands and my mother was never lazy. She had one spinning-wheel for wool, and another for flax and carding. She used to spin thread from her own spinning-wheel, which she often did for some hefty young women who weren't inclined to do it for themselves. Even if they had a mind to do it, they would have been still far too lazy.

Some ten years after my marriage I put up a new house. No one gave me a bit of help all the time I was doing it, and I roofed it myself. It's not a big house; all the same, if King George were to spend a whole month's holiday in the house, its ugliness wouldn't kill him. There was a felt roof on it, as on every house and shed in the area until the Board put up six slated houses. While the new house was being finished, a hen flew up onto the roof. My uncle Dermot was passing by, stopped to observe the hen, and saw the hard time it was having, trying to remain up on top. Eventually the slippery felt was too much for the hen and down she went.

"It serves you right; you've finally got your come-uppance," says Dermot.

Page 335

When I was small, Patrick Keane — and before him, Patrick Guithan — were the two leaders on the Island. I myself saw Patrick Keane, grandfather of the King we have now, as the owner of four or five milch cows. I didn't see the other man, the Guithan fellow, though his grandchildren were around in my time. I often heard that he had as many as eight to ten milch cows, a mare — a red mare she was — and a wooden plough. That mare was used for hauling gravel to the old tower[44] (whenever it was built) and he himself was a gilly from the age of sixteen. The poet Seán Dunleavy was still in his cradle at that time, so that means that the King's grandfather was sixteen years older than the poet. People like them had half a dozen houses that weren't too bad.

Those small houses used to have a sort of collapsible table — a table that had a flap all round it to stop the potatoes, or anything else on it, from falling off. It consisted of a frame with three legs under it, all of which could be folded up so that it could be hung on the wall until it was needed again.

One day my Uncle Liam came home from the strand, hungry and eager to eat. The tripod frame was standing, and the table was on it; it was loaded with potatoes and whatever other delicacies were with them. A large lump of potato fell from the table and off went the dog after it. He carried the frame and the table with him, and everything else that was on it he sent flying, all over the house. Off went the wife picking up the potatoes.

"Mary, Mother of God! little woman, it's a regular day at the fair for you!" says Liam.

In every house there'd be bowls and plates, wooden mugs, a couple of chairs and a couple of stools. The chair-seats used to be woven with hay-rope or straw.

Most houses used to have a pot-hanger over the fire for hanging things on, and there were tongs of some sort on the hearth.

[44] One of the Martello towers built in the time of Napoleon

Nowadays all the houses have cups and saucers, and the dressers are filled tastefully. It's only people that live in the houses now; and there are sheds outside for the animals and everything else.

The first form of lighting I ever saw was from cressets containing grease, tapers or wicks. As these burnt away, they would be replaced with new ones.

The grease used to come from scad and from pollocks. 'Dip' was the name we gave to the fat from the scad, and 'livers' was what we called the grease from the pollocks. These were melted down. Seal oil, too, was used for light, but very little of it was put on the cresset because people loved to gulp it down, dipped in some Indian meal bread, and I believe they needed that. Even when I was well up in my teens that method of lighting was still in use. *Page 336*

The cresset was a small metal vessel made in the shape of a boat or a currach, with one or two spouts on it, three or four legs under it and a little handle or lug on the side. They were eight or ten inches in length. Grease or seal oil used to be put in the cressets. They'd dip the reed or the wick into the grease and then stretch it out over the spout of the cresset to light it. As it was being consumed, they kept pushing the wick out. The wick was made from the white material found in reeds, or from a cord of soft cotton or linen. A large shell was often used instead of a cresset. I don't remember when paraffin arrived. I used to hear them say that a small sod of turf or a splinter of deal was used long before that.

I myself spent some of my youth on two meals a day. There was great work done each morning on the strand, on the hill or in the field. My morning meal was ready for me when the cows came in to be milked. I had my evening meal when the sun would be going down in the west. We didn't call the meals 'breakfast' or 'supper' at that time.

The food in those days consisted of potatoes and fish, sometimes with a drop of milk. When the potatoes were used up there was Indian meal to be had — mere husks really; and indeed no one today would have any truck with the kind of bread that used to be made from it, unless they had a good set of teeth to chew it. It's a pity that I don't have the same food today, now that I have health and teeth to grind it.

When I was young, two stone of flour used to come for Christmas. I was an adult before any tea came, and when a pound of it would arrive for Christmas it would be put aside and kept in safe keeping until the following Christmas.

Page 337

Nowadays our food is entirely different. We have bread-flour, tea and sugar. Some of them pick at their food four times a day. In those days I used to eat the same amount at each meal as is eaten now at these four meals. Then, if it was necessary, people used to last for two days on one such meal. Nowadays a man couldn't walk the length of a fork before he'd fall down on his backside, having had only a snack, instead of eating a proper meal.

Appendix 2

Education; Marriage; Drudgery; Seals; The fate of our family

[From the first edition, 162–4] *Page 339*

I went to school — whenever it was open — until I was eighteen. During that period I wasn't asked to do much at home, as my married brother was living in the house. His wife died and left two sons. My mother took them on until they were ready to move out, and my brother went to America.

I had to leave school then, because there was no one else in the house except my father. And so, three years after I left school I got married. I was twenty-one years of age. Up to then I had few responsibilities, but from that day on I had many. Indeed my whole life changed. Marriage is an important event in a person's life. One's attitude and perception change, but when all is said and done, marriage gives a man a zest for life. As they say, my life had been sheer paradise before that.

I really got stuck into things. Off I'd go to the beach to make fertiliser in order to sow more potatoes for the pigs. We used to have a couple of cows. At dawn I'd take off all my clothes except a pair of drawers, and wade out up to my neck, and gather seaweed with a rake. Then I'd bring it up to the top of the cliff, where I'd drag it out and spread it. I was always up early, without

Page 340

tea or sugar but only milk, bread and fish. Whether I was going to the beach or to the hills I'd be just as fast. I'd spend a while out at sea, a while fishing for seals and a while in the great seine-boats, each job requiring its own time.

The seals were dangerous enough. At a certain time of the year everyone used to be after them. There was that day of the great swell in Poolabasha cave where there was only enough room for one person to swim through the fissure, catch large seals, and bring them out through the same narrow opening. That day was a near thing for me, and could have been the end of me, when my uncle was drowning, and the rope had snapped on him.

Since I got married I tried my best to provide for the home, and to get my share of whatever was going. For a long time my father was a great help to me, both on the mainland and on the Island itself.

We had ten children altogether, but good fortune didn't follow them all, may God have mercy on us! My eldest son was seven or eight when he fell from a cliff and was killed. From then on, no sooner was one born but it was taken from us. Two died from measles, and there wasn't a disease around that didn't take one of them from me. Donal was drowned trying to rescue that lady on the White Strand. I also had another fine boy, who was just beginning to get close to me when he too was taken.

The sorrow of all these things weighed heavily on my poor wife, and so she too was taken from me. Up to this time I was always able to manage somehow. May God not leave us groping in the dark! A little baby was left after her, but luckily a young grown-up girl was there to care for her. That last daughter was called like the rest of them when she had just become a young adult. The daughter who brought her up and who married in Dunmore also passed away. She left six children behind. One boy has stayed at home with me, while another lad went to America. That's what has happened as regards my children. May the blessing of God be upon all those in the grave, and upon the poor woman whose spirit was broken on their account.

Appendix 3

*The story of Seán Dunleavy; The woman who put
an end to bailiffs and drivers; The biting song
Dunleavy composed about those who had
plundered his sheep*

[From the first edition, 234–5]
Since I've mentioned the poet Seán Dunleavy, I might as well tell
a story about him here.

It's about thirty-three years since Seán Dunleavy died. He died
on the Island after having been sick for a while. He didn't like the
fact that he had lived so long. As he said himself:

> *Living too long is worst of all*
> *No one cares or comes to call.*

The poet had a great outlook when he was young. I often used to
hear my mother talking about him; they were both of the same
generation. He had great vigour and energy. He used to jump over
every ditch going to Mass on Sundays, and was known by men
who were acquainted with him for his mettle and drive. I myself
knew more about his character than anyone else, even though he
was an old man in my time.

I believe that his first nest — i.e. his cradle — was in
Ballynaraha in Dunquin. He came to this Island having married

a woman from the Mannin family, who were farmers. She was a wonderful woman. She it was who put an end to the bailiffs and the drivers who were coming here every day, ruining the lives of the poor who were in dire need.

Page 342

The bailiff went up on to the roof of her house, and started knocking it down, and dropped a plank on top of her and on a group of feeble children. She grabbed hold of some new shears, which she opened — one prong out and one prong back. She was a strong woman, and she was furious. The bailiff didn't know what was happening until he felt a prong of the shears in his backside. It wasn't the roof of the house that went through the hole he'd made this time but a stream of his own blood. And that was the last bailiff we ever saw on this Island.

Dunleavy was not one bit pleased with those who had stolen his sheep, especially as they were earning more than he did, so he wrote a biting song about them. He spent part of his life in abject poverty, like many others. He never received a penny from anyone for his verses, but he was always the joker. God's blessing on them all.

Appendix 4

Matters concerning religion: Mass, confession and
the priest; Remembering the arrival of the bishop;
Stations of the Cross

[From the first edition, 258–9]
There used to be big problems regarding religion, as far as I can remember. To get to Mass, one had to cross three long miles of the Sound, over to Dunquin. In the winter it's very rare indeed that the Sound is suitable for a crossing, in which case we'd have to stay at home. We often used to go three months without Mass. On Sundays when we couldn't go over to the mainland we used to say the Rosary by ourselves at the time Mass was being celebrated on the mainland.

As regards confession, it was a rare person who used to go to Dunquin, as far as I remember, but once a year priests used to come to the Island. There used to be a large boat from Dunquin hired by the parish priest in order to bring him and those helping him over to the Island. Any money collected at the Stations would be given in payment. That's how it used to be until these large boats disappeared from both the Island and the mainland. Since then the Island currachs bring the priests over.

There isn't half the respect for the priest now that there used to be during my youth. At that time I well remember how it wouldn't have been considered a proper welcome for a priest, for a person not to genuflect after sweeping his cap clean off his head. Nowadays, if people meet a priest, the ones in the front will remove their caps, but those standing at the back would probably not remove theirs. No woman would be allowed in a boat with a priest, however great her need. No woman used to come close to the jetty. However, lately there seems to be no stopping them and the boats are full of women.

Page 344

One of my earliest memories is of having seen a bishop on the Blasket. I suppose he stood out because of the special cloak that he was wearing, though I wasn't very old at the time. I'm always quick to point out to anyone who wants to know where 'The Bishop's Seat' is located. He was walking along after he left the jetty until he came to a flat, grassy patch. There was a rock in the middle of this patch. The bishop stopped, looked around him, and then sat on the stone, gathering his cloak around him.

"This place is suitable enough, since the day is fine," says he.

I don't remember any other bishop coming since then. For a long time now, once every third year, the youths are asked to go over to the parish priest's house in Ballyferriter in order to get confirmed.

There used to be a house on the Island set aside especially for saying the Stations of the Cross every year when the priests used to come. But ever since the schoolhouse was built, they hold it there.

Appendix 5

An account of the day; The early woman;
The motor-boat at the White Strand, and
what brought them there

A Day in the Life of the Early-Rising Woman[45]

Page 345

They say that the woman I'm about to mention never goes to bed, and I don't find that hard to believe. Yesterday morning she was out at the crack of dawn, taking her cow to the field. When she returned home what did she see on the White Strand but fourteen motorboats going ceaselessly backwards and forwards, as if they were trying to race one another.

She ran as fast as her legs would carry her, although they were quaking from fear, because she thought that every man in them would be on shore before she had a chance to warn anyone in the village about them.

She had good reason for being alarmed because notices for rents, tax and dogs had come from the Government, and not one of them had been complied with. And so she thought that they were a search party from the Government that had come secretly

---

[45] On page 82 of the Seán Ó Coileáin edition of *An tOileánach*, the author notes that Tomás O'Crohan: … *has a small story here with the title:* 'Cuntas lae; an bhean mhoch' *which has been placed at the end as an Addendum* (pages 345–6); *since it is more consistent with* Allagar na hInse *than with* An tOileánach.

to take all the men with them, or all the women, whichever they happened to choose.

"I'm only sorry they wouldn't take all the women here with them!" said one man to her, as she told him what was happening.

"Oh, may sorrow be your reward!" she replied.

The reason for the hullabaloo with the boats was that one of them had been there two days earlier and had caught thirty *Page 346* pounds worth of fish and fifteen pounds worth on the second day. The first boat had done this unbeknownst to the others. They nearly killed the early woman for waking them so early while everybody else was snoring in bed.